HANDBOOK OF

PREACHING RESOURCES

FROM ENGLISH LITERATURE

THE MACMILLAN COMPANY
NEW YORK · CHICAGO
DALLAS · ATLANTA · SAN FRANCISCO
LONDON · MANILA

IN CANADA
BRETT-MACMILLAN LTD.
GALT, ONTARIO

HANDBOOK OF

PREACHING RESOURCES

FROM ENGLISH LITERATURE

Compiled and edited by

James Douglas Robertson

New York   THE MACMILLAN COMPANY   1962

A DIVISION OF THE CROWELL-COLLIER PUBLISHING COMPANY

First Printing

The Macmillan Company, New York
Brett-Macmillan, Ltd., Galt, Ontario

Printed in the United States of America

Library of Congress catalog card number: 62-8566

ACKNOWLEDGMENTS

Grateful acknowledgment is made to the following publishers, agents, authors, and copyright owners for permission to reprint in this volume from the works listed below:

Association for Promoting Christian Knowledge, "St. Patrick's Hymn Before Tara," translated by C. F. Alexander.

Ernest Benn, Ltd., from *The Locum Tenens* by V. L. Whitechurch.

A. & C. Black, Ltd., "The Rune of Hospitality," an anonymous poem arranged by Kenneth MacLeod in his *The Road to the Isles,* published by A. & C. Black, Ltd.

The Bodley Head, Ltd. (John Lane), from *Heretics* by G. K. Chesterton.

Curtis Brown, Ltd., from *History of Europe* by H. A. L. Fisher, published by Houghton Mifflin Co., Boston, and Eyre & Spottiswoode, Ltd., London.

Margaret V. Bryce, two excerpts from *Studies in Contemporary Biography* by James Bryce.

Burns Oates & Washbourne, Ltd., for selections from Francis Thompson.

Christy & Moore, Ltd., from "The Gate of the Year" by M. Louise Haskins.

James Clarke & Co., Ltd., two excerpts from *Christ in Shakespeare* by George Morrison.

Miss D. E. Collins, from *St. Francis of Assisi* by G. K. Chesterton, used also by permission of Hodder & Stoughton, Ltd. and A. P. Watt & Son.

Wm. Collins Sons & Co., Ltd., from *My Lady of the Chimney Corner* by Alexander Irvine.

A. J. Cronin, from "The Provost's Tale."

J. M. Dent & Sons, Ltd., from *Collected Essays and Addresses,* Vol. II, by Augustine Birrell.

Doubleday and Company, Inc., from *Books and Persons* by Arnold Bennett, copyright 1917 by George H. Doran Co., used also by permission of A. P. Watt & Son; from *Lord Jim* by Joseph Conrad, used also by permission of J. M. Dent & Sons, Ltd.; from *Youth* by Joseph Conrad, used also by permission of J. M. Dent & Sons, Ltd.; "Mother o' Mine" from *The Light That Failed* by Rudyard Kipling, used also by permission of Mrs. George Bambridge, the Macmillan Company of Canada, Ltd., and A. P. Watt & Son; "Recessional" from *The Five Nations* by Rudyard Kipling, used also by permission of Mrs. George Bambridge, Methuen & Co., Ltd., and A. P. Watt & Son; from *Mr. Maugham Himself* by W. Somerset Maugham (selected by John Beecroft); from *The Summing Up* by W. Somerset Maugham, copyright 1938 by W. Somerset Maugham; from *A Writer's Notebook* by W. Somerset Maugham, copyright 1949 by W. Somerset Maugham. The selections from W. Somerset Maugham are used also by permission of the author, William Heinemann, Ltd., and A. P. Watt & Son.

E. P. Dutton & Co., Inc., from *The Roadmender* by Michael Fairless, used also by permission of Wm. Collins Sons & Co., Ltd.; two excerpts from *Freedom and Growth and Other Essays* by Edmond G. A. Holmes, used also by permission of J. M. Dent & Sons, Ltd.; from *Not That It Matters* by A. A. Milne, used also by permission of Methuen & Co., Ltd.; from "Birds in Town and Country" in *The Best of W. H. Hudson* edited by Odell Shepard, used also by permission of The Royal Society for the Protection of Birds and The Society of Authors; from *Concerning the Inner Life* by Evelyn Underhill, used also by permission of Methuen & Co., Ltd.

The Executors of the Estate of H. G. Wells, from "Answer to Prayer," by H. G. Wells, in *The New Yorker* (May 1, 1937); and from *The World of William Clissold* by H. G. Wells; arrangements for both selections made through A. P. Watt & Son.

Harcourt, Brace and World, Inc., from *The Rock* by T. S. Eliot, copyright 1934 by Harcourt, Brace and Co., Inc., used also by permission of Faber and Faber, Ltd.; four excerpts from *Eminent Victorians* by G. Lytton Strachey, used also by permission of Chatto & Windus, Ltd.; from *Surprised by Joy* by C. S. Lewis, used also by permission of Geoffrey Bles, Ltd.

Harper & Brothers, from *Heaven and Hell, The Perennial Philosophy,* and *Proper Studies* by Aldous Huxley; from *Angel Pavement* and *English Journey* by J. B. Priestley; from "Faith" and "Indifference" in *The Sorrows of God* by G. A. Studdert-Kennedy, copyright 1924 by Harper & Brothers, used also by permission of Hodder & Stoughton, Ltd.

David Higham Associates, Ltd., from *The Greatest Story Ever Staged* by Dorothy Sayers, published by Hodder & Stoughton, Ltd.

Hodder & Stoughton, Ltd., two excerpts from *The Dark Mile* by John Hutton; from *Margaret Ethel MacDonald* by J. Ramsay MacDonald; from *Miscellanies* by Lord Rosebery; from "If I Had a Million Pounds" in *The Unutterable Beauty* by G. A. Studdert-Kennedy.

Henry Holt and Company, Inc., "Yonder See the Morning Blink" from *The Collected Poems of A. E. Housman,* copyright 1922, 1940 by Henry Holt and Company, Inc., copyright 1950 by Barclay's Bank, Ltd. Used also by permission of The Society of Authors, literary representative of the estate of the late A. E. Housman, and Jonathan Cape, Ltd.

Alfred A. Knopf, Inc., from *The Journal of Katherine Mansfield,* edited by J. Middleton Murry, used also by permission of The Society of Authors, literary representative of the estate of the late Katherine Mansfield.

J. B. Lippincott Company, from "Watchers of the Sky" in *Collected Poems in One Volume* by Alfred Noyes, used also by permission of Hugh Noyes.

Little, Brown and Company, from *Good-bye, Mr. Chips* by James Hilton, copyright 1934 by James Hilton, copyright renewed by Alice Hilton, used also by permission of the copyright owners; from *If Winter Comes* by A. S. M. Hutchinson, used also by permission of the author.

Longmans, Green & Co., Ltd., from *Personal Religion and the Life of Devotion* by W. R. Inge; two excerpts from *Speculum Animae* by W. R. Inge; from *Garibaldi's Defense of the Roman Republic* by G. M. Trevelyan.

Hugh MacDiarmid, "The Two Parents" by Hugh MacDiarmid.

Macmillan & Company, Ltd., from *Robert Browning* by G. K. Chesterton; from *The Hope of a New World* and from *Studies in the Spirit and Truth of Christianity* by William Temple.

The Macmillan Company, from "God's Funeral" in *Collected Poems* by Thomas Hardy, used also by permission of the trustees of the estate of Thomas Hardy and Macmillan & Company, Ltd.; "The Mystery" in *Poems* by Ralph Hodgson, used also by permission of Macmillan & Company, Ltd.; from *The Everlasting Mercy* and *The Trial of Jesus* by John Masefield, used also by permission of The Society of Authors and Dr. John Masefield, O.M.; from *The Secret Woman* by Eden Phillpotts, used also by permission of Hughes Massie, Ltd.

McGraw-Hill Book Company, Inc., two excerpts from *Boswell's London Journal 1762-1763*, edited by Frederick A. Pottle, copyright 1950 by Yale University.

Harold Matson Company, from *The Magnetic Mountain*, Part III, by C. Day Lewis, copyright 1935 by C. Day Lewis. Used also by permission of Jonathan Cape, Ltd.

Methuen & Co., Ltd., from *Happy England* by Robert Lynd.

Mrs. John Morley, from *Life of William Ewart Gladstone* by John Morley, arrangements made by Gamlen, Bowerman, and Forward.

John Murray, Ltd., from *Recollections of a Long Life*, Vol. II, by Lord Brougham; from *Modern Poets of Faith, Doubt, and Paganism* by Arthur T. Lyttelton; from *The Faith of Edward Wilson* by George Seaver.

The New York Times, from two essays by Ivor Brown in *Highlights of Modern Literature*, edited by Francis Brown. Used also by permission of Ivor Brown.

Miss Theo. Oxenham, "After Work," "Seeds," and "Faith" by John Oxenham; "The Pilgrim Way," "The Ways," and "Your Place" from *Bees in Amber* by John Oxenham, published by the Fleming H. Revell Company.

Oxford University Press, Inc., from *William Temple, His Life and Letters* by F. A. Iremonger.

G. P. Putnam's Sons, two excerpts from *Blood, Sweat, and Tears* by Winston S. Churchill, copyright 1941 by Winston S. Churchill, used also by permission of Cassell and Company, Ltd. and McClelland and Stewart, Ltd.; two excerpts from *Mrs. Gladstone* by Mary Drew.

Random House, Inc., from *For the Time Being*, "A Christmas Oratorio," by W. H. Auden, copyright 1944 by W. H. Auden, used also by permission of Faber and Faber, Ltd.; from *Holes in the Sky* by Louis MacNeice, copyright 1948 by Louis MacNeice, used also by permission of Faber and Faber, Ltd.

Routledge and Kegan Paul, Ltd., from *Carlyle to Threescore-and-Ten* by D. A. Wilson.

Charles Scribner's Sons, from *Courage* and *Margaret Ogilvie* by James M. Barrie, used also by permission of Hodder & Stoughton, Ltd.; three excerpts from *Father and Son* by Edmund Gosse, copyright 1907 by Charles Scribner's Sons, renewal copyright 1935 by Philip Gosse, used also by permission of William Heinemann, Ltd.; from *The Country House* and *The Man of Property* by John Galsworthy; "Valley of the Shadow" from *A Sheaf* by John Galsworthy, copyright 1916 by Charles Scribner's Sons, renewal copyright 1944 by Ada Galsworthy. The Galsworthy selections are used also by permission of William Heinemann, Ltd.

Sidgwick & Jackson, Ltd., from "A Prayer" in *Poems 1902-19* by John Drinkwater.

The Society of Authors and the Public Trustee, from *Saint Joan* by George Bernard Shaw.

Sylvan Press, Ltd., from *Ideas and Beliefs of the Victorians*.

The *Times* (London), from "Life's True Values" in *Selected Essays from the Times*.

Mr. G. M. Trevelyan, from *Life of John Bright* by G. M. Trevelyan.

The Trustees of the Estate of Lord Tweedsmuir (John Buchan), from *A Lodge in the Wilderness, Pilgrim's Way*, and *The Three Hostages* by John Buchan, used also by permission of Hodder & Stoughton, Ltd., and A. P. Watt & Son.

A. Watkins, Inc., from *Father Malachy's Miracle* by Bruce Marshall, copyright 1948 by Bruce Marshall.

Henry Williamson, from *The Wet Flanders Plain* by Henry Williamson.

CONTENTS

INTRODUCTION

By Andrew W. Blackwood

This volume should help to meet a pressing need among pastors and seminary students today. The need appears in a helpful book, *Concerning Preaching,* by John Oman, of Cambridge. In a chapter about "Reading" he says: "Inspiration comes largely from keeping company with the inspired. . . . [Among] all kinds of defects in our present system of theological education . . . the chief defect . . . I take to be ignorance of literature, particularly English literature."

The principle here applies most of all to Holy Scripture. The present volume rightly assumes that in every sermon the warp should come from the inspired Book of Books. But the woof may well come from the interpretation of life in the Western world. Where better than in the noblest works of prose and poetry can any spokesman for God find what he needs to fill out the pattern of many a sermon while yet on the loom? Better still, in such a book one can see how to approach and deal with many a difficult and perplexing truth or duty. Best of all, the volume encourages the man of God to spend time every day with what is well written and well worth reading.

From all these points of view the compiler and interpreter has done his work well. The resulting volume seems to me the best of its kind. Through the years this editor has "traveled in realms of God." Day by day he has stored countless treasures. Many of them he now shares with lovers of truth and beauty. More than other anthologists this friend has a keen sense of literary, moral, and spiritual values. He also has an eye for things practical. To facilitate speedy reference and use of the 657 items, he has listed them under clear headings. These he has arranged alphabetically, with adequate cross reference, equally free from confusion. Wherever necessary he has introduced a quotation with a brief statement telling the reader what he needs to know, or perhaps recall.

The resulting book stands ready to supply what a man needs to lighten up a dark corner in a coming sermon. Better still, a given excerpt may suggest or show how to deal with a truth or a duty that vitally concerns every hearer of the message. Best of all, the book should affect countless others as it has affected me. It has made me feel ashamed and sorry for spending too many of my waking moments on television entertainment and on reading what has not been well written. Surely I ought now to renew my friendship with Bunyan, Dickens, and many another of those "friends in books' clothing." I ought likewise to know and love "new" friends whose written work the world will never let die. How else can a minister keep his place among men of education and culture, all for the glory of God through His blessing on the hearers of sermons?

PREFACE

This collection of moral and spiritual materials quarried from the mine of English literature issues from my readings, casual and intense, over a number of years. The most obvious advantage of a work of this nature is that it offers in accessible form values from books too numerous and too voluminous to have always at hand. No collection of excerpts can of course substitute for direct acquaintance with the originals. Yet in pointing out the sources from which the selections are taken I hope that the reader may on occasion be stimulated to further pursuit. No pretense is made to having drawn everything from primary sources. Yet in most instances where values come from secondary sources I have been able to check with the originals. In the main the selections are brief, tailored to meet pulpit needs. If a favorite passage is missing, the omission may be in part owing to the bias of the compiler.

The task of providing topic headings was not an easy one; for not infrequently a given selection might have been placed appropriately under different headings. Where deemed advisable I have prefaced a selection with a brief word relating to the larger context from which it is taken. Where there are several selections under a topic, I have sought to introduce each with a word or phrase descriptive of its relationship to the topic. In this connection uniformity of expression has sometimes been sacrificed for clarity of statement. To increase the usefulness of the volume, I have frequently listed alongside main topics, related topics for further reading. In a selection where a fictional character is speaking, the name of the character is in parenthesis at the end.

Conscientious effort has been made to communicate with all copyright owners and to respect their rights. If anyone has been overlooked, I shall see to it that a future edition remedies the omission. I am particularly grateful to the librarians of Edinburgh

University who went out of their way to facilitate my access to the resources of the library, and to the staff of the library of The British Museum for their courteous service. My thanks also to Mrs. Dwight Meier for her very efficient typing of the manuscript.

J. D. R.

HANDBOOK OF

PREACHING RESOURCES

FROM ENGLISH LITERATURE

PREACHING RESOURCES
FROM ENGLISH LITERATURE

ADVERSITY   *see also* COURAGE, SORROW, SUFFERING
courage in

1.   *(When Martin Chuzzlewit learns that the fifty-acre tract in America in which he had invested all his savings, and Mark Tapley's too, turns out to be a hideous swamp, he sinks into a fever. Mark, however, refusing to be overpowered by the calamity, takes himself in hand thus:)*

"Now, Mr. Tapley," said Mark, giving himself a tremendous blow on the chest by way of reviver, "just you attend to what I've got to say. Things is looking as bad as they *can* look, young man. You'll not have such another opportunity for showing your jolly disposition, my fine fellow, as long as you live. And, therefore, now's the time to come out strong; or Never!"

Dickens, Martin Chuzzlewit

2.   *(The night John Stuart Mill came, pale as death, to tell Carlyle that the manuscript of the first volume of* The French Revolution, *which Carlyle had lent him, had been accidentally burned, its author's first concern was to relieve Mill's suffering. Carlyle pretended to make light of the loss. Actually, he did not have the original draft to fall back on. It was at this time that he made the following entry in his diary:)*

Oh, that I had faith! Oh, that I had! Then were there nothing too hard or heavy for me. Cry silently in thy inmost heart for it. Surely He will give it thee. At all events, it is as if my invisible schoolmaster had torn my copybook when I showed it, and said,

"No, boy! Thou must write it better." What can I, sorrowing, do but obey—obey and think it the best? To work again; and oh! may God be with me, for this earth is not friendly. On, in His name!

J. A. Froude, *Thomas Carlyle, A History of His Life*
in London, Vol. I

using

3.   Then, welcome each rebuff
                     That turns earth's smoothness rough
              Each sting that bids nor sit nor stand but go!
                     Be our joys three parts pain!
                     Strive, and hold cheap the strain;
              Learn, nor account the pang; dare, never grudge
                     the throe!

Browning, "Rabbi Ben Ezra"

without God

4.   *(The cashier in the city office lives in constant dread of unemployment. When at length it does come he has no inner resources to fall back on. The mood he expresses is characteristic of many who find themselves in like circumstances.)*

"You go on for years and years building up a position for yourself until at last you have a place of your own. Then in less than six months' time, without your having any hand or say in it [it is all suddenly taken away from you]. What was the good of trams going up and down the City Road? What was the good of having a City Road at all with shops opening and policemen keeping the traffic right? What was the good of paying taxes and going round to doctors and dentists and reading newspapers and voting, if this is what can happen any minute? My God!—what was the good of it all?"

J. B. Priestley, *Angel Pavement*

AMBITION   *see also* PRIDE
the cruelty of selfish

5.   *(Learning of King Duncan's approaching visit to Macbeth's castle, Lady Macbeth, fiercely ambitious for her husband, steels herself for her role in the murder of Duncan:)*

The raven himself is hoarse
That croaks the fatal entrance of Duncan
Under my battlements. Come, you spirits,
That tend on mortal thoughts, unsex me here,
And fill me from the crown to the toe top-full
Of direst cruelty! make thick my blood;
Stop up the access and passage to remorse,
That no compunctious visitings of nature
Shake my fell purpose, nor keep peace between
The effect and it! Come to my woman's breasts
And take my milk for gall, you murdering ministers,
Wherever in your sightless substances
You wait on nature's mischief! Come, thick night,
And pall thee in the dunnest smoke of hell,
That my keen knife see not the wound it makes;
Nor heaven peep through the blanket of the dark,
To cry, "Hold, Hold!"

Shakespeare, *Macbeth*, Act I, Sc. 5

the folly of worldly

6. Cromwell, I charge thee, fling away ambition:
    By that sin fell the angels; how can man then,
    The image of his Maker, hope to win by it?

                    ❋   ❋   ❋

                    Be just and fear not:
    Let all the ends thou aim'st at be thy country's,
    Thy God's, and truth's; then if thou fall'st, O Cromwell,
    Thou fall'st a blessed martyr!

                    ❋   ❋   ❋

                    O Cromwell, Cromwell!
    Had I but served my God with half the zeal
    I served my king, he would not in mine age
    Have left me naked to mine enemies.

Shakespeare, *King Henry VIII*,
Act III, Sc. 2 (Cardinal Wolsey)

the power of worldly

7. My friends, do you remember the old Scythian custom, when
the head of a house died? How he was dressed in his finest dress, and

set in his chariot, and carried about to his friends' house; and each of them placed him at his tables' head, and all feasted in his presence? Suppose it were offered to you in plain words, as it is offered to you in dire facts, that you should gain this Scythian honor, gradually, while you yet thought yourself alive. Suppose the offer were this: You shall die slowly; . . . but day by day your body shall be dressed more gaily, and set in higher chariots, and have more orders on its breast—crowns on its head, if you will. Men shall bow before it, stare and shout around it, crowd after it up and down the streets; build palaces for it, feast with it at their tables' heads all the night long; . . . Would you take the offer, verbally made by the death-angel? Would the meanest among us take it, think you? Yet practically and verily we grasp at it, every one of us, in a measure; many of us grasp at it in its fullness of horror. Every man accepts it who desires to advance in life without knowing what life is; who means only that he is to get more horses, and more footmen, and more fortune, and more public honor, and—*not* more personal soul. He only is advancing in life whose heart is getting softer, whose blood warmer, whose brain quicker, whose spirit is entering into living peace.

Ruskin, *Sesame and Lilies*

APATHY
the sin of

see also INDIFFERENCE

8. It is better to emit a scream in the shape of a theory than to be entirely insensible to the jars and incongruities of life and take everything as it comes in a forlorn stupidity. Some people swallow the universe like a pill; they travel on through the world like smiling images pushed from behind. For God's sake, give me the young man who can make a fool of himself! As for the others, the irony of facts shall take it out of their hands, and make fools of them in downright earnest, ere the farce be over. There shall be such a mopping and a mowing at the last day, and such blushing and confusion of countenance for all those who have been wise in their own esteem, and have not learnt the rough lessons that youth hands on to age. If we are indeed here to perfect and complete our own natures, and grow larger, stronger, more sympathetic against a nobler career

in the future, we had all best bestir ourselves to the utmost while
we have time. *To equip a dull, respectable person with wings would
make a parody of an angel.*

R. L. Stevenson, *Virginibus Puerisque,*
"Crabbed Youth and Age"

9.   Pitiful is the case of the blind, who cannot read the face;
pitiful that of the deaf, who cannot follow the changes of the voice.
And there are others also to be pitied; for there are some of an inert,
uneloquent nature, who have been denied all the symbols of communication, who have neither a lively play of facial expression, nor
speaking gestures, nor a responsive voice, nor yet the gift of frank
explanatory speech: people truly made of clay, people tied for life
into a bag which no one can undo. They are poorer than the gypsy,
for their heart can speak no language under heaven.

R. L. Stevenson, *Truth of Intercourse*

ASPIRATION
not in vain

10.   *(Abt Vogler, the inspired musician, extemporizing on his
instrument, regrets that the music cannot be recalled. But he con-
soles himself with the fact that it still persists; for it is an "echo of
the eternal life, a pledge of the continuance of whatever good has
existed.")*

All we have willed or hoped or dreamed of good shall exist;
Not its semblance, but itself; no beauty, nor good, nor power
Whose voice has gone forth, but each survives for the melodist
When eternity affirms the conception of an hour.
The high that proved too high, the heroic for earth too hard,
The passion that left the ground to lose itself in the sky,
Are music sent up to God by the lover and the bard;
Enough that he heard it once: we shall hear it by-and-by.

Browning, "Abt Vogler"

BACKSLIDING
consequences of

11.   The penalty of backsliding is not something unreal and vague,
some unknown quantity which may be measured out to us dispro-
portionately, or which, perchance, since God is good, we may

altogether evade. The consequences are already marked within the structure of the soul. So to speak, they are physiological. The thing effected by our indifference or by our indulgence is not the book of final judgment, but the present fabric of the soul.

Henry Drummond, *Natural Law in the Spiritual World*

THE BIBLE
in devotional life

12.   I have sometimes seen more in a line of the Bible than I could well tell how to stand under; and yet at another time the whole Bible hath been to me as dry as a stick; or rather my heart hath been so dead and dry unto it that I could not conceive the least dram of refreshment, though I have looked it all over.

Bunyan, *Grace Abounding*

influence of

13.   No greater moral change ever passed over a nation than passed over England during the years which parted the middle of the reign of Elizabeth from the Long Parliament. England became the people of a book, and that book was the Bible. It was read at churches and read at home, and everywhere its words, as they fell on ears which custom had not deadened, kindled a startling enthusiasm. As a mere literary monument, the English version of the Bible remains the noblest example of the English tongue. But far greater was the effect of the Bible on the character of the people. Elizabeth might silence or tune the pulpits, but it was impossible for her to silence or tune the great preachers of justice and mercy and truth who spoke from the book. The whole temper of the nation felt the change. A new conception of life and of man superseded the old. A new moral and religious impulse spread through every class.

John Richard Green, *A Short History of the English People*

man's responsiveness to

14.   I've noticed that in these villages where the people lead a quiet life among the green pastures and still waters, tilling the ground and tending the cattle, there's a strange deadness to the Word, as different as can be from the great towns, like Leeds, where

I once went to visit a holy woman who preaches there. It's wonderful how rich is the harvest of souls up those high-walled streets, where you seemed to walk as in a prison yard, and the ear is deafened with the sound of worldly toil. I think maybe it is because the promise is sweeter when this life is so dark and weary, and the soul gets more hungry when the body is ill at ease.

George Eliot, *Adam Bede*

the Word of God

15.   Within that awful volume lies
            The mystery of mysteries!
            Happiest they of human race
            To whom God has granted grace
            To read, to fear, to hope, to pray,
            To lift the latch, and force the way;
            And better had they not been born
            Who read to doubt or read to scorn.

Sir Walter Scott, written in his Bible

BLINDNESS   *see also* PREACHERS AND PREACHING—
spiritual   ministerial blindness, SIN

16.   I would, sir, prefer my blindness to yours; yours is a cloud spread over the mind, which darkens both the light of reason and of conscience. Mine keeps from my view only the colored surfaces of things, while it leaves me at liberty to contemplate the beauty and stability of virtue and of truth. . . . Let me then be the most feeble creature alive, as long as that feebleness serves to invigorate the energies of my rational and immortal spirit; as long as in that obscurity, in which I am enveloped, the light of the divine presence more clearly shines.

Milton, "Defensio Secunda pro Populo Anglicano"

CENSORIOUSNESS   *see also* CENSURE, TONGUE

17.   Miss Mann was a perfectly honest, conscientious woman, who had performed duties in her day from which many a one would have shrunk appalled. She had passed along through protracted scenes of suffering, exercised rigid self-denial, made large sacrifices

of time, money, health, for those who repaid her only by ingratitude; and now her main—almost her sole—fault was that she was censorious. Censorious she certainly was. . . . She dissected impartially almost all her acquaintances; she made few distinctions; she allowed scarcely any one to be good.

Charlotte Brontë, *Shirley*

CENSURE
great men victims of

see also TONGUE

18.   Censure, says a late ingenious author, is the tax a man pays to the public for being eminent. It is a folly for an eminent man to think of escaping it, and a weakness to be affected with it. All the illustrious persons of antiquity, and indeed of every age in the world have passed through this fiery persecution. There is no defense against reproach but obscurity; it is a kind of concomitant to greatness, as satires and invectives were an essential part of a Roman triumph.

Addison, *The Spectator*, No. 101

indiscriminate

19.   Then gently scan your brother man,
            Still gentler sister woman;
        Tho' they may gang a kennin' wrang,
            To step aside is human.
        One point must still be clearly dark,
            The moving *Why* they did it;
        And just as lamely can ye mark
            How far perhaps they rue it.

        Who made the heart, 'tis He alone
            Decidedly can try us;
        He knows each chord, its various tone,
            Each spring, its various bias.
        Then at the balance let's be mute,
            We never can adjust it;
        What's done we partly may compute,
            But know not what's resisted.

Burns, "Address to the Unco Guid" (the "rigidly righteous")

20. Nice distinctions are so troublesome. It is so much easier to say that a thing is black than to discriminate the particular shade of brown, blue, or green, to which it really belongs. It is so much easier to make up your mind that your neighbor is good for nothing than to enter into all the circumstances that would oblige you to modify that opinion.

George Eliot, *Amos Barton*

CHEERFULNESS   *see also* THANKSGIVING

21. Cheerfulness keeps up a kind of daylight in the mind, filling it with a steady and perpetual serenity. . . . An inward cheerfulness is an implicit praise and thanksgiving to Providence under *all* dispensations. It is a kind of acquiescence in the state wherein we are placed, and a secret approbation of the Divine Will in His conduct towards man.

Addison, *The Spectator*, No. 381

CHILDREN
education of

22. It is a pity that commonly more care is had, and that among very wise men, to find out a cunning man for their horse than a cunning man for their children. To the one they will gladly give a stipend of 200 crowns a year, yet loth to offer the other 200 shillings. God, that sitteth in heaven, laugheth their choice to scorn, and rewardeth them liberally accordingly; for He permitteth them to have tame and well-ordered horses but wild and undisciplined children.

Roger Ascham, *The Schoolmaster*

23. Thelwall thought it very unfair to influence a child's mind by inculcating any opinions before it had come to years of discretion to choose for itself. I showed him my garden, and told him it was a botanical garden. "How so?" said he; "it is covered with weeds." "Oh," I replied, "*that* is only because it has not yet come to its age of discretion and choice. The weeds, you see, have taken the liberty to grow, and I thought it unfair in me to prejudice the soil towards roses and strawberries."

Coleridge, *Table Talk*

24.   (*The writer speaks of his mother.*)

Her little folks were treasures given to her to guard and pro-
tect, not to mould into her own image. They had personalities of
their own, and inheritances of their own. They were individuals, not
appendages; and it was her duty, she thought, to enrich them by
teaching them how to use their own talents and faculties. Hers was
to provide an atmosphere for them to breathe, a purity for them to
feel, a liberty for them to employ. She seemed to say: "I am at
hand to hold and to help you *if necessary,* but I want you to develop
your own little selves so that when you are men and women you
will be persons of a free will and not creatures of circumstance."

J. Ramsay MacDonald, *Margaret Ethel MacDonald*

exploited by parents   *see also* SELF-CENTEREDNESS

25.   I have no patience with those fathers and mothers who make
of their children's sense of duty to them a daily scourge for the
backs of their children, and who deliberately forget and ignore the
fact that they have a duty to their children. Cannibals, I call them,
who live on the flesh and blood of their own offspring.

Stopford Brooke, *Diary*

CHOICE   *see also* INDECISION, PROCRASTINATION, WILL
determines destiny

26.   To every man there openeth
                     A Way, and Ways, and a Way,
                     And the High Soul climbs the High Way,
                     And the Low Soul gropes the Low,
                     And in between on the misty flats
                     The rest drift to and fro.
                     But to every man there openeth
                     A High Way and a Low,
                     And every man decideth
                     The Way his soul shall go.

John Oxenham, "The Ways"

life, a series of choices

27.   The saint is one who knows that every moment of our human
life is a moment of crisis; for at every moment we are called upon

to make an all-important decision—to choose between the way that leads to death and spiritual darkness and the way that leads to light and life; between interests exclusively temporal and the eternal order; between our personal will or the will of some projection of our personality, and the will of God.

         Aldous Huxley, *The Perennial Philosophy*

CHRIST
the Cross of

28.   "I have seen with a new clearness the meaning of those words, 'If any man love me, let him take up my cross.' I have heard this enlarged on as if it meant the troubles and persecutions we bring on ourselves by confessing Jesus. But surely this is a narrow thought. The true cross of the Redeemer was the sin and sorrow of the world—*that* was what lay heavy on his heart—and that is the cross we shall share with him; that is the cup we must drink with him, if we would have any part in that Divine Love which is one with his sorrow."

         George Eliot, *Adam Bede*
         (Dinah Morris, the Methodist preacher)

the love of   *see also* LOVE, GOD SEEKING MAN

29.   *(David, seeking with harp and song to restore King Saul from madness, reaches a climax when he prophesies of Christ's love: If David, a mere man, would give his life for the King, what of Christ's love for him?)*

     " 'Tis not what man Does which exalts him, but what man
             Would do!
See the King—I would help him but cannot, the Wishes fall through.
Could I wrestle to raise him from sorrow, grow poor to enrich,
To fill up his life, starve my own out, I would—knowing which,
I know that my service is perfect. Oh, speak through me now!
Would I suffer for him that I love? So wouldst thou—so wilt thou!
So shall crown thee the topmost, ineffablest, uttermost crown—
And thy love fill infinitude wholly, nor leave up nor down
One spot for the creature to stand in! . . .

               *   *   *

                         O Saul, it shall be

A Face like my face that receives thee; a Man like to me,
Thou shalt love and be loved by, forever: a Hand like this hand
Shall throw open the gates of new life to thee! See the Christ stand!"

Browning, "Saul"

the revolutionary

30. Longinus. He believed that he was God, they say.
Procula. What do you think of that claim?
Longinus. If a man believes anything up to the point of dying for it, he will find others to believe it.
Procula. Do you believe it?
Longinus. He was a fine young fellow, my lady, not past the middle age. And he was all alone and defied all the Jews and all the Romans, and when we had done with him, he was a poor broken-down thing, dead on the cross.
Procula. Do you think he is dead?
Longinus. No, lady, I don't.
Procula. Then where is he?
Longinus. Let loose in the world, lady, where neither Roman nor Jew can stop his truth.

John Masefield, "The Trial of Jesus"

31. The people who hanged Christ never accused Him of being a bore—on the contrary; they thought Him too dynamic to be safe. It has been left for later generations to mufflle up that shattering personality and surround Him with the atmosphere of tedium. We have very efficiently pared the claws of the Lion of Judah, certified Him "meek and mild," and recommended Him as a fitting household pet for pale curates and pious old ladies. To those who knew Him, however, He in no way suggested a milk-and-water person; *they* objected to Him as a dangerous firebrand. True, He was tender to the unfortunate, patient with honest inquirers and humble before Heaven; but He insulted respectable clergymen by calling them hypocrites; He referred to King Herod as "that fox"; He went to parties in disreputable company and was looked upon as a "gluttonous man and a winebibber, a friend of publicans and sinners"; He insulted indignant tradesmen and threw them and their belongings out of the Temple; . . . He showed no proper deference for wealth or social position; when confronted with neat

dialectical traps, He displayed a paradoxical humor that affronted serious-minded people, and He retorted by asking disagreeable questions that could not be answered by rule of thumb. . . . But He had "a daily beauty in his life that made us ugly," and official-dom felt that the established order of things would be more secure without Him. So they did away with God in the name of peace and quietness.

> Dorothy Sayers, *The Greatest Drama Ever Staged*

salvation in

32.　*(The allusion is to Samuel Johnson.)*

He talked often to me about the necessity of faith in the *sacrifice* of Jesus, as necessary, beyond all good works whatever, for the salvation of mankind.

He pressed me to study Dr. Clarke and to read his sermons. I asked him why he pressed Dr. Clarke, an Arian. "Because," said he, "he is fullest on the *propitiatory sacrifice*."

> Boswell, *Life of Johnson*

33.　　I remember that one day as I was musing on the wickedness and blasphemy of my heart, and considering the enmity that was in me to God, that the Scripture came into my mind, "He hath made peace through the blood of his cross"—by which I was made to see again and again that God and my soul were friends by his blood—yea, I saw that the justice of God and my sinful soul could embrace and kiss each other through his blood. This was a good day to me; I hope I shall never forget it.

> Bunyan, *Grace Abounding*

the Second Coming of

34.　　Ah! what time wilt Thou come? when shall that crie
　　　'The Bridegroome's coming!' fill the skie?
　　　Shall it in the evening run
　　　When our words and works are done?
　　　Or will Thy all-surprising light
　　　Break at midnight . . . ?
　　　　　　*　　*　　*
　　　Or shall these early, fragrant hours
　　　Unlock Thy bowers?
　　　　　　*　　*　　*

Let my course, my aim, my love,
And chief acquaintance be above;
So when that day and hour shall come,
In which Thyself shall be the sun,
Thou'lt find me drest and on my way,
Watching the break of Thy great day.

Henry Vaughan, "The Dawning"

our sufficiency

35.   He is a path, if any be misled;
He is a robe, if any naked be;
If any chance to hunger, He is bread;
If any be a bondman, He is free;
If any be but weak, how strong is He!
To dead men, life is He; to sick men, health;
To blind men, sight; and to the needy, wealth;
A pleasure without loss; a treasure without stealth.

Giles Fletcher, "Christ's Victory and Triumph"

36.   Christ, as a light,
Illumine and guide me!
Christ, as a shield, o'ershadow and cover me!
Christ, be under me! Christ, be over me!
    Christ, be beside me
    On left hand and right!
Christ, be before me, behind me, about me!
Christ, this day be within and without me!

"St. Patrick's Hymn Before Tara"
(from the Irish), translated by C. F. Alexander

CHRISTIAN LIFE   *see also* CHRISTIANS, LOVE, SERVICE,
"kept by the power of God"   SOCIAL CONCERN

37.   If I forget,
Yet God remembers! If these hands of mine
Cease from their clinging, yet the hands divine
Hold me so firmly that I cannot fall;
And if sometimes I am too tired to call
For him to help me, then he reads the prayer
Unspoken in my heart, and lifts my care.

I dare not fear, since certainly I know
That I am in God's keeping, shielded so
From all that else would harm, and in the hour
Of stern temptation strengthened by his power;
I tread no path in life to him unknown;
I lift no burden, bear no pain, alone;
My soul a calm, sure hiding-place has found:
The everlasting arms my life surround.

God, thou art love! I build my faith on that.
I know thee who hast kept my path, and made
Light for me in the darkness, tempering sorrow
So that it reached me like a solemn joy
It were too strange that I should doubt thy love.

Browning, "Paracelsus"

motive in the

38.   Far above all other motives was his love to Christ. That
was the root of his life, and the life of all his effort. It was a
conscious, personal, realized devotion. It was too hallowed a feeling
for him to speak much of. It colored and pervaded every thought;
was an unceasing presence with him; lay at the foundation of every
endeavor, and was brought to bear on every action in life, on
every book he read, and almost on every word he spoke.

Stopford A. Brooke, *Life and Letters of F. W. Robertson*

nature of the

39.   Religion is not ours till we live by it, till it is the religion
of our thoughts, words, and actions, till it goes with us into every
place, sits uppermost on every occasion, and forms and governs
our hopes and fears, our cares and pleasures. He is the religious
man who watches and guards his spirit, and endeavors to be always
in the temper of religion; who is as fearful of foolish thoughts,
irregular tempers, and vain imaginations at one time as another;
who is wise and heavenly at home or in the field as in the house of
God. For when once religion has got possession of man's heart,
and is become his ruling temper, it is agreeable to such a one in all

places and at all times to speak and act according to its direc-
tions.

William Law, *Serious Call*

one way of resolving problems of faith

40. In the midst of our difficulties I have one ground of hope,
just one stay, but as I think, a sufficient one. It serves me in the
stead of all arguments whatever; it hardens me against criticism;
it supports me if I begin to despond; and to it I ever come round.
It is the decision of the Holy See; Saint Peter has spoken.

John Henry Newman

a perversion of the

41. About half-way between our village and the town there lay a
comfortable villa inhabited by a retired solicitor, whom I shall
call Mr. Dormant. We often called at his half-way house, and
although he was a member of the town-meeting, he not infrequently came to us for "the breaking of bread." He was extremely
fluent and zealous in using the pious phraseology of the sect. . . .
Mr. Dormant was not very well off, and had persuaded an aged
gentleman of wealth to come and board with them. When in the
course of the winter the gentleman died, much surprise was felt·
at the report that he had left almost his entire fortune to Mr.
Dormant.

Much surprise—for the old gentleman had a son to whom he had
always been warmly attached, who was far away, I think in South
America. . . . Now Mr. Dormant came into his fortune, and began
to make handsome gifts to missionary societies and to his own
meeting in the town. . . . But in process of time we heard that the
son had come back from the Antipodes, and was making investiga-
tions. Before we knew where we were, the news burst upon us
like a bombshell that Mr. Dormant had been arrested on a criminal
charge and was now in gaol at Exeter.

Sympathy was at first much extended amongst us to the prisoner.
But it was soon lessened when we understood that the old gentleman had been "converted" while under Dormant's roof, and had
been given the fact that his son was an "unbeliever" as a reason
for disinheriting him. All doubt was set aside when it was divulged,

under pressure, by the nurse who attended on the old gentleman,
herself one of the "saints," that Dormant had traced the signature
to the will by drawing the fingers of the testator over the document
when he was already and finally comatose.

Dormant could be induced to exhibit no species of remorse; and,
to the obvious anger of the judge himself, stated that he had only
done his duty as a Christian, in preventing this wealth from coming
into the hands of an ungodly man, who would have spent it in the
service of the flesh and of the devil.

Edmund Gosse, *Father and Son*

a series of resurrections

42.   The whole history of the Christian life is a series of resurrec-
tions. Every time a man bethinks himself that he is not walking in
the light, that he has been forgetting himself, and must repent;
that he has been asleep and must awake; that he has been letting
his garments trail, and must gird up the loins of his mind; every
time this takes place there is a resurrection in the world. Yes, every
time a man finds that his heart is troubled, that he is not rejoicing
in God, a resurrection must follow; a resurrection out of the night
of troubled thought into the gladness of truth. For the truth is,
and ever was, and ever must be, gladness, however much the souls
on which it shines may be obscured by the clouds of sorrow,
troubled by fears, or shot through with the lightnings of pain.

George MacDonald,
Selection from the Writings of, ed. by E. Dewey

shallowness in the

43.   A shallow religiousness, the tendency to be content with a
bright ethical piety wrongly called practical Christianity, a nice
brightly-varnished this-world faith, seems to me to be one of the
defects of institutional religion at the present time. We are drifting
towards a religion which consciously or unconsciously lays all the
stress on service, and hardly any of the stress on awe; and that is
a type of religion which in practice does not wear well. It does little
for the soul in those awful moments when the pain and mystery
of life are most deeply felt. It does not provide a place for that

profound experience which Tauler called "Suffering in God." It does not lead to sanctity; and sanctity after all, is the religious goal.

Evelyn Underhill, *Concerning the Inner Life*

spiritual fluctuations of the

44.   I have wondered much at this one thing that though God doth visit my soul with never so blessed a discovery of Himself, yet I have found again that such hours have attended me afterwards that I have been in my spirit so filled with darkness that I could not so much as once conceive what that God and that comfort was with which I have been refreshed.

Bunyan, *Grace Abounding*

CHRISTIANS   *see also* CHRISTIAN LIFE, DISSENSION, INDIF-
fair-weather   FERENCE

45.   Sunday, 21 November. I got up well and enjoyed my good situation. I had a handsome dining room and bed-chamber, just in Pall Mall, the finest part of town; I was in pursuit of my commission, which I was vastly fond of; and I had money enough to live like a gentleman.

I went to Mayfair Chapel and heard prayers and an excellent sermon from the book of Job on the comforts of piety. I was in fine frame. And I thought that God really designed us to be happy. I shall certainly be a religious man. I was so much so in youth. I have now and then flashes of devotion, and it will one day burn into a steady flame.

Boswell's London Journal, 1762-1763

46.   (*Christian and Hopeful overtake Mr. By-ends, who describes the people of the town of Fair-speech, from whence he comes:*)
"Tis true, we somewhat differ in religion from those of the stricter sort, yet but in two small points: first, we never strive against wind and tide; secondly, we are always most zealous when Religion goes in his silver slippers; we love much to walk with him in the street if the sun shines and the people applaud him."

To which Christian replies, "If you will go with us you must go against wind and tide; you must also own your Religion in his rags as well as when in his silver slippers; and stand by him, too, when bound in irons as well as when he walketh the streets with applause."

Then By-ends makes his decision. "I shall never desert my old principles, since they are harmless and profitable." So Christian and Hopeful part company with him, and he is joined by three other companions whose names are Mr. Hold-the-World, Mr. Money-Love, and Mr. Save-All.

Bunyan, Pilgrim's Progress (adapted)

lukewarm

47.   And we,
   Light half-believers of our casual creeds,
     Who never deeply felt, nor clearly willed,
  Whose insight never has borne fruit in deeds,
     Whose vague resolves never have been fulfilled;
       For whom each year we see
  Breeds new beginnings, disappointments new;
     Who hesitate and falter life away,
     And lose tomorrow the ground won today.

Matthew Arnold, "The Scholar Gypsy"

"respectable"

48.   They had all done so well for themselves, these Forsytes, that they were all what is called "of a certain position." Originally, perhaps, members of some primitive sect, they were now in the natural course of things members of the Church of England, and caused their wives and their children to attend with some regularity the more fashionable churches of the Metropolis. To have doubted their Christianity would have caused them both pain and surprise. Some of them paid for pews, thus expressing in the most practical form their sympathy with the teachings of Christ.

John Galsworthy, The Man of Property

superficial

49.   Religious doctrines had taken no hold on Hetty's mind; she was one of those numerous people who have had godfathers and godmothers, learned their catechism, been confirmed, and gone to

church every Sunday and yet, for any practical result of strength in life or trust in death, have never appropriated a single Christian idea or Christian feeling.

George Eliot, *Adam Bede*

50.   There is a religion which is too superficial to reach the heart. It is rather slight than false. It has discernment enough to distinguish sin, but not firmness enough to oppose it; compunction sufficient to soften the heart, but not vigor sufficient to reform it. It laments when it does wrong, and performs all the functions of repentance of sin except forsaking it. It has everything of devotion except the stability, and gives everything to religion except the heart. This is a religion of times, events, and circumstances; it is brought into play by accidents, and dwindles away with the occasion which called it out.

Hannah More, *Practical Piety*

worldly-minded   *see also* WORLDLINESS IN RELIGION

51.   "A good sermon of Mr. Gifford's at our church upon 'Seek ye first the kingdom of heaven.' A very excellent and persuasive, good and moral sermon. He showed, like a wise man, that righteousness is a surer moral way of being rich than sin or villainy." [Thus Stevenson quotes Samuel Pepys, and he adds:]

It is thus that respectable people desire to have their Greathearts address them, telling, in mild accents, how you may make the best of both worlds, and be a moral hero without courage, kindness, or troublesome reflection; and thus the Gospel becomes a manual of worldly prudence, and a handy-book for Pepys and the successful merchant.

R. L. Stevenson, *Familiar Studies of Men and Books*

THE CHURCH
and its contribution to society

52.   Surely no achievements of the Christian Church are more truly great than those which it has effected in the sphere of charity. For the first time in the history of mankind it has inspired many thousands of men and women, at the sacrifice of all worldly interests, and often under circumstances of extreme discomfort or danger, to devote their entire lives to the single object of assuaging

the sufferings of humanity. It has covered the globe with countless institutions of mercy, absolutely unknown to the whole pagan world. It has indissolubly united in the minds of men the idea of supreme goodness with that of active and constant benevolence.

W. E. H. Lecky, *History of European Morals*

not a place of relaxation

53.   "Well, Master Jackson," said the minister, walking home after service with an industrious laborer, who was a constant attendant, "well, Master Jackson, Sunday must be a blessed day of rest for you, who work so hard all week! And you make good use of the day, for you are always to be seen at church." "Aye, sir," replied Jackson, "it is indeed a blessed day; I works hard enough all week; and then I comes to church o' Sundays, and sets me down and thinks o' nothing."

Robert Southey, *The Doctor*

COMFORT
in modern life

54.   Comfort is a thing of recent growth, younger than steam, a child when telegraphy was born, only a generation older than radio. The invention of the means of being comfortable and the pursuit of comfort as a desirable end are modern phenomena, unparalleled in history since the time of the Romans. Like all phenomena with which we are extremely familiar, we take them for granted, as a fish takes the water in which it lives, not realizing the oddity and novelty of them, not bothering to consider their significance. The padded chair, the well-sprung bed, the sofa, central heating, and the regular hot bath—these and a host of other comforts enter into the daily lives of even the most moderately prosperous of the Anglo-Saxon bourgeoisie. Three hundred years ago they were unknown to the greatest kings.

Aldous Huxley, *Proper Studies*

CONFESSION   *see also* REMORSE, REPENTANCE
a long-delayed

55.   "Everything comes to light, Nancy, sooner or later. When God Almighty wills it our secrets are found out. I've lived with a secret on my mind, but I'll keep it from you no longer. I wouldn't have you know it by somebody else, and not by me—I wouldn't have

you find it out after I'm dead. I'll tell you now. It's been 'I will'
and 'I won't' with me all my life—I'll make sure of myself now."

George Eliot, *Silas Marner* (Godfrey Cass)

the therapeutic value of

56.   *(Lucy, a Protestant English governess in Belgium, is ill and
lonely. Hearing bells, she makes her way to an old church where
for some reason the urge to make confession suddenly grips her.
Slowly she moves toward the confessional.)*

The priest within the confessional never turned his eye to regard
me; he only quietly inclined his ear. He might be a good man, but
this duty had become a sort of form; he went through it with a
phlegm of custom. I hesitated; of the formula of confession I was
ignorant; instead of commencing with the usual prelude, I said,
"Mon père, Je suis Protestante." He inquired, not unkindly, why,
being a Protestant, I came to him. I told him I was perishing for a
word of advice and comfort. I had been living alone for weeks, had
been ill, and had a pressure of affliction on my mind. "Was it a
sin, a crime?" he asked startled. I assured him on that point, and
gave him an outline of my experience. He looked surprised and
puzzled, and said, "You take me unawares. I have not had such a
case as yours. Ordinarily we know our routine. On no account would
I lose sight of you. Go, my daughter, for the present, but return
again to me." Of course, I had not expected more. But the mere
relief of communication in an ear which was human and sentient,
yet consecrated, had done me good. I was already solaced, and I
returned to him no more.

Charlotte Brontë, *Villette*

CONSCIENCE   *see also* CONVICTION, REMORSE
afraid of

57.   The most frequent impediment to men's turning the mind
inward upon themselves is that they are afraid of what they shall
find there. There is an aching hollowness in the bosom, a dark cold
speck at the heart, an obscure and boding sense of something that
must be kept *out of sight* of the conscience; some secret lodger,
whom they can neither resolve to reject nor retain.

Coleridge, *Aids to Reflection*

in dying men

58. It chills the blood to hear the dearest secrets of the heart—the pent-up, hidden secrets of many years—poured forth by the unconscious, helpless being before you. Strange tales have been told in the wanderings of dying men; tales so full of guilt and crime that those who stood by the sick person's couch have fled in horror and affright, lest they should be scared to madness by what they heard and saw; and many a wretch has died alone, raving of deeds the very name of which has driven the boldest man away.

Dickens, *Sketches by Boz*

the flexibility of

59. Conscience is an elastic and flexible article, which will bear a great deal of stretching and adapt itself to a great variety of circumstances. Some people by prudent management and leaving it off piece by piece, like a flannel waistcoat in warm weather, even contrive, in time, to dispense with it altogether; but there be others who can assume the garment and throw it off at pleasure; and this, being the greatest and most convenient improvement, is the one most in vogue.

Dickens, *The Old Curiosity Shop*

the impact of

60. *(When the slayer is rebuked for not keeping his foul deed secret, he cries:)*

"My secret! Mine! It was a secret any breath of air could whisper at will! The stars had it in their twinkling, the water in its flowing, the leaves in their rustling, the seasons in their return! It lurked in strangers' faces, and their voices! Everything had lips on which it trembled.—My secret!"

Dickens, *Barnaby Rudge*

61. Nowhere in our literature is the power of conscience more superbly pictured than in Shakespeare. Think for instance of Macbeth immediately after the murder of Duncan. He hears the watchmen asking God to bless them, and he cannot say Amen. It is one of the profoundest touches in the drama, that Macbeth awakes to the consciousness of guilt through the discovery that he cannot say Amen. He feels that to say it would be a mockery, and he feels so because he is a murderer. Had he been saving Duncan's life instead of taking it, the word would never have stuck fast in his throat. It is Shakespeare teaching us through conscience that even villainy is conscious that God is on the side of what is good.

G. H. Morrison, *Christ in Shakespeare*

62. *(As they are about to murder the sleeping Duke of Clarence the second murderer is troubled by conscience.)*

Second murderer: A man cannot steal but it accuseth him: he cannot swear but it checks him: 'tis a blushing, shame-faced spirit that mutinies in a man's bosom; it fills one full of obstacles; it once made me restore a purse of gold that I found: it beggars any man that keeps it; it is turned out of all towns and cities for a dangerous thing.

First murderer: Zounds! It is even now at my elbow.

Shakespeare, *King Richard III*, Act I, Sc. 4

63. *(On the night before the Battle of Bosworth Field—where he is to meet his Nemesis—the evil Richard is awakened in his sleep, startled by a dream that has stirred the conscience. Guilty of the most brutal crimes, including the murder of the young princes in the Tower, the wretched king for the first time experiences the anguish of a revolted conscience.)*

O coward conscience, how thou dost afflict me!
The light burns blue. It is now dead midnight.
Cold, fearful drops stand on my trembling flesh.

＊　＊　＊

My conscience hath a thousand several tongues,
And every tongue brings in a several tale,
And every tale condemns me.

＊　＊　＊

All several sins . . .
Throng to the bar crying all Guilty! Guilty!

Shakespeare, *King Richard III*, Act V, Sc. 3

64.
I sat alone with my conscience
In a place where time had ceased,
And I thought of my former living
In the land where the years increased.

The ghost of forgotten actions
   Came floating before my sight,
And things that I thought were dead things
   Were alive with a terrible might.

And I know of the future judgment,
   How dreadful so e'er it be,
To sit alone with my conscience
   Will be judgment enough for me.
                William Stubbs, "Castles in the Air"

nature evokes

65.   One summer evening, I found
A little boat tied to a willow tree
Within a rocky cove, its usual home.
Straight I unloosed her chain, and stepping in
Pushed from the shore. It was an act of stealth
And troubled pleasure, nor without the voice
Of mountain-echoes did my boat move on;
             ❋   ❋   ❋
I dipped my oars into the silent lake,
And, as I rose upon the stroke, my boat
Went heaving through the water like a swan;
When, from behind a craggy steep till then
The horizon's bound, a huge peak, black and huge,
As if with voluntary power instinct,
Upreared its head. I struck and struck again,
And growing still in stature the grim shape
Towered up between me and the stars, and still,
For so it seemed, with purpose of its own
And measured motion like a living thing,
Strode after me. With trembling oars I turned,
And through the silent water stole my way
Back to the covert of the willow tree;
There in her mooring-place I left my bark,—
And through the meadow homeward went, in grave
And serious mood; but after I had seen
That spectacle, for many days . . . o'er my thoughts

There hung a darkness, call it solitude
Or blank desertion.

Wordsworth, *The Prelude*, Bk. I

no human remedy for a guilty

66. *(From her part in the murder of Duncan, Lady Macbeth is sick in mind. Following her sleepwalking scene Macbeth entreats the waiting physician:)*

Canst thou not minister to a mind diseased,
Pluck from the memory a rooted sorrow,
Raze out the written troubles of the brain
And with some sweet oblivious antidote
Cleanse the stuff'd bosom of that perilous stuff
Which weighs upon the heart?

Shakespeare, *Macbeth*, Act V, Sc. 3

the strength of a good

67. What stronger breastplate than a heart untainted!
Thrice is he armed that hath his quarrel just;
And he but naked, though locked up in steel,
Whose conscience with injustice is corrupted.

Shakespeare, *King Henry VI*, Part 2, Act III, Sc. 2

trifling with

68. "I don't remember ever being see-saw when I'd made up my mind that a thing was wrong. It takes the taste out of my mouth for things, when I know I should have a heavy conscience after 'em. I've seen pretty clear . . . as you can never do what's wrong without breeding sin and trouble more than you can ever see. It's like a bit o' bad workmanship—you never see the end o' the mischief it'll do. And it's a poor look-out to come into the world to make your fellow-creatures worse off instead o' better."

George Eliot, *Adam Bede* (Adam)

CONTENTMENT   *see also* HAPPINESS, REST
and great men

69. Great men, with hardly an exception, nauseate their greatness for not being of the particular sort they most fancy. The poet

Gray was passionately fond of military history; but he took no Quebec. General Wolfe took Quebec, and whilst he was taking it, recorded the fact that he would sooner have written Gray's "Elegy"; and so Carlyle—who panted for action, who hated eloquence, whose heroes were Cromwell and Wellington; who beheld with pride and no ignoble envy the bridge at Auldgarth his mason-father had helped to build half a century before, and then exclaimed, "A noble craft, that of a mason; a good building will last longer than most books—than one book in a million"; who despised men of letters and abhorred the "reading public"; whose gospel was Silence and Action—spent his life in talking and writing; and his legacy to the world is thirty-four volumes octavo.

Augustine Birrell, Obiter Dicta

a lesson in

70.　Jupiter made a proclamation that all mortals should bring their griefs and woes on a certain day, and throw them in a heap on a certain great plain. The human family marched in a line, each person casting his peculiar burden on the mounting pile. One poor soul from under her cloak threw a bundle named poverty. Another dragged along a heavy burden which when opened turned out to be his wife. Old women cast in their wrinkles. Others threw in their gray hair, bad teeth, and bald heads. Oddly enough, no one thought it fit to throw away a vice, a frailty, or a passion. It was always some affliction or remorse.

A second edict of the god announced that there should be an exchange, since everyone must carry some burden. At this, the hurry and excitement became intense. Some who had brought sickness went away with poverty. Some who had carried hunger went away with thirst. One lady exchanged a birthmark for a bad reputation. Another lady who came with a lock of gray hair took home the asthma. The whole plain was filled with murmurings and discontent. All agreed on one thing: the new affliction was worse than the old. "I learned a lesson," says the essayist, "that our Heavenly Father knows best, and assigns to each soul the sphere for which it is best fitted, and the burden it can most patiently bear."

Addison, The Spectator, No. 558

71. Theocrite was a poor Italian boy who worked diligently at his chores in the monastery, and who never failed—morning, noon and night—to sing God's praises. Yet he was unhappy. If only he could serve God as Pope! Then he could sing God's praises grandly! How the lad longed to change his status in life. So much did he pine after the papal throne that God eventually granted Theocrite his wish. Gabriel the archangel came to earth to care for the monastic chores, and Theocrite sat on the throne. But in his new role the boy was more miserable than ever. God, too, was sad because he missed the little human praise that came regularly from the monastery. "The silence of that one weak voice had stopped the chorus of creation." Angelic song could not replace human praise. And so it was that the unhappy Theocrite was more than glad to return to the monastery and resume his chores and his humble songs of praise to God.

Browning, "The Boy and the Angel" (adapted)

72. There was a Pig that sat alone
Beside a ruined Pump:
By day and night he made his moan—
It would have stirred a heart of stone
To see him wring his hoofs and groan,
Because he could not jump.

There was a Frog that wandered by—
A sleek and shining lump:
Inspected him with fishy eye,
And said, "O Pig, what makes you cry?"
And bitter was that Pig's reply,
"Because I cannot jump!"

That Frog he grinned a grin of glee,
And hit his chest a thump:
"O Pig," he said, "be ruled by me,
And you shall see what you shall see.
This minute, for a trifling fee,
I'll teach you how to jump!

"My fee shall be a mutton chop
My goal this ruined Pump:
Observe with what an airy flop
I plant myself upon the top!
Now bend your knees and take a hop,
For that's the way to jump!"

Uprose that Pig, and rushed full whack
Against the ruined Pump:
Rolled over like an empty sack
And settled down upon his back,
While all his bones at once went "Crack!"
—It was a fatal jump.

Lewis Carroll, "The Pig-Tale"

a questionable

73.   I am not content to pass away "like a weaver's shuttle." These
metaphors solace me not, nor sweeten the unpalatable draught of
mortality. I care not to be carried with the tide that smoothly bears
human life to eternity. I am in love with this green earth: the face
of town and country, the unspeakable rural solitudes, and the sweet
security of streets. I would set up my tabernacle here. I am content
to stand still at the age to which I am arrived; I, and my friends;
to be no younger, no richer, no handsomer. I do not want to drop,
like mellow fruit into the grave.

Charles Lamb, Essays of Elia, "New Year's Eve"

CONVERSION   see also GOD SEEKING MAN

74.   (Saul Kane, the one-time pugilist, finds his whole outlook
changed at the time of his conversion.)
O glory of the lighted mind,
How dead I'd been, how dumb, how blind.
The station brook, to my new eyes,
Was babbling out of Paradise;
The waters rushing from the rain
Were singing Christ has risen again.
I thought all earthly creatures knelt
From rapture of the joy I felt.

John Masefield, "The Everlasting Mercy"

CONVERTS
the Church's assimilation of

75.   The ignorant enthusiast whom the Anglican Church makes
an enemy the Catholic Church makes a champion. She bids him
nurse his beard, covers him with a gown and hood of coarse dark
stuff, ties a rope around his waist, and sends him forth to teach in
her name. . . . All his influence is used to strengthen the Church
of which he is a minister. To that Church he becomes as strongly
attached as any of the cardinals whose scarlet carriages and liveries
crowd the entrance of the palace of the Pope. In this way the
Church of Rome unites in herself all the strength of establishment
and all the strength of dissent.

Macaulay, *Ranke's History of the Popes*

CONVICTION
of sin
see also CONSCIENCE, REMORSE, SIN

76.   I walked to a neighboring town, and sat down upon a settle
in the street, and fell into a very deep pause about the most fearful
state my sin had brought me to; and, after long musing, I lifted
my head; but methought I saw as if the sun that shineth in the
heavens did grudge to give me light; as if the very stones in the
street, and tiles upon the houses, did band themselves against me.
Methought that they all combined together to banish me out of
the world. I was abhorred of them, and unfit to dwell among them,
because I had sinned against the Saviour.

Bunyan, *Grace Abounding*

77.   The scene is Glamis Castle, Macbeth's fortress in Scotland.
Without, the air is sweet and wholesome; within, the stillness is
intense and oppressive. Macbeth has just murdered his guest, the
sleeping King Duncan. Immediately following the work of exter-
mination there is heard a loud knocking at the gate. The sensation
it produces is weird and unearthly. It all depends upon reaction.
In the breast of the murderer rages the tempest, in the castle
reigns the quietness of the deep. De Quincey makes this "loud
knocking at the gate" the subject of one of his most famous essays.
He sees two worlds represented in a clash: Duncan's world of
everyday happenings has suddenly been arrested by Macbeth's

world of fiendishness and passion. When the world of darkness
vanishes, the poet makes us sensible of the return of the ordinary
by a reaction—the knocking! It signifies the return of life to
normalcy. It acts like a dash of cold water on the face of a man
in a swoon. Cannon Farrar calls the scene literature's classic illustration of conviction of sin.

Shakespeare, *Macbeth,* Act II (adapted)

78.   Come down, O Christ, and help me! reach Thy hand,
For I am drowning in a stormier sea
Than Simon on the lake of Galilee:
The wine of life is spilt upon the sand,
My heart is as some famine-murdered land
Whence all good things have perished utterly,
And well I know my soul in hell must lie
If I this night before God's throne should stand.

Oscar Wilde, "E Tenebris"

CONVICTIONS   *see also* Preachers and Preaching—cour-
courage of   age in

79.   Luther's appearance before the Diet of Worms, on the 17th
of April, 1521, may be considered the greatest scene in modern
European history, the point indeed, from which the whole subse-
quent history of civilization takes its rise. The world's pomp and
power sits there on this hand: on that stands up for God's truth
one man, the son of the poor miner, Hans Luther. It is the greatest
moment in modern history. English Puritanism, England and its
parliaments, the Americas, the French Revolution, Europe and its
work everywhere at present—the germ of it all lay there; had
Luther in that moment done other, it had all been otherwise.

Carlyle, *Heroes and Hero-Worship*

essential to happiness

80.   "Do you seriously believe that happiness can be obtained by
ignoring one's convictions?"
"But what if you have no convictions?"
"Then you are incapable of happiness in any worthy sense! You
may graze but you will never feast!"

George Gissing, *Born to Exile*

a man without

81.
> I am a man apart:
> A mouthpiece for the creeds of all the world;
> A soulless life that angels may possess
> Or demons haunt, wherein the foulest things
> May loll at ease among the loveliest;
> A martyr for all mundane moods to tear;
> The slave of every passion; and the slave
> Of heat and cold, of darkness and of light;
> A trembling lyre for every wind to sound.
>
> John Davidson, "A Ballad in Blank Verse"

COURAGE   *see also* COWARDICE, PREACHERS AND PREACHING
indomitable   —courage in, SUFFERING—courage in

82.   We shall go on to the end, we shall fight in France, we shall fight on the seas and oceans, we shall fight in the air, we shall defend our Island, whatever the cost may be, we shall fight on the beaches, we shall fight on the landing grounds, we shall fight in the fields and in the streets, we shall fight in the hills; we shall never surrender. . . .

Winston S. Churchill, *Blood, Sweat, and Tears*

the loneliness of

83.   I thought France would have friends at the court of the king of France; and I find only wolves fighting for pieces of her poor torn body. I thought God would have friends everywhere, because He is the friend of everyone; and in my innocence I believed that you who now cast me out would be like strong towers to keep harm from me. But I am wiser now. . . . Do not think you can frighten me by telling me that I am alone. France is alone; and God is alone; and what is my loneliness before the loneliness of my country and my God? I see now that the loneliness of God is His strength. Well, my loneliness shall be my strength too: it is better to be alone with God: His friendship will not fail me. . . . In His strength I will dare, and dare, and dare, until I die.

G. B. Shaw, *Saint Joan* (Joan of Arc)

to stand alone

84.   Can numbers then change nature's stated laws?
           Can numbers make the worse the better cause?
           Vice must be vice, virtue be virtue still,
           Though thousands rail at good and practise ill.
                              *   *   *

           Unawed by numbers, follow Nature's plan;
           Assert the rights, or quit the name of man.
           Consider well, weigh strictly right and wrong;
           Resolve not quick, but once resolved, be strong.
                              *   *   *

           Rather stand up, assured with conscious pride,
           Alone, than err with millions on thy side.
                                        Charles Churchill, "Night"

COWARDICE   *see also* COURAGE, ESCAPISM
moral

85.   *(The Countess of Derby gains audience with Charles II. She
seeks protection for the persecuted Catholics. But the King fears
to show them any favor:)*
       "There is no steering the vessel in the face of the tempest; we
must run for the nearest haven, and happy if we reach one," said he.
       "This is cowardice, my liege," said the Countess. "There is but
one right and one wrong, one honorable and forward course; all
others are deviate and unworthy."
                                        Scott, *Peveril of the Peak*

86.   There was some juggling among the officials to avoid taxation; and Pepys, with a noble impulse, growing ashamed of this
dishonesty, designed to charge himself with 1000 pounds; but finding none to set him an example, "nobody of our ablest merchants"
with their moderate liking for clean hands, he judged it "not
decent"; he feared it would "be thought vain glory"; and, rather
than appear singular, cheerfully remained a thief. One able merchant's countenance, and Pepys had dared to do an honest act!
Had he found one brave spirit, properly recognized by society, he
might have gone far as a disciple.
                       R. L. Stevenson, *Familiar Studies of Men and Books*

COWARDS

87.   How many cowards, whose hearts are all as false
As stairs of sand, wear yet upon their chins
The beards of Hercules and frowning Mars;
Who, inward searched, have livers white as milk.

Shakespeare, *The Merchant of Venice,*
Act III, Sc. 2 (Bassanio)

CRUELTY
of silence

88.   The worst thing you can do to an author is to be silent as to his works. An assault upon a town is a bad thing, but starving it is still worse; an assault may be unsuccessful, you may have more men killed than you kill, but if you starve the town you are sure of victory.

Boswell, *Life of Johnson* (Dr. Johnson)

DEATH
"Any man's death diminishes me."

89.   *(It was formerly the custom in England to toll the bell of the parish church at someone's death, on which occasion general inquiry would be made to find out who had just passed away. The Dean of St. Paul's has this custom in mind when he says:)*

No man is an island entire of itself; every man is a piece of a continent, a part of the main. If a clod be washed away by the sea, Europe is the less. . . . Any man's death diminishes me, because I am involved in mankind; and therefore never send to know for whom the bell tolls; it tolls for thee!

John Donne, *Devotions upon Emergent Occasions*

of birds

90.   The bird, however hard the frost may be, flies briskly to his customary roosting place, and, with beak tucked into his wing, falls asleep. He has no apprehensions; only the hot blood grows colder and colder, the pulse feebler as he sleeps, and at midnight, or in the early morning, he drops from his perch—dead.

Yesterday he lived and moved, responsive to a thousand external influences, reflecting earth and sky in his small brilliant brain as in a looking-glass; also he had a various language, the inherited knowledge of his race, and the faculty of flight, by means of which he could shoot, meteor-like, across the sky, and pass swiftly from place to place; and with it such perfect control over all his organs, such marvellous certitude in all his motions, . . . Now, on this morning, he lies stiff and motionless; if you were to take him up and drop him from your hand he would fall to the ground like a stone or a lump of clay—so easy and swift is the passage from life to death in wild nature! But he was never miserable.

W. H. Hudson, *The Best of,* ed. by Odell Shepard

a blow to man's pride

91.   *(Dickens in the Alps visited the St. Bernard convent, located on one of the highest mountains in the world.)*

Beside the convent in a little outhouse with a grated iron door are the bodies of people found in the snow which have never been claimed and are withering away—not laid down or stretched out, but standing up, in corners and against walls; some erect and horribly human, with distinct expressions on their faces; some sunk down on their knees; some dropping over on one side; some tumbled down altogether, and presenting a heap of skulls and fibrous dust. There is no other decay in that atmosphere; and there they remain during the short days and the long nights, the only human company out of doors, withering away by grains, and holding ghastly possession of the mountain where they died.

Dickens, in a letter to John Foster, 1846

a child's view of   *see also* FUNERAL, IMMORTALITY

92.   I met a little cottage girl:
                She was eight years old, she said;
                Her hair was thick with many a curl
                That clustered round her head.

                        *   *   *

                "Sisters and brothers, little maid,
                How many may you be?"
                "How many? Seven in all," she said,
                And wondering looked at me.

"And where are they? I pray you tell."
She answered, "Seven are we;
And two of us at Conway dwell,
And two are gone to sea."

"Two of us in the churchyard lie,
My sister and my brother;
And in the churchyard cottage I
Dwell near them with my mother."
＊　＊　＊

"You run about, my little maid,
Your limbs they are alive;
If two are in the churchyard laid,
Then ye are only five."
＊　＊　＊

"How many are you, then," said I,
"If they two are in heaven?"
Quick was the little maid's reply,
"O master, we are seven."

"But they are dead; those two are dead!
Their spirits are in heaven!"
'Twas throwing words away; for still
The little maid would have her will,
And say, "Nay, we are seven!'

Wordsworth, "We Are Seven"

and the Christian's hope

93.   The more we sink into the infirmities of age, the nearer we
are to immortal youth. All people are young in the other world.
That state is an eternal spring ever fresh and flourishing. Now, to
pass from midnight into noon on the sudden; to be decrepit one
minute and all spirit and activity the next, must be a desirable
change. To call this dying is an abuse of language.

Jeremy Taylor, *Holy Dying*

a crossing of the bar

94.   Sunset and evening star,
             And one clear call for me!

And may there be no moaning of the bar,
   When I put out to sea,

But such a tide as moving seems asleep,
   Too full for sound and foam,
When that which drew from out the boundless
   deep
Turns again home.

Twilight and evening bell,
   And after that the dark!
And may there be no sadness of farewell
   When I embark;

For tho' from out our borne of Time and Place
   The flood may bear me far,
I hope to see my Pilot face to face
   When I have crossed the bar.
                Tennyson, "Crossing the Bar"

the great leveler

95.   The boast of heraldry, the pomp of power,
       And all that beauty, all that wealth e'er gave,
     Await alike the inevitable hour.
     The paths of glory lead but to the grave.
     Thomas Gray, "Elegy Written in a Country Churchyard"

a happy release

96.   *(The death of little Nell)*
    She was dead. There upon her little bed she lay at rest. She
was dead. No sleep so beautiful and calm, so free from trace of
pain, so fair to look upon. She seemed a creature fresh from the
hand of God, and waiting for the breath of life; not one who had
lived and suffered death. . . .
    And as the schoolmaster kissed her he said, "Think what earth
is compared with the world to which her young spirit has winged
its early flight; and say, if one deliberate wish expressed in solemn

terms above this bed could call her back to life, which of us would utter it?"

Dickens, The Old Curiosity Shop

man's indifference to the imminence of   see also LIFE—the
uncertainty of

97.   In old age we live under the shadow of Death, which, like the sword of Damocles, may descend at any moment; but we have so long found life to be an affair of being rather frightened than hurt that we have become like the people who live under Vesuvius, and chance it without much misgiving.

Samuel Butler, The Way of All Flesh

98.   Although few things are spoken of with more fearful whisperings than this prospect of death, few have less influence on conduct under healthy circumstances. We have all heard of cities in South America built upon the side of fiery mountains, and how, even in this horrible neighborhood, the inhabitants are not a jot more impressed by the solemnity of mortal conditions than if they were delving gardens in the greenest corner of England. There are serenades and suppers and much gallantry among the myrtles overhead: and meanwhile the foundations shudder underfoot, the bowels of the mountains growl, and at any moment ruin may leap sky-high into the moonlight, and tumble man and his merry-making in the dust. . . . There is something indescribably reckless and desperate in such a picture.

And yet, when one comes to think upon it calmly, the situation of these South American citizens forms only a very pale figure for the state of ordinary mankind.

R. L. Stevenson, Virginibus Puerisque, "Aes Triplex"

man soon forgotten after   see also HUMAN NATURE—the self-
centeredness of

99.   The pathetic exhortation on country tombstones, "Grieve not for me, my wife and children dear," etc., is for the most part speedily followed to the letter. We do not leave so great a void in society as we are inclined to imagine, partly to magnify our own importance, and partly to console ourselves by sympathy. Even in the same family the gap is not so great; the wound closes up sooner than we

should expect. Nay, *our room* is not infrequently thought better than *our company*. People walk along the streets the day after our death just as they did before, and the crowd is not diminished. While we were living, the world seemed in a manner to exist only for us, for our delight and amusement, because it contributed to them. But our hearts cease to beat, and it goes on as usual, and thinks no more about us than it did in our lifetime.

Hazlitt, *Table Talk*, "On the Fear of Death"

preserved in

100.   I remember the strange Alpine story of the youth who fell down a glacier and was lost, and of how a scientific companion, one of several who accompanied him, all young, computed that the body would again appear on a certain date and place many years afterwards. When that time came round some of the survivors returned to the glacier to see if the prediction would be fulfilled; all old men now; and the body reappeared as young as the day he left them.

Sir J. M. Barrie, *Courage*

resignation in the face of   *see also* SUBMISSION

101.   (*A few weeks before her death Anne Brontë wrote these words to a friend:*)

"I have no horror of death; if I thought it inevitable, I think I could quietly resign myself to the prospect, in the hope that you, dear Miss _____, would give as much of your company as you possibly could to Charlotte, and be a sister to her in my stead. But I wish it would please God to spare me, not only for papa's and Charlotte's sakes, but because I long to do some good in the world before I leave it. I have many schemes in my head for future practice—humble and limited indeed—but still I should not like them all to come to nothing, and myself to have lived to so little purpose. But God's will be done."

Quoted in Mrs. Elizabeth Gaskell, *Life of Charlotte Brontë*

settles destiny

102.   Some men find fault with death because no experiment can be made of it without an absolute dissolution: they would die

twice, to try what kind of state it is, that they might be fitly furnished against the second time, when they must die in earnest. But this is madness, and were it granted them, the good they pretend would not be performed. For he that will cast away one life without preparing for death will not fear to hazard another; desperate malefactors will take no warning by reprieves.

Henry Vaughan,
Two Excellent Discourses of Life and Death (1654)

triumphant in

103.   (The allusion is to Mr. Valiant-for-Truth.)

When that day that he must go hence was come, many accompanied him to the Riverside, into which as he went he said, "Grave, where is thy victory?" So he passed over, and all the trumpets sounded for him on the other side.

Bunyan, *Pilgrim's Progress*

104.   [John Knox] had a sore fight of an existence, wrestling with Popes and Principalities; in defeat, contention, life-long struggle; rowing as a galley-slave, wandering as an exile. A sore fight, but he won it! "Hast thou hope?" they asked him in his last moment, when he could no longer speak. He lifted his finger and pointed upward. And so he died. Honor to him! His works have not died. The letter of his work dies, but the spirit of it never!

Carlyle, *Heroes and Hero-Worship*

victory over

105.   Fear death?—to feel the fog in my throat,
     The mist in my face,
When the snows begin, and the blasts denote
     I am nearing the place,
The power of the night, the press of the storm,
     The post of the foe;
Where he stands, the Arch Fear in a visible form,
     Yet the strong man must go:
For the journey is done and the summit attained,
     And the barriers fall,
Though a battle's to fight ere the guerdon be gained,
     The reward of it all.

I was ever a fighter, so—one fight more,
   The best and the last!
I would hate that death bandaged my eyes, and
     forbore,
   And bade me creep past.
No! let me taste the whole of it, fare like my peers
   The heroes of old,
Bear the brunt, in a minute pay life's glad arrears
   In pain, darkness, and cold.
For sudden the worst turns the best to the brave,
   The black minute's at end,
And the elements rage, the fiend-voices that rave,
   Shall dwindle, shall blend,
Shall change, shall become first a peace out of pain,
   Then a light, then my breast,
O thou soul of my soul! I shall clasp thee again,
   And with God be at rest!

Browning, "Prospice"

of the young

106.   When Death strikes down the innocent and the young, for
every fragile form from which he lets the panting spirit free, a
hundred virtues rise in shapes of mercy, charity, and love, to walk
the world, and bless it. Of every tear that sorrowing mortals shed
on such green graves, some good is born, some gentler nature comes.
In the Destroyer's steps there spring up bright creations that defy
his power; and his dark path becomes a way of light to Heaven.

Dickens, *The Old Curiosity Shop*

DEBT   *see also* ESCAPISM, PARASITE

107.   *(Mr. Micawber, always in debt, seeks to discharge his obligations in the grand manner.)*

  "To leave this metropolis," said Mr. Micawber, "and my friend
Mr. Thomas Twaddles, without acquitting myself of the pecuniary
part of this obligation, would weigh upon my mind to an unsupport-
able extent. I have, therefore, prepared for my friend, Mr. Thomas
Twaddles, and I now hold in my hands a document which ac-
complishes the desired object. I beg to hand to my friend, Mr.

Thomas Twaddles, my I.O.U. for forty-one, ten, eleven and a half, and I am happy to recover my moral dignity, and to know that I can once more walk erect before my fellow-man!" With this introduction (which greatly affected him) Mr. Micawber placed his I.O.U. in the hands of Mr. Twaddles, and said he wished him well in every relation of life. I am persuaded, not only that this was quite the same to Mr. Micawber as paying the money, but that Mr. Twaddles himself hardly knew the difference until he had had time to think about it. Mr. Micawber walked so erect before his fellow-man, on the strength of this virtuous action, that his chest looked half as broad again when he lighted down from the stairs.

Dickens, *David Copperfield*

DESPONDENCY *see also* DISAPPOINTMENT
how one man sought to drown his

108. Some men in his blighted position would have taken to drinking; but on receiving the news that Sophy Wackles was lost to him for ever, Mr. Swiveler only took to playing the flute; thinking after mature consideration that it was a good, sound, dismal occupation, not only in unison with his own sad thoughts, but calculated to awaken a fellow-feeling in the bosoms of his neighbors. The air was, "Away with Melancholy"—a composition which, when played very slowly, and especially by a gentleman but imperfectly acquainted with the instrument, has not a lively effect. Yet for half the night Mr. Swiveler played the unhappy tune over and over again. It was not until he had breathed into the flute his whole sentiment, and had nearly maddened the people next door and over the way, that he shut up the music box, extinguished the candle, and finding himself greatly lightened and relieved in his mind, turned around and fell asleep.

Dickens, *The Old Curiosity Shop*

yielding to

109. *(Thrown into the dungeon of the Castle of Chillon for his faith, Bonnivard has been captive so long that when freedom at last does come, it finds him bereft of all capacity to enjoy it:)*

> At last men came to set me free;
> I ask'd not why, I reck'd not where;

It was, at length the same to me
Fettered or fetterless to be.

I learned to love despair.
And thus, when they appeared at last,
And all my bonds aside were cast,
These heavy walls to me had grown
A hermitage—and all my own. . . .

My very chains and I grew friends,
So much a long communion tends
To make us what we are;—even I
Regain'd my freedom with a sigh.

Byron, "The Prisoner of Chillon"

DISAPPOINTMENT
see also DESPONDENCY
hiding our

110.   We mortals, men and women, devour many a disappointment between breakfast and dinnertime; keep back the tears and
look a little pale about the lips, and in answer to inquiries say, "Oh,
nothing!" Pride helps us; and pride is not a bad thing when it only
urges us to hide our own hurts—not to hurt others.

George Eliot, *Middlemarch*

DISCIPLINE
of self

111.   [Cromwell] first acquired discipline of himself, and over
himself acquired the most signal victories; so that on the first day
he took the field against the external enemy, he was a veteran in
arms, consummately practised in the toils and exigencies of war.

Milton, "Defensio Secúnda pro Populo Anglicano"

112.   *(The allusion is to Florence Nightingale.)*
It was not by gentle sweetness and womanly self-abnegation
that she had brought order out of chaos in the Scutari Hospitals,
that from her own resources she had clothed the British Army,
that she had spread her dominion over the serried and reluctant
powers of the official world; it was by strict method, by stern

discipline, by rigid attention to detail, by ceaseless labor, by the fixed determination of an indomitable will. Beneath her cool and calm demeanor lurked fierce and passionate fires.

Lytton Strachey, *Eminent Victorians*

DISSENSION *see also* ZEAL
over trifles

113. Religion should extinguish strife,
And make a calm of human life;
But friends that chance to differ
On points which God has left at large,
How fiercely will they meet and charge!
No combatants are stiffer.

Cowper, "Friendship"

114. Alas— how light a cause may move
Dissension between hearts that love!
Hearts that the world in vain had tried;
And sorrow had more closely tied;
That stood the storm when waves were rough.
Yet in a sunny hour fall off
Like ships that have gone down at sea
When heaven was all tranquility.

Thomas Moore, *Lalla Rookh*

115. *(Gulliver among the Lilliputians)*
It is allowed on all hands that the primitive way of breaking eggs before we eat them, was upon the larger end: but his present Majesty's grandfather, while he was a boy going to eat an egg, and breaking it in accordance to the ancient practice, happened to cut one of his fingers. Whereupon the Emperor, his father, published an edict commanding all his subjects, upon great penalties, to break the smaller end of their eggs. The people so highly resented this law that our histories tell us there have been six rebellions raised on that account; wherein one Emperor lost his life, and another his crown. It is computed that eleven thousand persons have at several times suffered death rather than submit to break their eggs at the smaller end. Many hundred large volumes have been published upon this controversy.

Swift, *Gulliver's Travels*

the zeal of

116.   I have known, and still know, many Dissenters who profess
to have a zeal for Christianity; and I dare say they have. But I
have known very few Dissenters indeed, whose hatred of the Church
of England was not a much more active principle of action with
them than their love for Christianity. The Wesleyans in uncor-
rupted parts of the country are nearly the only exceptions. There
never was an age since the days of the Apostles in which the
Catholic spirit of religion was so dead, and put aside for the love
of sects and parties, as at present.

Coleridge, Table Talk

DOGMATISM
one kind of

117.   "There's glory for you!"

"I don't know what you mean by 'glory,'" Alice said.

"I mean, there's a nice knock-down argument for you!"

"But 'glory' doesn't mean a 'nice knock-down argument,'" Alice
objected.

"When *I* use a word," Humpty Dumpty said, in a rather scornful tone, "it means just what I choose it to mean,—neither more nor
less."

Lewis Carroll, Through the Looking-Glass

DOUBT   see also FAITH
the agony of

118.
> To spend uncounted years of pain,
> Again, again, and yet again,
> In working out in heart and brain
>   The problem of our being here:
> To gather facts from far and near,
> Upon the mind to hold them clear,
> And, knowing more may yet appear
> Unto one's latest breath to fear,
> The premature result to draw—
> Is this the object, end, and law,
>   And purpose of our being here?

Arthur Hugh Clough,
"Perche Pensa? Pensando S'Invecchia"

an antidote to

119. Times of doubt and discouragement, when we seem to have lost our way, must reckon with those mountain-top experiences during which God and Heaven were glorious realities. "When I was on the top of Mt. Clear," wrote Bunyan, "I saw the shining minarets of the Celestial City."

Bunyan, *Pilgrim's Progress* (adapted)

120. Most true it is, as a wise man teaches us, that doubt of any sort cannot be removed except by action. On which ground, too, let him who gropes painfully in darkness or uncertain light, and prays vehemently that the dawn may ripen into day, lay this other precept well to heart, which to me was of invaluable service: "Do the Duty which lies nearest thee," which thou knowest to be a duty! Thy second Duty will already have become clearer.

Carlyle, *Sartor Resartus*

121. God has spoken to us all, once or twice or more often, as a man speaketh unto his friend. There have been moments in the lives of each one of us, in which the spirit's true endowments stand out plainly from its false ones and apprise it if pursuing the right or the wrong way, to its triumph and undoing. We must "cherish these best hours of the mind," as Bacon says, and not let them slip from us. We shall find them very helpful in moments of doubt and despondency.

William Ralph Inge, *Speculum Animae*

122. Our love to God does not depend upon the emotions of the moment. If you fancy you do not love Him enough, above all when Satan tempts you to look inward, go immediately and minister to others; visit the sick, perform some act of self-sacrifice or thanksgiving. Never mind how *dull* you may feel while doing it; the fact of your *doing* it proves that your will, your spiritual part, is on God's side, however tired or careless the poor flesh may be.

Charles Kingsley, *Daily Thoughts*

123. But there are hours, and they come to us all at some period of life or other, when the hand of Mystery seems to be heavy on the soul—when some life-shock scatters existence, . . . hours when the feeling of personal worthlessness, the uncertainty and meanness of all human aims, and a doubt of all human goodness, unfix the soul from all its old moorings—and leave it drifting—drifting over the vast Infinitude, with an awful sense of solitariness. Then the man whose faith rested on outward authority and not on inward life will find it give way: the authority of the priest, the authority of the Church, or merely the authority of a document proved by miracles and backed by prophecy; the soul—conscious life here-after—God—will be an awful desolate Perhaps. Well! in such moments you doubt all—whether Christianity be true, whether Christ was man or God or a beautiful fable. . . . In such an hour what remains? I reply, Obedience. Leave those thoughts for the present. Act—be merciful and gentle—honest: force yourself to abound in little services: try to do good to others: be true to the Duty that you know. *That* must be right whatever else is uncertain. And by all the laws of the human heart, by the word of God, you shall not be left in doubt. Do that much of the will of God which is plain to you, and "you shall know of the doctrine, whether it be of God."

F. W. Roberston, Sermons

cleaving to the sunnier side of

124.   Thou canst not prove the nameless, O my son,
           Nor canst thou prove the world thou movest in,
           Thou canst not prove that thou art body alone,
           Nor canst thou prove that thou art spirit alone,
           Nor canst thou prove that thou art both in one.
           Thou canst not prove thou art immortal, no,
           Nor yet that thou art mortal. . . .
           For nothing worthy proving can be proven,
           Nor yet disproven. Wherefore thou be wise,
           Cleave ever to the sunnier side of doubt,
           And cling to Faith beyond the forms of Faith!

Tennyson, "The Ancient Sage"

deliverance from

125.   Now there was, not far from the place where they lay, a castle called Doubting Castle; the owner thereof was Giant Despair.

The giant, finding them next morning, put them into a very dark
dungeon, where they lay from Wednesday till Saturday without
food. On Thursday morning Giant Despair returned to beat them
till they were unable to move. The following morning he advised
them to suicide, assuring them that they would never leave this
place alive. When he was gone, Christian groaned, "For my part
I know not whether it is best to live thus or die. My soul chooseth
strangling rather than life." Whereupon Hopeful encouraged his
companion to patience. Next day Giant Despair took his prisoners
into the castleyard and showed them the bones and skulls of those
whom he had already despatched. When this was unavailing, he
beat them all the way into the dungeon. On Saturday night about
midnight, they began to pray, and continued in prayer till almost
break of day. Now a little before day Christian cried, "What a fool
am I to lie in a dungeon when I may as well walk at liberty! I have
a key in my bosom, called Promise, that will open any lock in
Doubting Castle." Then with it he turned the lock, and the door
flew open with ease, and Christian and Hopeful both came out.
Then they went on, and came to the King's highway, and so were
safe.

Bunyan, Pilgrim's Progress

in doubt of

126.   *(If the life of the believer is beset by doubt, the life of the
unbeliever is beset by faith. The bishop is reasoning with a skeptic:)*
    Just when we're safest, there's a sunset touch,
    A fancy from a flower-bell, some one's death,
    A chorus-ending from Euripides,—
    And that's enough for fifty hopes and fears
    As old and new at once as Nature's self,
    To rap and knock and enter in our soul,
    Take hands and dance there a fantastic ring
    Round the ancient idol, on his base again,—
    The grand perhaps!
✿   ✿   ✿

    What think ye of Christ, friend? When all's done and said,
    Like you this Christianity or not?

It may be false, but will you wish it true?
Has it your vote to be so if it can?
                        Browning, "Bishop Blougram's Apology"

in praise of

127.   You tell me, doubt is Devil-born.

            I know not: one indeed I knew
                In many a subtle question versed,
                Who touch'd a jarring lyre at first,
            But ever strove to make it true;

            Perplex'd in faith but pure in deeds,
                At last he beat his music out.
                There lives more faith in honest doubt,
            Believe me, than in half the creeds.
                                Tennyson, "In Memoriam"

the resolving of

128.   I know not why the Evil,
            I know not why the Good, both mysteries
            Remained unsolved, and both insoluble.
            I know that both are there, the battle set,
            And I must fight on this side or on that.
            I can't stand shiv'ring on the bank, I plunge
            Head first. I bet my life on Beauty, Truth,
            And Love, not abstract but incarnate Truth,
            Not Beauty's passing shadow but its Self.
            Its very self made flesh, Love realized.
            I bet my life on Christ—Christ Crucified.
                        *   *   *
                        You want to argue? Well,
            I can't. It is a choice. I choose the Christ.
                        G. A. Studdert-Kennedy, "Faith"

in spite of

129.   I have a life with Christ to live,
                But, ere I live it, must I wait

Till learning can clear answer give
Of this and that book's date?

I have a life in Christ to live,
I have a death in Christ to die;—
And must I wait till science give
All doubts a full reply.

Nay rather, while the sea of doubt
Is raging wildly round about,
Questioning of life and death and sin,
Let me but creep within
Thy fold, O Christ, and at Thy feet
Take but the lowly seat,
And hear Thine awful voice repeat
In gentlest accents, heavenly sweet,
Come unto Me, and rest:
Believe Me, and be blest.

John Campbell Shairp

DUTY   *see also* OBEDIENCE
devotion to

130.   A life regardful of duty is crowned with an object, directed
by a purpose, inspired by an enthusiasm, till the very humblest
routine, carried out conscientiously for the sake of God is elevated
into moral grandeur: and the very obscurest office, filled conscientiously at the bidding of God, becomes an imperial stage on
which all the virtues play. To one who lives thus the insignificant
becomes important, the unpleasant delightful, the evanescent
eternal.

F. W. Faber, *Treasure Thoughts of,* ed. by Rose Porter

ENCOURAGEMENT   *see also* FAILURE, INFLUENCE, THANKS-
GIVING

131.   *(The poet refers to his father, the revered Dr. Thomas
Arnold, headmaster of Rugby.)*
At your voice,
Panic, despair, flee away.
Ye move through the ranks, recall

The stragglers, refresh the outworn,
Praise, reinspire the brave!
Order, courage, return.
Eyes rekindling, and prayers,
Follow your steps as ye go.
Ye fill up the gaps in our files,
Strengthen the wavering line,
'Stablish, continue the march,
On, to the bound of the waste,
On, to the city of God.

                          Matthew Arnold, "Rugby Chapel"

132.   *(Charles Lamb, who seems to have borne more than his
share of sorrow and suffering, wrote these words to a friend:)*
You say that this world to you seems drained of its sweets. O,
Robert, I don't know what you call sweet. Honey and the honey-
comb, roses and violets, are yet in the earth. The sun and moon yet
reign in Heaven, and the lesser lights keep up their pretty twin-
klings. Meats and drinks, sweet sights and sweet smells, a country
walk, spring and autumn have all a sweetness by turns. Good
humor and good nature, friends at home that love you, friends
abroad that miss you—you possess all these things, and more in-
numerable. You may extract honey from everything.

                          Charles Lamb, *Letters*, Vol. I

ENEMY   *see also* STRUGGLE
his power not to be measured by the loudness of his clamor

133.   Because half-a-dozen grasshoppers under a fern make the
field ring with their importunate chink, whilst thousands of great
cattle, reposing beneath the shadow of the British oak, chew the
cud and are silent, pray do not imagine that those who make the
noise are the only inhabitants of the field; or that they are many
in number; or that, after all, they are other than the little shrivelled,
meager, hopping, though loud and troublesome, insects of the hour.

                          Edmund Burke, *Reflections on the Revolution in France*

ENVY   *see also* JEALOUSY
the persistence of

134.   Mr. Badman's envy was so rank and strong that if it at any
time turned its head against a man, it would hardly ever be pulled

in again. He would watch over that man to do him mischief, as the
cat watches over the mouse to destroy it; yea, he would wait seven
years, but he would have an opportunity to hurt him, and when he
had it, he would make him feel the weight of his envy.

Bunyan, Grace Abounding

ESCAPISM   *see also* COWARDICE
brings death

135. *(The road and the river which run to "many-towered
Camelot," where King Arthur holds court, pass by the Lady's
silent bower. No one has ever seen the Lady of Shalott, but the
reapers in the field have heard the echo of her song. Aloft she sits,
weaving in a magic web the life of the outside world—but only
as she sees it reflected through her mirror. She fears to look at life
directly lest a curse fall on her. But she grows weary of the un-
reality of her existence—"I am half sick of shadows," said the Lady
of Shalott. One day Sir Lancelot rides past, toward Camelot, and
flashes into the crystal mirror. The sight is too much for her. She
turns from the mirror and faces reality—and death.)*

> She left the web, she left the loom,
> She made three paces through the room,
> She saw the water lily bloom,
> She saw the helmet and the plume,
>   She looked down to Camelot.
>
> Out flew the web and floated wide;
> The mirror cracked from side to side;
> 'The curse is come upon me,' cried
>   The Lady of Shalott.

Tennyson, "The Lady of Shalott"

a form of

136. Mr. Skimpole then betook himself to lying down on his
back under a tree, and looking at the sky. "Enterprise and effort,"
he would say to us (on his back), "are delightful to me. I have
the deepest sympathy with them. I lie in a shady place like this and
think with admiration of adventurous spirits going to the North
Pole, or penetrating to the heart of the Torrid Zone."

Dickens, Bleak House

137.   Mr. Podsnap settled that whatever he put behind him he put
out of existence. . . . Mr. Podsnap had even acquired a peculiar
flourish of his right arm in often clearing the world of its most
difficult problems, by sweeping them behind him. (i.e. "pod-
snappery.")

Dickens, *Our Mutual Friend*

by projecting the blame

138.   Why slander we the times?
                        What crimes
                Have days and years, that we
                Thus charge them with iniquity?
                    If we would rightly scan,
                It's not the times are bad, but man.
                    If thy desire it be
                        To see
                The times prove good, be thou
                But such thyself, and surely know
                    That all thy days to thee
                Shall spite of mischief happy be.

Joseph Beaumont

139.   This is the excellent foppery of the world, that when we are
sick in fortune,—often the surfeit of our own behaviour,—we make
guilty of our disasters the sun, the moon, and the stars: as if we were
villains by necessity; fools by heavenly compulsion; knaves, thieves,
and treachers by spherical predominance; drunkards, liars, and
adulterers, by an enforced obedience of planetary influence.

Shakespeare, *King Lear*, Act I, Sc. 2 (Edmund)

EXCESS
sin of

140.   To gild refined gold, to paint the lily,
            To throw a perfume on the violet,
            To smooth the ice, or add another hue
            Unto the rainbow, or with taper-light
            To seek the beauteous eye of heaven to garnish,
            Is wasteful and ridiculous excess.

Shakespeare, *King John*, Act IV, Sc. 2 (Earl of Salisbury)

FAILURE *see also* ENCOURAGEMENT
Browning's doctrine of success through

141.   Better have failed in the high aim, as I,
           Than vulgarly in the low aim succeed.

                                        "The Inn Album"

           'Tis not what man does which exalts him, but
           What he would do!

                                                "Saul"

           That low man seeks a little thing to do,
               Sees it and does it:
           This high man, with a great thing to pursue,
               Dies e'er he knows it.

                                    "A Grammarian's Funeral"

a parable of

142.   I stand amid the dust of moulded years—
           My mangled youth lies dead beneath the heap.
           My days have crackled and gone up in smoke,
           Have puffed and burst as sun-starts on a stream.
               Yea, faileth now even the dream
           The dreamer, and the lute the lutinist;
           And now my heart is as a broken fount,
           Wherein tear-drippings stagnate, spilt down ever
               From the dank thoughts that shiver
           Upon the sighful branches of my mind.
               Such is; what is to be?

                        Francis Thompson, "The Hound of Heaven"

FAITH *see also* DOUBT, TRUST
the confidence of

143.   I go to prove my soul!
           I see my way as birds their trackless way.
           I shall arrive! what time, what circuit first,

I ask not. . . .
In some time, his good time, I shall arrive:
He guides me and the bird. In his good time.

Browning, "Pauline"

144.   One who never turned his back but marched breast forward,
       Never doubted clouds would break,
       Never dreamed, though right were worsted, wrong would
           triumph,
       Held we fall to rise, are baffled to fight better,
                        Sleep to wake.

Browning, "Asolando"

consequence of loss of   *see also* LIFE—the meaninglessness of

145.   *(One of the best-known poems of the nineteenth century
represents the main movement of mind in the last quarter of the century: it is an expression of the emptiness of life when Christian faith
is gone. It is nighttime—the moon is out, the tide is full and the sea is
calm. From the English coast the poet, with his companion, stands
gazing across the Straits to the shores of France. Wistfully he
muses:)*

                        . . . The sea of faith
       Was once, too, at the full, and round earth's shore
       Lay like the folds of a bright girdle furl'd;
       But now I only hear
       Its melancholy, long, withdrawing roar,
       Retreating, to the breath
       Of the night-wind, down the vast edges drear
       And naked shingles of the world.

                        Ah, love, let us be true
       To one another! For the world which seems
       To lie before us like a land of dreams,
       So various, so beautiful, so new,
       Hath really neither joy, nor love, nor light,
       Nor certitude, nor peace, nor help for pain;
       And we are here as on a darkling plain

Swept with confused alarms of struggle and flight,
Where ignorant armies clash by night.
> Matthew Arnold, "Dover Beach"

146. *(The poet, visiting the chief seat of the Carthusian monks, high in the French Alps, wistfully describes its silent courts, the chapel, the halls, the gardens. He expresses longing for the spiritual peace of these simple anchorites. But the Apostles of the Enlightenment have shaken his faith in the Christianity in which he was nurtured—they seized his youth:)*

And purged its faith, and trimm'd its fire,
Show'd me the high white star of Truth,
There bade me gaze and there aspire.

(But that which reason rejects, the heart cries after. Frustration and longing are expressed in these lines:)

Wandering between two worlds, one dead,
The other powerless to be born,
With nowhere yet to rest my head,
Like these on earth, I wait forlorn.
Their faith, my tears, the world deride—
I come to shed them at your side.

Oh, hide me in your gloom profound,
Ye solemn seats of holy pain!
Take me, cowled forms, and fence me round
Till I possess my soul again!
> Matthew Arnold, "Stanzas from the Grand Chartreuse"

147. *(Hardy saw more clearly than most Victorians the real drift and significance of the new knowledge concerning the earth's past and concerning the natural history of man. To accept it and all its implications meant, for many, stripping man of that faith and hope which gave meaning to this life and comforting assurance of future existence. Life, as he sees it, is now become a meaningless riddle, and God has ceased to be a reality. Wistfully the poet sees the "passing" of God.)*

I saw a slowly stepping train
Lined on the brows, scoop-eyed and bent and hoar,

Following in files across a twilit plain;
A strange and mystic form the foremost bore.

      ❋   ❋   ❋

O man-projected figure, of late
Imaged as we, thy knell, who shall survive?
Whence came it we were tempted to create
One whom we can no longer keep alive?

      ❋   ❋   ❋

How sweet it was in years far hied
To start the wheels of day with trustful prayer!
To lie down liegely at the eventide
And feel a blest assurance He was there.

            Thomas Hardy, "The Funeral of God"

148.   *("A man and his wife, having lost faith in God and hope
of a life to come, and being utterly miserable in this life, resolve
to end themselves by drowning."—Tennyson's prefatory note.)*

Lightly step over the sands! The waters—you hear
    them call!
Life with its anguish, and horrors, and errors—away
    with them all!
And she laid her hands in my own—she was always
    loyal and sweet—
Till the points of the foam in the dusk came playing
    about our feet.
There was a strong sea-current would sweep us out to
    the main.
Ah, God, though I felt as I spoke, I was taking the
    name in vain—
Ah, God, and we turned to each other, we kissed, we
    embraced, she and I,
Knowing the life we believed everlasting, would die:
We had read their know-nothing books, and we lean'd
    to the darker side—
Ah, God! should we find Him, perhaps, perhaps, if
    we died!
We never found Him on earth, this earth is a father-
    less hell—

Dear love, forever and ever, forever and ever farewell!
Never a cry so desolate, not since the world began,
Never a kiss so sad, no, not since the coming of man.

Tennyson, "Despair"

the courage of

149. Faith reels not in the storm of warring words,
    She brightens at the clash of "Yes" and "No,"
    She sees the best that glimmers thro' the worst,
    She feels the sun is hid but for a night,
    She spies the summer thro' the winter bud,
    She tastes the fruit before the blossom falls,
    She finds the fountain where they wail'd "Mirage!"

Tennyson, "The Ancient Sage"

the force of

150. The real force of demonstration for Savonarola lay in his own burning indignation at the sight of wrong; in his fervent belief in an Unseen Justice that would put an end to the wrong, and in an Unseen Purity to which lying and uncleanness were an abomination. To his ardent, power-loving soul, believing in great ends, and longing to achieve those ends by the exertion of its own strong will, the faith in a supreme and righteous Ruler became one with the faith in a speedy Divine interposition that would punish and reclaim.

George Eliot, Romola

losing faith in a fellow man

151. No one who has ever known what it is to lose faith in a fellow-man, whom he has profoundly loved and reverenced, will lightly say that the shock leaves the faith in the Invisible Goodness unshaken. With the sinking of high human trust, the dignity of life sinks too; we cease to believe in our better self, since that also is part of our common nature which is degraded in our thought; and all the finer impulses of the soul are dulled.

George Eliot, Romola

perfect

152.   That man is perfect in faith who can come to God in the
utter dearth of his feelings and desires, without a glow or an aspiration, with the weight of low thoughts, failures, neglects, and wandering forgetfulness, and say to Him, "Thou art my refuge."

George MacDonald, *Unspoken Sermons*

presumptuous

153.   Mahomet made the people believe that he would call a hill
to him, and from the top of it offer up his prayers for the observers
of his law. The people assembled; Mahomet called the hill to him,
again and again, and when the hill stood still, he was never a bit
abashed, but said, if the hill will not come to Mahomet, Mahomet
will go to the hill.

Francis Bacon, *Essays*, "Of Boldness"

the simplicity of

154.   Lord, give me faith!—to live from day to day,
        With tranquil heart to do my simple part,
        And, with my hand in thine, just go Thy way.

        Lord, give me faith!—to trust, if not to know;
        With quiet mind in all things Thee to find,
        And, child-like, go where Thou wouldst have me go.

        Lord, give me faith!—to leave it all to Thee,
        The future is Thy gift, I would not lift
        The veil Thy love has hung 'twixt it and me.

John Oxenham, "Faith"

a sustaining

155.   I dare not fear, since certainly I know
        That I am in God's keeping, shielded so
        From all that else would harm, and in the hour
        Of stern temptation strengthened by his power;
        I tread no path in life to him unknown;
        I lift no burden, bear no pain, alone;

My soul a calm, sure hiding-place has found:
The everlasting arms my life surround.
God, thou art love! I build my faith on that.
I know thee who hast kept my path, and made
Light for me in the darkness, tempering sorrow
So that it reached me like a solemn joy;
It were too strange that I should doubt thy love.

Browning, "Paracelsus"

tested   *see also* ADVERSITY, STRUGGLE, TEMPTATION

156.   It is a dreadful night.
                       But by and by
                  The clouds will lift,
                  And the wild storm will drift
                  Towards the horizon yonder.
                  The light will shine;
                  I shall then see my way—
                  I only tarry for the break of day.

James Douglas, "Expectancy"

157.   Thrice blest is he to whom is given
                       The instinct that can tell
                  That God is on the field when He
                       Is most invisible.

                  He hides Himself so wondrously
                       As though there were no God;
                  He is least seen when all the powers
                       Of ill are most abroad.

                  Or He deserts us at the hour
                       The fight is all but lost
                  And seems to leave us to ourselves
                       Just when we need Him most.

F. W. Faber, from a hymn

158.   I falter where I firmly trod,
                       And falling with my weight of cares
                       Upon the great world's altar stairs
                  That slope through darkness up to God,

I stretch lame hands of faith and grope,
And gather dust and chaff, and call
To what I feel is Lord of all,
And faintly trust the larger hope.
                    Tennyson, "In Memoriam"

in time of sorrow

159.   (*After the death of her sister Emily, and with her youngest sister, Anne, dying of tuberculosis, Charlotte Brontë wrote to a friend:*)
    "I avoid looking forward or backward, and try to keep looking upward. . . . The days pass in a slow, dark march; the nights are the test; the sudden wakings from restless sleep, the revived knowledge that one lies in her grave, and another not at my side but in a separate and sick bed. However, God is over all."
                    Quoted in Mrs. Elizabeth Gaskell,
                    The Life of Charlotte Brontë

validated by personal experience

160.   There is no substitute for first-hand experience in the spiritual life. We must believe the explorers of the high places of the unseen world when they tell us that they have been there, and found what they sought. But they cannot really tell us *what* they found; if we wish to see what they have seen, we must live as they have lived.
                    William Ralph Inge,
                    Personal Religion and the Life of Devotion

the vision of   *see also* VISION

161.   That is not faith, to see God only in what is strange and rare; but this is faith, to see God in what is most common and simple, to know God's greatness not so much from disorder as from order, not so much from those strange sights in which God seems (but only seems) to break His laws, as from those common ones in which He fulfills His laws.
                    Charles Kingsley, *Daily Thoughts*

162.   I have seen
        A curious child, who dwelt upon a tract
        Of inland ground, applying to his ear

The convolutions of a smooth-lipped shell;
To which, in silence hushed, his very soul
Listened intently; and his countenance soon
Brightened with joy; for from within were heard
Murmurings whereby the monitor expressed
Mysterious union with its native sea.

Even such a shell the Universe itself
Is to the ear of Faith: and there are times,
I doubt not, when to you it doth impart
Authentic tidings of invisible things.

Wordsworth, *The Excursion*, Book IV

FAITHFULNESS   *see also* WORK—the stewardship of

163.   Is your place a small place?
                        Tend it with care;—
                          He set you there.

                     Is your place a large place?
                        Guard it with care!—
                          He set you there.

                     Whate'er your place, it is
                        Not yours alone, but His
                          Who set you there.

John Oxenham, "Your Place"

in little things   *see also* GREATNESS—in obscurity

164.   Little faithfulnesses are not only the preparation for great
ones, but little faithfulnesses are in themselves the great ones. . . .
The essential fidelity of the heart is the same whether it be exercised
in two mites or in a regal treasury; the genuine faithfulness of the
life is equally beautiful whether it be displayed in governing an
empire or in writing an exercise. . . . It has been quaintly said that
if God were to send two angels to earth, the one to occupy a throne,
and the other to clean a road, they would each regard their em-
ployments as equally distinguished and equally happy.

F. W. Faber, *Treasure Thoughts of*, ed. by Rose Porter

THE FALL
inspired by Satan

165. *(The poet envisions Satan and his peers, after their Fall, holding council in Hell, debating whether another battle should be hazarded for the recovery of Heaven. Beelzebub finally tenders a proposal, first devised by Satan, to search the truth of a tradition in Heaven concerning another world and another kind of created being:)*

> There is a place
> . . . another world, the happy seat
> Of some new race call'd *Man* . . .
>
> *   *   *
>
> Thither let us bend our thoughts, to learn
> What creatures there inhabit, of what mould,
> Or substance, how endued, and what their power
> And where their weakness; how attempted best,
> By force or subtlety . . .
>   This would surpass
> Common revenge, and interrupt his joy
> In our confusion, and our joy upraise
> In his disturbance; when his darling sons,
> Hurl'd headlong to partake with us, shall curse
> Their frail original and faded bliss,
> Faded so soon! . . .
>   Thus Beelzebub
> Pleaded his devilish counsel . . .
>   Done all to spite
> The great Creator.

Milton, *Paradise Lost,* Book II

FAME
         see also AMBITION, GREATNESS—the emptiness of earthly

a matter of God's judgment

166.   Fame is no plant that grows on mortal soil,
           Nor in the glistering foil
           Set off to the world, nor in broad rumor lies,
           But lives and spreads aloft by those pure eyes

And perfect witness of all-judging Jove:
As he pronounces lastly on each deed,
Of so much fame in heaven expect thy meed.

Milton, "Lycidas"

the thirst for

167.   I used to know a man who carried always with him a Russian novel in the original; not because he read Russian, but because a day might come when, as a result of some accident, the "pocket of the deceased" would be exposed in the public press. He said, you never know; but the only accident which happened to him was to be stranded for twelve hours in August at a wayside station in the Highlands. After this he maintained that the Russians were overrated.

A. A. Milne, Not That It Matters

FATHER
"Honor thy Father"

168.   Of her father, Mrs. Carlyle always spoke with reverence; he was the only person who had any real influence over her. But however wilful or indulged she might be, obedience to her parents —unquestioning and absolute—lay at the foundation of her life. She was accustomed to say that this habit of obedience to her parents was her salvation through life,—that she owed all that was of value in her character to this habit as the foundation. Her father, from what she told me, was a man of strong and noble character,— very true, and hating all that was false. She always spoke of any praise he gave her as of a precious possession. She loved him with a deep reverence; and she never spoke of him except to friends whom she valued. It was the highest token of her regard when she told any one about her father.

Carlyle, Reminiscences, Vol. I

FEAR AND ANXIETY
dispelled

169.   The little cares that fretted me
I lost them yesterday,

Among the fields above the sea,
Among the winds at play;
Among the lowing of the herds,
The rustling of the trees;
Among the singing of the birds,
The humming of the bees.

The foolish fears of what might happen,
I cast them all away
Among the clover-scented grass,
Among the new-mown hay;
Among the husking of the corn
Where drowsy poppies nod,
Where ill thoughts die and good are born—
Out in the fields with God!

"The Little Cares That Fretted Me"
Attributed to Elizabeth Barrett Browning

170.   *(If ever anyone knew the pain of sleepless nights it was Robert Louis Stevenson. Even as a child he would wake up from a brief slumber with the sweat of a nightmare on his brow, to lie awake and listen, and long for the first signs of life among the silent streets.)*

It was my custom as the hours dragged on, to repeat the question, "When will the carts come in?" The road before our house is a great thoroughfare for early carts. I know not what they carry, whence they come, or whither they go. But I know that e'er dawn, and for hours together, they stream continuously past, and with the same rolling and jerking of wheels and the same clink of horses' feet. They are really the first throbbings of life, the harbingers of day; and it pleases you so much to hear them as it must please a shipwrecked seaman once again to grasp a hand of flesh and blood after years of miserable solitude. They have the freshness of the daylight about them. You can hear the carters cracking their whips and crying hoarsely to their horses or to one another; and sometimes even the peal of healthy, harsh horse-laughter comes up to you through the darkness. There is now an end of mystery and fear.

R. L. Stevenson, *Lay Morals and Other Papers*

FLATTERY
the absurdities of

171. The body of Constantine, adorned with the vain symbols of greatness, the purple and diadem, was deposited on a golden bed in one of the apartments of the palace, which for that purpose had been splendidly furnished and illuminated. Every day, at the appointed hours, the principal officers of the state, the army, and the household, approaching the person of their sovereign with bended knees and a composed countenance, offered their respectful homage as seriously as if he had been still alive. From motives of policy, this theatrical representation was for some time continued; nor could flattery neglect the opportunity of remarking that Constantine alone, by the peculiar indulgence of Heaven, had reigned after his death.

Gibbon, Decline and Fall of the Roman Empire

an irresistible

172. He knew his uncle repeated all compliments to the persons for whose use they were meant; and he found by experience the great impressions which they made on the philosopher as well as on the divine: for, to say the truth, there is no kind of flattery so irresistible as this at second hand.

Henry Fielding

man's susceptibility to

173. Men are most and best flattered upon those points where they wish to excel, and yet are doubtful whether they do or not. As for example, Cardinal Richelieu, who was undoubtedly the ablest statesman of his time, had the idle vanity of being thought the best poet too. He envied the great Corneille his reputation, and ordered a criticism of him to be written. Those, therefore, who flattered skillfully, said little to him of his abilities in state affairs. But the incense which they gave him, the smoke of which they knew would turn his head in their favor, was as a *bel esprit* and a poet. Why? Because he was sure of one excellency, and distrustful as to the other.

Lord Chesterfield, *Advice to His Son*

the servile spirit of

174.   God help the man, condemn'd by cruel fate,
       To court the seeming, or the real great!
       Much sorrow shall he feel, and suffer more
       Than any slave who labors at the oar:
       By slavish methods must he learn to please,
       By smooth-tongued flattery, that cursed court-disease;
       Supple to every wayward mood strike sail,
       And shift with shifting humor's peevish gale.
       To nature dead, he must adopt vile art,
       And wear a smile, with anguish in his heart.

                              Charles Churchill, "Night"

FORGIVENESS   *see also* LOVE, MERCY, RESENTMENT, RE-
                                                    TALIATION

the costliness of

175.   "Forgiveness," said Mr. Pecksniff, "entire and pure forgiveness, is not incompatible with a wounded heart; perchance when
the heart is wounded forgiveness becomes a greater virtue. With
my breast still wrung and grieved to its inmost core by the ingratitude of that person, I am proud and glad to say that I forgive
him."

                              Dickens, *Martin Chuzzlewit*

forgiving others

176.   Let not the sun go down upon thy wrath, but write thy
wrong in ashes. Draw the curtain of night upon injuries, and shut
them up in the tower of oblivion, and let them be as though they
had not been. To forgive our enemies, yet hope that God will
punish them, is not to forgive enough. To forgive them ourselves,
and not to pray God to forgive them, is a partial piece of charity.
Forgive thine enemies totally, without any reserve.

                              Sir Thomas Browne, *Christian Morals*

177.   It is not because a brother does many things which we may
think wrong, or which may in themselves deserve the heaviest
punishment, that he is to be disowned and renounced: the obliga-

tion to treat him as a brother uninterruptedly subsists; it is limited only by our power to render kindly offices, and his capacity to receive them; and the active exercise of its functions can never be suspended, except only when and in so far as he refuses to accept them, or is incapable of profiting by them.

Gladstone, *The Might of Right*

God's

178. *(Salome had robbed Ann of her husband, and after his death the two women happened to meet in the churchyard. It was winter.)*

Salome whispered to Ann, "There are some things too small for God to heed, and my broken life is one of them."

"Never, never," cried Ann, "all, to the pattern of the frost on these dear graves, be the thought invention of our God. Nought's too small for Him and nought too great. I've larned that, and I've larned what God's forgiveness means. Ours be but the shadow of His. He comes three parts of the way." Ann's eyes blazed into a sudden passion of faith and love. "The haste o' God. Quicker'n lightning. A sigh of sorrow brings Him or one humble thought."

Eden Phillpotts, *The Secret Woman*

a magnanimous

179. *(Lachlan Campbell was a strict Presbyterian of the old school, a man of iron principle. When his young, motherless girl ran off to London he disowned her and struck her name off the old family Bible. In the months that followed, as his Highland neighbors watched the old man go about his farm chores they knew that behind the grim exterior was a broken heart. As Marget Howe put it, "It was waesome tae see the auld man gatherin' his bit things wi' a shakin' hand, and speakin' tae me aboot the weather, an' a' the time his eyes were sayin' 'Flora, Flora!'" At Marget's pleading the poor girl was persuaded to come back to the Glen. In fear and trembling she reached Drumtochty. It was nighttime, and the Glen was bathed in the light of the harvest moon.)*

A turn of the path brought her within sight of the cottage, and her heart came into her mouth, for the kitchen window was a blaze of light. . . . But when she reached the door her strength had departed, and she was not able to knock. But there was no need, for the dogs, who never forget nor cast off, were bidding her welcome

with short joyous yelps of delight, and she could hear her father
feeling for the latch, which for once could not be found, and saying
nothing but "Flora, Flora!"

She had made up some kind of speech, but the only word she
ever said was "Father"; for Lachlan, who had never even kissed
her all the days of her youth, clasped her in his arms and sobbed
out blessings over her head, while the dogs licked her hands with
their soft, kindly tongues.

"It is a pity you have not the Gaelic," Flora said to Marget
afterwards; "it is the best of all languages for loving. There are
fifty words for darling, and my father would be calling me every
one that night I came home."

Ian Maclaren, Beside the Bonnie Briar Bush

of self

180.   *(The pastor is telling of one who, unable to forgive himself
for his sin, finally took his own life:)*

[He]

> Against his conscience rose in arms, and, braving
> Divine displeasure, broke the marriage vow.
> That which he had been weak enough to do
> Was misery in remembrance; he was stung,
> Stung by his inward thoughts, and by the smiles
> Of wife and children stung to agony.
> Wretched at home, he gained no peace abroad;
> Ranged through the mountains, slept upon the earth,
> Asked comfort of the open air, and found
> No quiet in the darkness of the night,
> No pleasure in the beauty of the day.
> His flock he slighted: his paternal fields
> Became a clog to him, whose spirit wished
> To fly—but whither!

*   *   *

> Much to the last remained unknown: but this
> Is sure, that through remorse and grief he died;
> Though pitied among men, absolved by God,
> He could not find forgiveness in himself;
> Nor could endure the weight of his own shame.

Wordsworth, The Excursion, Bk. VI

an unforgiving spirit

181.   *(Two maiden sisters, who lived in Edinburgh, refused to have any dealings with each other.)*

The pair inhabited a single room. From the facts it must have been double-bedded; and it may have been of some dimensions; but when all is said, it was a single room. Here our two spinsters fell out—on some point of controversial divinity belike; but fell out so bitterly that there was never a word spoken between them, black or white, from that day forward. You would have thought that they would separate; but no, whether from lack of means or the Scottish fear of scandal, they continued to keep house together where they were. A chalk line drawn upon the floor separated the two domains; it bisected the doorway and the fireplace, so that each could go out and in, and do her own cooking without violating the territory of the other. So, for years they co-existed in a hateful silence; their meals, their ablutions, their friendly visitors, exposed to an unfriendly scrutiny; and at night, in the dark watches, each could hear the breathing of her enemy. Never did four walls look down upon an uglier spectacle than these sisters rivalling in un-sisterliness.

R. L. Stevenson, Edinburgh: Picturesque Notes

182.   *(The husband was grievously wronged by his wife whom he practically worshiped. After long years of separation he almost unwittingly discovers her, only to find her in a dying state. She begs his forgiveness.)*

"You . . . you . . . loved me once."

He stood like a statue in a flood of sunlight.

"I ask . . . too hard a thing . . . You cannot forgive?"

He suddenly straightened himself, but he never uttered a word. He never looked at her again or so much as turned his head. He walked quickly across the room, opened the door, and was gone. She watched him to the last, her eyes starting from her head, her breath coming in choking sobs, her hands clutching each other convulsively. . . .

V. L. Whitechurch, The Locum Tenens

FRIENDSHIP
the security of

183.   Oh, the comfort—the inexpressible comfort of feeling
            safe with a person,
        Having neither to weigh thoughts,
        Nor measure words—but pouring them
        All right out—just as they are—
        Chaff and grain together—
        Certain that a faithful hand will
        Take and sift them—
        Keep what is worth keeping—
        And with the breath of kindness
        Blow the rest away.

                            Dinah Maria Mulock Craik, *Poems*

FUNERAL   *see also* DEATH
of a man of faith

184.   Servant of God, well done!
                    Rest from thy loved employ:
            The battle fought, the victory won,
                    Enter thy Master's joy.

            The pains of death are past,
                Labor and sorrow cease,
            And Life's long warfare closed at last,
                Thy soul is found in peace.

                                    James Montgomery

FUTURE LIFE   *see also* IMMORTALITY
knowledge of the

185.   "I cannot see what harm would come of letting us know a
little—as much as might serve to assure us that there was more of
something on the other side."—Just this: that, their fears allayed,
their hopes encouraged from any lower quarter, men would (as
usual) turn away from the Fountain, to the cistern of life. . . .
That there are thousands who would forget God if they could but
be assured of a tolerable state of things beyond the grave as even
this wherein we live, is plainly to be anticipated from the fact that

the doubts of so many in respect of religion concentrate themselves
now-a-days upon the question whether there is any life beyond
the grave; a question which does not immediately belong to religion
at all. Satisfy such people, if you can, that they shall live, and what
have they gained? A little comfort perhaps—but a comfort not from
the highest source, and possibly gained too soon for their well-
being. Does it bring them any nearer to God than they were before?
Is He filling one cranny more of their hearts in consequence?

George Macdonald, Thomas Wingfield, Curate

GIVING   see also SERVICE
genuine

186.   For the real good of every gift it is essential, first, that the
giver be in the gift—as God always is, for He is love—and next, that
the receiver know and receive the giver in the gift. Every gift of
God is but a harbinger of His greatest and only sufficing gift—that
of Himself. No gift unrecognized as coming from God is at its own
best: therefore many things that God would gladly give us must
wait until we ask for them, that we may know whence they come.
When in all gifts we find Him, then in Him we shall find all things.

George MacDonald, Second Series,
"The Word of Jesus on Prayer"

GOD   see also NATURE—God revealed in
the evidence for

187.   I have some favorite flowers in spring, among which are the
mountain daisy, the foxglove, the wild-brier rose and the hoary
hawthorne, that I view and hang over with particular delight. I
never heard the loud, solitary whistle of the curlew in a summer
noon, or the wild mixing cadence of a troop of gray plovers in an
autumnal morning, without feeling an elevation of soul. Tell me,
my dear friend, to what can this be owing? Are we a piece of
machinery, which, like the Aeolian harp, passive, takes the impres-
sion of the passing accident? Or do these workings argue something
within us above the trodden clod? I own myself partial to such
proofs of those awful and important realities—a God that made all
things, man's immaterial and immortal nature, and a world of weal
or woe beyond death and the grave.

Burns, in a letter, New Year's Day morning, 1789

188.   I look out of myself into a world of men and there I see a sight which fills me with unspeakable distress. The world seems simply to give the lie to that great truth, of which my whole being is so full, the fact of God's [existence]. If I looked into a mirror and did not see my face, I should have the sort of feeling which actually comes upon me when I look into this living busy world and see no reflection of its Creator. Were it not for this voice, speaking so clearly in my conscience and my heart, I should be an atheist, or a pantheist, or a polytheist when I looked into the world.

John Henry Newman,
"God, the World, and the Church" (an essay)

189.   What can be more foolish than to think that all this rare fabric of heaven and earth could come by chance, when all the skill of art is not able to make an oyster? To see rare effects, and no cause; a motion, without a mover; a circle, without a center; a time, without an eternity; a second, without a first. These are things so against philosophy and natural reason that he must be a beast in understanding who can believe in them. The thing formed says that nothing formed it; and that which is made, is, while that which made it is not! This folly is infinite.

Jeremy Taylor, *Sermons for the Winter Half-Year*

190.   I found Him in the shining of the stars,
                 I mark'd Him in the flowering of His fields,
                 But in His ways with men I find Him not.

Tennyson, "Guinevere"

the immanence of   *see also* PROVIDENCE, VISION—the blessed-
                                                           ness of

191.   As gently as falls an autumn leaf she laid her hand on Eliza's head: "Ah, wumin, God isn't a printed book to be carried aroun' by a man in fine clothes, not a gold cross to be danglin' at the watch-chain of a priest. God's spirit comes in as many ways as there's need fur it comin', and that's quite a wheen. . . . God takes a hand wherever He can find it. Sometimes He takes a Bishop's hand and lays it on a child's head in benediction, then He takes the hand of a doctor to relieve pain, the hand of a mother to guide a child, and sometimes He takes the hand of a poor old craither like me to give comfort to a neighbor. But they're all hands touched by His Spirit, and His Spirit is everywhere lukin' for hands to use."

Alexander Irvine, *My Lady of the Chimney Corner*

192.   Speak to Him, thou, for He hears, and Spirit with Spirit can meet—
Closer is He than breathing, and nearer than hands and feet.

Tennyson, "The Higher Pantheism"

in man's image

193.   "O God, put away justice and truth for we cannot understand them and we do not want them. Eternity would bore us dreadfully. Leave Thy heavens and come down to our earth of water-clocks and hedges. Become our uncle. Look after baby, amuse Grandfather . . . help Willie with his homework, introduce Muriel to a handsome naval officer. Be interesting and weak like us, and we will love you as we love ourselves."

W. H. Auden, "For the Time Being," A Christmas Oratorio

the only satisfaction

194.   In having all things, and not Thee, what have I?
Not having Thee what have my labors got?
Let me enjoy but Thee, what further crave I?
And having Thee alone, what have I not?
    I wish nor sea nor land; nor would I be
Possess'd of heaven, heaven unpossess'd of Thee.

Francis Quarles

presumptuous inquiry into the mystery of

195.   O awful, awful name of God! Light unbearable! Mystery unfathomable! Vastness immeasurable! Who are these who come forward to explain the mystery, and gaze unblinking into the depths of the light, and measure the immeasurable vastness to a hair? O Name, that God's people of old did fear to utter! O Light, that God's prophet would have perished had he seen! Who are these that are now so familiar with it?

Thackeray, *The Paris Sketch Book*

196.   Dangerous it were for the feeble brain of man to wade far
into the doings of the Most High; whom although to know be life,
and joy to make mention of his name, yet our soundest knowledge
is to know that we know him not as indeed he is, neither can know
him; and our safest eloquence is our silence, when we confess without confession that his glory is inexplicable, his greatness above our
capacity and reach.

Richard Hooker, *Ecclesiastical Polity*, Bk. I, Ch. 2

the vision of

197.   When Gerontius arrives in the other world he begs to be
admitted into the Divine Presence. He is impatient to behold the
Beatific Vision. In spite of the angel's efforts to dissuade him he
persists, until at last the eager spirit "with the intemperate energy
of Love" darts into the Presence—only to fall, blinded and seared
by the Divine Glory. Trembling, he cries,

"Take me away, and in the lowest deep
There let me be. . . ."

John Henry Newman, "The Dream of Gerontius" (adapted)

GOD SEEKING MAN   *see also* Love—the sacrifice of,
Sorrow, Suffering

the Divine condescension

198.   God who registers the cup
Of mere cold water, for His sake
To a disciple rendered up—
Disdains not His own thirst to slake
At the poorest love was ever offered:
And because it was my heart I proffered,
With true love trembling at the brim,
He suffers me to follow Him
For ever.

Browning, "Christmas Eve"

199.   You must picture me alone in that room in Magdalen, night
after night, feeling whenever my mind lifted even for a second from
my work, the steady, unrelenting approach of Him whom I so
earnestly desired not to meet. That which I greatly feared had

at last come upon me. In the Trinity Term of 1929 I gave in, and
admitted that God was God, and knelt and prayed: perhaps, that
night, the most dejected and reluctant convert in all England. I
did not then see what is now the most shining and obvious thing;
the Divine humility which will accept a convert on such terms.
The Prodigal Son at least walked home on his own feet. But who
can duly adore that Love which will open the high gates to a
prodigal who is brought in kicking, struggling, resentful, and darting
his eyes in every direction for a chance to escape? The words
compelle intrare, compel them to come in, have been so abused by
wicked men that we shudder at them; but, properly understood,
they plumb the depth of Divine mercy. The hardness of God is
kinder than the softness of men, and His compulsion is our libera-
tion.

C. S. Lewis, *Surprised by Joy*

the Divine courtesy

200.   Nor will God force any door to enter in. He may send a
tempest about the house; the wind of His admonishment may burst
doors and windows, yea, shake the house to its foundations; but
not then, not so, will He enter. The door must be opened with
the willing hand, ere the foot of Love will cross the threshold. He
watches to see the door move from within. Every tempest is but
an assault in the siege of love. The terror of God is but the other
side of His love; it is love outside, that would be inside—love that
knows no house, only a place, until it enter.

George Macdonald, *The Cause of Spiritual Stupidity*

the Divine persistence

201.   *(Because none has come to help him in his hour of distress
the hero of the poem grows embittered toward all men:)*
> This bitter night
> I will make fast my door
> That hollow friends may trouble me no more.
(But in the night a knock is heard, and a Voice pleads:)
> Rise, let me in. . . .
> My Feet bleed, see my Face,
> See my Hands bleed that bring thee grace,

My heart doth bleed for thee,
Open to Me.
(All night long the knocking continues—till at daybreak the wretched man hears the footsteps fade away, "echoing like a sigh." On opening the door he sees)
Each footprint marked in blood and on my door
The mark of blood forevermore.
Christina Rossetti, "Despised and Rejected" (adapted)

202. *(To gratify his father's ambition Francis Thompson (d. 1907) embarked on a medical career—and failed to pass his final examinations. Seeking refuge from reproach, he lived a life of obscurity in London, at first selling books and later working for the book trade. Failing in both of these enterprises he enlisted as a soldier, but was discharged for incompetence. Thereafter he lived in the lowest conceivable kind of poverty, selling matches in the daytime and sleeping on the Thames Embankment at night. By now he was in poor health and addicted to laudanum. He tried writing. His first brief compositions eventually found an editor in Wilfred Meynell, husband of the poet Alice Meynell. The Meynells, impressed by the merit of the fragments, were able to locate their author only after much difficulty. Shocked when they first saw him—emaciated and in rags—they restored him to health and helped him find religious faith.*

"The Hound of Heaven," which Coventry Patmore declared "one of the very few great odes the language can boast," has been more widely read than any other religious poem of the century. It is the story of a man running from God.)
(1. He retreats within himself:)
I fled Him, down the nights and down the days;
I fled Him, down the arches of the years;
I fled Him, down the labyrinthine ways
Of my own mind; and in the midst of tears
I hid from Him . . .
(2. Forced to look beyond himself, the hunted soul seeks security in human love:)
I pleaded, outlaw-wise,
By many a hearted casement, curtained red.

(3. He tries to lose himself in the wonders of the universe:)
Across the margent of the world I fled,
And troubled the gold gateways of the stars,
                          ❋   ❋   ❋
Clung to the whistling mane of every wind.

(4. He seeks a hiding-place in the fellowship of little children:)
They at least are for me, surely for me!

(5. He finally seeks consolation in the nature scene:)
Against the red throb of its sunset heart
        I laid my own to beat.

(6. But the fleeing soul knew that there was no ultimate escape
from those strong Feet that followed:)
        But with unhurrying chase,
        And unperturbèd pace,
Deliberate speed, majestic instancy,
        They beat—and a Voice beat
        More instant than the Feet:
"All things betray thee, who betrayest Me."
                          ❋   ❋   ❋
That Voice is round me like a bursting sea . . .
"Lo, all things fly thee, for thou flyest Me!
        Strange, piteous, futile thing!
                          ❋   ❋   ❋
        Ah, fondest, blindest, weakest,
        I am He Whom thou seekest!
Thou dravest love from thee, who dravest Me."
                    Francis Thompson, "The Hound of Heaven"

the Divine withholding

203.   When God at first made man,
        Having a glass of blessings standing by;
        Let us (said He) pour on him all we can:
        Let the world's riches, which dispersèd lie,
            Contract into a span.

            So strength first made a way;
        Then beauty flowed, then wisdom, honour, pleasure.
        When almost all was out, God made a stay,

Perceiving that alone of all His treasure
　　Rest in the bottom lay.

　For if I should (said He)
Bestow this jewel also on my creature,
He would adore my gifts instead of me,
And rest in Nature, not the God of Nature.
　　So both should losers be.

　Yet let him keep the rest,
But keep them with repining restlessness:
Let him be rich and weary, that at least,
If goodness lead him not, yet weariness
　　May toss him to My breast.

George Herbert, "The Pulley"

in manifold ways

204.　　　　　　　　　　As men from men
　　Do, in the constitution of their souls,
　　Differ, by mystery not to be explained;
　　And as we fall by various ways, and sink
　　One deeper than another, self-condemned,
　　Through manifold degrees of shame;
　　So manifold and various are the ways
　　Of restoration, fashioned to the steps
　　Of all infirmity, and tending all
　　To the same point, attainable by all—
　　Peace in ourselves, and union with our God.

Wordsworth, The Excursion, Bk. IV

GOODNESS
instinctive

205.　　I called upon Dr. Johnson. He said he did not like Dempster. He said he had not met any man in a long time who had given him such general displeasure. That he was totally unfixed in his principles, and wanted to puzzle other people. I told him that Dempster's principles were poisoned by David Hume, but that he was a good, benevolent sort of man. "Sir," said Johnson, "I can lay but little stress upon that instinctive constitutional goodness that

is not founded upon principle. I grant you that such a man may be
a very good member of society. I can conceive him doing no harm.
But if such a man stood in need of money, I should not like to
trust him."

Boswell's London Journal, 1762-1763

GREATNESS *see also* AMBITION, FAME
the emptiness of earthly

206. When the shadows lengthen and the sun is going down,
earthly greatness fades to tinsel, and nothing is any longer beautiful
to look back upon but the disinterested actions, many or few, which
are scattered over the checkered career. Disraeli like many other
distinguished men had to pay the penalty of his character. A fool
may have his vanity satisfied with garters and peerages; Disraeli
must have been conscious of their emptiness.

J. A. Froude, *The Earl of Beaconsfield*

207. *(The allusion is to Frederick the Great.)*
What is greatness? What is glory? These are the questions which
arise on a contemplation of Frederick's life. He indeed had his full
measure of glory and is usually designated as "Great." But his death
was preceded by scores of thousands of others for which he was
solely responsible, a gloomy and sorrowful procession of plain folk
slaughtered because "ambition, interest, the desire to make people
talk about me" had let him seize without provocation or justification a province from a young woman unable at the moment to defend it. These souls surely await him at the gates of the future.

Lord Rosebery, *Miscellanies, Literary and Historical,* Vol. I

208.   Farewell! a long farewell, to all my greatness!
This is the state of man: today he puts forth
The tender leaves of hope; tomorrow blossoms,
And bears his blushing honors thick upon him;
The third day comes a frost, a killing frost;
And, when he thinks, good easy man, full surely
His greatness is a-ripening, nips his root,
And then he falls, as I do.

Shakespeare, *King Henry VIII,*
Act III, Sc. 2
(Cardinal Wolsey)

the humility of true

209.   *(The writer is speaking of Gladstone, one of Britain's great prime ministers.)*

Could any scene be more compelling than the incident my brother Alfred told me of a walk he took with the Grand Old Man at Hawarden, when, soon after the start, the latter interrupted the copious talk by stopping outside a cottage in which an old laborer lay dying? From outside Alfred saw the picture of the white-haired statesman kneeling by the sick man's bedside, and with the beautiful face uplifted, while words simple, stately, and sincere were being uttered in the deep expressive tones that had touched the hearts of listening millions in every corner of the land. But more impressive, more eloquent of the higher life, was the utterly genuine self-forgetfulness with which he presently rose up and resumed his conversation, wholly unconscious that he had been acting differently from the common run of men.

Edward Lyttelton, *Memories and Hopes*

in obscurity   *see also* INFLUENCE

210.   I believe there are quiet victories and struggles, great sacrifices of self, and noble acts of heroism—even in many of its apparent lightnesses and contradictions—not the less difficult to achieve because they have no earthly chronicle or audience—done every day in nooks and corners, and in little households, and in men's and women's hearts—any one of which might reconcile the sternest man to such a world, and fill him with belief and hope in it, though two-fourths of its people were at war, and another fourth at law.

Charles Dickens, *The Battle of Life*

211.   Not a day passes over the earth but men and women of no note do great deeds, speak great words, and suffer noble sorrows. Of these obscure heroes, philosophers, and martyrs, the greater part will never be known till that hour when many that are great shall be small, and the small great.

Charles Reade, *The Cloister and the Hearth*

GREED   *see also* MONEY

212.   Gold! gold! gold! gold!
             Bright and yellow, hard and cold,

> Molten, graven, hammered and rolled,
> Heavy to get, and light to hold;
> Hoarded, bartered, bought and sold,
> Stolen, borrowed, squandered, doled;
> Spurned by the young, but hugged by the old
> To the very verge of the churchyard mold;
> Price of many a crime untold.

Thomas Hood, "Gold"

213.   A miser, being dead and fairly interred, comes to the banks of the Styx desiring to be ferried over along with the other ghosts. Charon demands his fare, and is surprised to see the miser, rather than pay it, throw himself into the river and swim over to the other side, notwithstanding all the clamor and opposition that could be made to him. All hell was in an uproar; and each of the judges was meditating some punishment suitable to a crime of such dangerous consequence to the infernal revenues. Shall he be chained to the rock with Prometheus? or tremble below the precipice in company with the Danaïdes? No, says Minos, none of these. We must invent some severer punishment. Let him be sent back to earth to see the use his heirs are making of his riches.

David Hume, Essays, "Of Avarice"

214.   Avarice is rarely the vice of a young man: it is rarely the vice of a great man: but Marlborough was one of the few who have, in the bloom of youth, loved lucre more than wine and women, and who have, at the height of greatness, loved lucre more than power or fame. All the precious gifts which nature had lavished on him he valued chiefly for what they would fetch. At twenty he made money of his beauty and vigor. At sixty he made money of his genius and glory.

Macaulay, History of England

GUIDANCE   *see also* CHRIST—our sufficiency, PROVIDENCE
dependence only on God for

215.   My parents founded every action, every attitude, upon their interpretation of the Scriptures, and upon the guidance of the Divine Will as revealed to them by direct answer to prayer. Their ejaculation in the face of any dilemma was, "Let us cast it before the Lord!"

So confident were they of the reality of their intercourse with
God, that they asked for no other guide. They recognized no
spiritual authority among men, they subjected themselves to no
priest or minister, they troubled their consciences about no current
manifestation of "religious opinion." They lived in an intellectual
cell, bounded at its sides by the walls of their own house, but open
above to the very heart of the uttermost heavens.

Edmund Gosse, *Father and Son*

HAPPINESS   *see also* CONTENTMENT
an atttitude of mind

216.   Hazlitt in one of his essays relates how he went on foot from
one great man's house to another in search of works of art. In the
end he discovered that he triumphed over these noble and wealthy
owners because he was more capable of enjoying their costly posses-
sions than they were; they had paid the money and he had received
the pleasure. While one man worked to buy the picture, the other
enjoyed the fruit of his labor.

R. L. Stevenson, *Virginibus Puerisque*, "Ordered South"

not found in escape   *see also* ESCAPISM

217.   Rasselas, son of the emperor of Abyssinia, was confined in a
palace until he should succeed to the throne. It was situated in
a fertile valley enclosed by high mountains and entered only by a
canyon cut through a rock which was guarded by high iron gates.
Never was more scenic setting than this valley! Mountain slopes
with trees of every leaf, a lake that was a fisherman's paradise,
gardens that scented the air with the most delicate fragrance! The
youth Rasselas had everything necessary to happiness, yet he was
not happy. For three long years he explored the mountains, seeking
escape from what to him was an intolerable existence. At length,
with the help of his tutor, Imlac, he discovered a cleft in a rock
that led to the rim of the vast outer world. Soon, far below them
ran the Nile, winding its snake-like course. Through the world the
two roamed, studying human life in all its phases. They visited
the temple of mirth where St. Cecilia sang, the temple of wisdom
where Democritus lived, the temple of justice where Aristides sat,

the temple of wisdom where Solomon dropped his mantle. But nowhere did Rasselas find happiness.

"Ye who listen with credulity," adds Johnson, "to the whispers of fancy, and pursue with eagerness the phantoms of hope; who expect that age will perform the promises of youth, and that the deficiencies of the present day will be supplied by the morrow,— attend to the history of Rasselas, Prince of Abyssinia."

Samuel Johnson, Rasselas (adapted)

the search for see also MAN—the seeker

218. From the winter of 1821, when I first read Bentham, I had what might truly be called an object in life: to be a reformer of the world. My conception of my own happiness was entirely identified with this object. . . . But the time came when I awakened from this as from a dream. It was in the autumn of 1826. I was in a dull state of nerves, such as everybody is occasionally liable to; one of those moods when what is pleasure at other times becomes insipid or indifferent. . . . The lines of Coleridge exactly describe my case:

> "A grief without a pang, void, dark and drear,
> A drowsy, stifled, unimprisoned grief,
> Which finds no natural outlet or relief
> In word, or sigh, or tear."

(From this state Mill was aroused by a passage in his readings. It caused him to revise his idea of happiness, which he states as follows:)

Those only are happy who have their minds fixed on some object other than their own happiness; on the happiness of others, on the improvement of mankind, even on some art or pursuit, followed not as a means but as itself an ideal end. Aiming thus at something else, they find happiness by the way. . . . Ask yourself whether you are happy, and you cease to be so. The only chance is to treat, not happiness, but some end external to it, as the purpose of life.

John Stuart Mill, Autobiography

springs from within

219. The fountain of content must spring up in the mind, and he who has so little knowledge of human nature as to seek happiness

by changing anything but his own disposition will waste his life
in fruitless efforts and multiply the griefs which he purposes to
remove.

Samuel Johnson

the way to

220.   We can only have the highest happiness, such as goes along
with being a great man, by having wide thoughts and much feeling for the rest of the world as well as ourselves; and this sort of
happiness often brings much pain with it. . . . There are so many
things wrong and difficult in the world, that no man can be great
unless he gives up thinking much about pleasure and rewards, and
gets strength to endure what is hard and painful.

George Eliot, Romola

the world's failure to minister to man's   *see also* WORLD

221.   (*Abd al-Rahman, the famed monarch of Cordova, reputedly
uttered these words:*)
    "I have now reigned above fifty years in victory or peace;
beloved by my subjects, dreaded by my enemies, and respected by
my allies. Riches and honors, power and pleasure, have waited on
my call; nor does any earthly blessing appear to have been want-
ing to my felicity. In this situation I diligently numbered ᴜᴇ days
of pure and genuine happiness which have fallen to my lot; they
amount to Fourteen: O man, place not thy confidence in this present
world!"

Quoted in Gibbon, Decline and Fall of the Roman Empire

HEAVEN
an intolerable place to the irreligious

222.   If a man without religion were admitted into heaven, doubtless he would sustain a great disappointment. He would perceive
himself to be an isolated being, cut away by Supreme Power from
those objects which were still entwined about his heart. Nay, he
would be in the presence of that Supreme Power, whom he never
on earth could bring himself steadily to think upon, and whom he
now regards only as the destroyer of all that was precious and dear
to him. Heaven is not a place of happiness except to the holy.
    Nay, I will venture to say more than this;—it is fearful but it is
right to say it—that if we wish to imagine a punishment for an

unholy, reprobate soul, we perhaps could not fancy a greater than
to summon it to heaven. Heaven would be hell to an irreligious
man.

John Henry Newman, *Parochial Sermons*

HEREDITY
need not determine destiny

223. Lord, I find the genealogy of my Saviour strangely
chequered with four remarkable changes in four generations. Ro-
boam begat Abia—a bad father begat a bad son. Abia begat Asa—
a bad father and a good son. Asa begat Josaphat—a good father
and a good son. Josaphat begat Joram—a good father and a bad son.
I see, Lord, from hence that my father's piety cannot be entailed;
that is bad news for me. But I see also that actual impiety is not
hereditary; that is good news for my son.

Thomas Fuller, *Good Thoughts in Bad Times*

HOME   *see also* CHILDREN
religion in the

224. But the real strength of Evangelicalism lay not in the pulpit
or the platform, but in the home. . . . To judge from memoirs and
biographies, the Evangelical families of England were conspicu-
ously happy families, and it was in hearts of Victorian mothers
that the Evangelical piety won the most signal and the most gracious
of its triumphs. The characteristic religious observance of the
Victorian home was family prayers, which, as the then Archbishop
of Canterbury reminded us ten years ago, brought remembrance
of God right into the heart of the home life from beginning to
end. The Evangelical was not shy about his religion because he had
grown up into it from his mother's knee. Puritanism, it has been
said, was the religion of the State: Methodism the religion of the
heart: the Oxford Movement the religion of the Church: but
Evangelicalism was the religion of the home.

Harman Grisewood, ed., *Ideas and Beliefs of the Victorians*

tyrants in the

225. "Anyone who watches the world must think with trembling
sometimes of the account which many a man will have to render.

For in our society there's no law to control the King of the Fireside. He is master of property, happiness—life almost. He is free to punish, to make happy or unhappy, to ruin or torture. He may kill a wife gradually, and be no more questioned than the Grand Seignor who drowns a slave at midnight. He may make slaves and hypocrites of his children; or drive them into revolt and enmity against the natural law of love. When the annals of each little reign are shown to the Supreme Master, under whom we hold sovereignty, histories will be laid bare of household tyrants as savage as Nero."

Thackeray, Henry Esmond (Lady Esmond)

HOSPITALITY   see also KINDNESS
the Rune of

226.   I saw a stranger yestreen;
            I put food in the eating place,
            Drink in the drinking place,
            Music in the listening place,
            And, in the sacred name of the Father,
            He blessed myself and my house,
            My cattle and my dear ones.
            And the lark sang in her song,
                Often, often, often,
            Goes the Christ in the stranger's guise;
                Often, often, often,
            Goes the Christ in the stranger's guise.

Anonymous; old Gaelic rune recovered by
Kenneth MacLeod, The Road to the Isles

HUMAN NATURE   see also HYPOCRISY, MAN, SELF-
the capriciousness of   CENTEREDNESS

227.   It is now sixteen or seventeen years since I saw the Queen of France, then the Dauphiness, at Versailles; and surely never lighted on this orb, which she hardly seemed to touch, a more delightful vision. I saw her just above the horizon, decorating and cheering the elevated sphere she had just begun to move in— glittering like the morning star, full of life, and splendor, and joy. . . . Little did I dream that I should have lived to see disasters

fallen upon her in a nation of gallant men, in a nation of men of honour, and of cavaliers. I thought ten thousand swords must have leaped from their scabbards to avenge even a look that threatened her with insult. But the age of chivalry is gone.

Edmund Burke, *Reflections on the Revolution in France*

228. At these times Mr. Micawber, when pestered by creditors, would be transported with grief and mortification, even to the length (as I was once made aware by the screams of his wife) of making motions at himself with a razor; but within half-an-hour afterwards, he would polish up his shoes with extraordinary pains, and go out, humming a tune with a greater air of gentility than ever. Mrs. Micawber was quite as elastic. I have known her to be thrown into fainting fits by the king's taxes at three o'clock, and to eat lamb-chops, breaded, and drink warm ale (paid for with two teaspoons that had gone to the pawnbrokers) at four. On one occasion, when an execution had just been put in, coming home through some chance as early as six o'clock, I saw her lying under the grate in a swoon, with her hair full torn about her face; but I never heard her more cheerful than she was that very same night, over a veal-cutlet before the kitchen fire telling me stories about her papa and mama, and the company they used to keep.

Dickens, *David Copperfield*

229. I think what has chiefly struck me in human beings is their lack of consistency. I have never seen people all of a piece. It has amazed me that the most incongruous traits should exist in the same person and for all that yield a plausible harmony. I have often asked myself how characteristics, seemingly irreconcilable, can exist in the same person.

W. Somerset Maugham, *The Summing Up*

230. *(It had ever been Lady Castlewood's disposition to devise kindnesses and scheme benevolences for those about her. But when word reached her that her husband had been killed in a duel, of his own provoking, her ladyship's reaction was sudden and remarkable.)*

The widow of the slain nobleman showed an extraordinary spirit, and declared she would have revenge on her husband's murderer. So much and suddenly had grief, anger, and misfortune appeared to change her. But fortune good or ill, does not change men or women. It but develops character. . . . The heart is a secret even to him who has it in his own breast. Who hath not found himself surprised into revenge, or action, or passion, for good or evil, whereof the seeds lay within him, latent and unsuspected, until the occasion called them forth.

Thackeray, *Henry Esmond*

the credulity of

231.   But half the opinions and prejudices of mankind, those which they hold in the most unqualified approbation and which have been instilled into them under the strongest sanctions, are opinions, not which they have ever thought, known, or felt one tittle about, but which they have taken up on trust from others, which have been palmed on their understandings by fraud or force, and which they continue to hold at the peril of life, limb, property, and character, with as little warrant from common sense in the first instance as appeal to reason in the last.

Hazlitt, *Table Talk*, "On Genius and Common Sense"

the self-centeredness of   *see also* SELF-CENTEREDNESS

232.   *(The subject of the extract is the poet Swinburne.)*
   As I stood watching autobus after autobus swing round in a fearful semicircle to begin a new journey, I gazed myself into a mystic comprehension of the significance of what I saw. A few yards beyond where the autobuses turned was a certain house with lighted upper windows, and in that house the greatest lyric versifier that England ever had, and one of the greatest poets of the whole world and of all the ages, was dying: a name immortal. But nobody looked; nobody seemed to care; I doubt if any one thought of it. This enormous negligence appeared to me to be . . . magnificently human.

Arnold Bennett, *Books and Persons*

233.   How very little one human being generally cares for another! How very little the world misses anybody! How soon the chasm left by the best and wisest men closes! Our own selfishness when others are taken away ought to teach us how little others

will suffer at losing us. There are not ten people in the world whose deaths would spoil my dinner.

Macaulay, in a letter to Hannah M. Macaulay, July 31, 1833

the self-deceptiveness of *see also* HYPOCRISY

234. A somewhat amazing fact in the strange and contradictory character of Samuel Pepys is the constant element of subtlety which blends with so much frankness. He wants to do wrong in many different ways but he wants still more to do it with propriety, and to have some sort of plausible excuse which will explain it in a respectable light. Nor is it only other people whom he is bent on deceiving. Were that all, we should have a very simple type of hypocritical scoundrel, which would be as different as possible from the extraordinary Pepys. There is a sense of propriety in him, and a conscience of obeying the letter of the law and keeping up appearances even in his own eyes. If he can persuade himself that he has done that, all things are open to him. He will receive a bribe, but it must be given in such a way that he can satisfy his conscience with ingenious words. The envelope has coins in it, but then he opens it behind his back and the coins fall out upon the floor. He has only picked them up when he found them there, and can defy the world to accuse him of having received any coins in the envelope. Thus, along the whole course of life, he cheats himself continually. It is a curious question what idea of God can be entertained by a man who plays tricks with himself in this fashion. Of Pepys certainly it cannot be said that God "is not in all his thoughts," for the name and the remembrance are constantly recurring. Yet God seems to occupy a quite hermetically sealed compartment of the universe; for His servant in London shamelessly goes on with the game he is playing, and appears to take a pride in the very conscience he systematically hoodwinks.

John Kelman, *Among Famous Books*

the weakness of

235. (*Patrick Branwell, the only brother of the three Brontë sisters, lived to bring much suffering into the home. His early death was an added blow. Charlotte speaks of it in these words:*)

When I looked on the face and forehead of my dead brother, and asked myself what had made him go ever wrong, tend ever downwards, when he had so many gifts to induce to and aid in, an upward course, I seemed to receive an oppressive revelation of the feebleness of humanity—of the inadequacy of even genius to lead to true greatness if unaided by religion and principle.

                        Charlotte Brontë, in a letter to W. S. Williams

236.   She was tired, she was sick of that barren exhortation—Do right, and keep a clear conscience, and God will reward you, and your troubles will be easier to bear. She wanted *strength* to do right —she wanted something to rely on besides her own resolutions; for was not the path behind her all strewn with *broken* resolutions? How could she trust in new ones?

                        George Eliot, *Janet's Repentance*

HUMILITY   *see also* GREATNESS, PRIDE
breeds contentment

237.   Now as they were going along and talking, they espied a boy feeding his father's sheep. The boy was in very mean clothes, but of a fresh and well-favored countenance; and as he sat by himself he sang:

>   "He that is down, need fear no fall;
>   He that is low, no pride;
>   He that is humble ever shall
>   Have God to be his guide."

Then said Mr. Greatheart to Christian, "Do you hear him? I will dare to say this boy lives a merrier life, and wears more of that herb called heart's-ease in his bosom than he that is clad in silk and velvet."

                        Bunyan, *Pilgrim's Progress*

the cultivation of

238.   Let every day be a day of humility; condescend to all the weaknesses and infirmities of your fellow-creatures, cover their frailties, love their excellencies, encourage their virtues, relieve their wants, rejoice in their prosperities, compassionate their distress, receive their friendship, overlook their unkindness, forgive their malice, be a servant of servants, and condescend to do the lowest offices to the lowest of mankind.

                        William Law, *Serious Call*

HYPOCRISY   *see also* HUMAN NATURE—the self-deceptiveness of, HYPOCRITE, INSINCERITY, LYING—the
sin of

239. *(The poet satirizes religious hypocrisy:)*
Lord, mind Gawn Hamilton's deserts,
He drinks, an' swears, an' plays at cartes;

❄ ❄ ❄

An' when we chasten'd him therefor,
Thou kens how he bred sic a splore [made sport of it],
As set the warld in a roar
                    O' laughin' at us;
Curse thou his basket and his store,
                    Kail and potatoes!

❄ ❄ ❄

But, Lord, remember me and mine,
Wi' mercies temp'ral and divine,
That I for gear and grace may shine,
                    Excell'd by nane;
An' a' the glory shall be thine,
                    Amen, Amen!
                    Burns, "Holy Willie's Prayer"

240.   Keep up appearances; there lies the test;
The world will give thee credit for the rest.
Outward be fair, however foul within;
Sin, if thou wilt; but then, in secret, sin.
This maxim's into common favor grown,
Vice is no longer vice unless 'tis known.
                    Charles Churchill, "Night"

241. *(On the eve of King Duncan's fatal visit to Macbeth's castle
Lady Macbeth schools her husband on his treacherous role:)*
                    To beguile the time,
Look like the time; bear welcome in your eye,
Your hand, your tongue; look like the innocent flower,
But be the serpent under 't.
                    Shakespeare, *Macbeth*, Act I, Sc. 5

242.   Mark you this, Bassanio:
        The devil can cite Scripture for his purpose.
        An evil soul, producing holy witness,
        Is like a villain with a smiling cheek;
        A goodly apple rotten at the heart.
        Oh, what a goodly outside falsehood hath.
                          Shakespeare, *The Merchant of Venice*,
                                  Act III, Sc. 1 (Shylock)

243.   The world is still deceiv'd with ornament.
        In law, what plea so tainted and corrupt
        But, being season'd with a gracious voice,
        Obscures the show of evil? In religion,
        What damned error, but some sober brow
        Will bless it and approve it with a text,
        Hiding the grossness with fair ornament?
        There is no vice so simple but assumes
        Some mark of virtue in its outward parts.
                          Shakespeare, *The Merchant of Venice*,
                                  Act III, Sc. 2 (Bassanio)

without

244.   When he was envious, instead of affecting indifference, instead of damning with faint praise, instead of doing injuries slily
and in the dark, he told everybody that he was envious. "Do not,
pray, do not talk of Johnson in such praiseworthy terms," he said
to Boswell; "you harrow up my very soul." Other men were far too
cunning to say such a thing. They would have echoed the praises
of the man whom they envied, and then have sent to the newspapers
anonymous libels upon him. . . . He was neither ill-natured enough,
nor long-headed enough, to be guilty of any malicious act which
required contrivance and disguise.
                          Macaulay, "Oliver Goldsmith"

HYPOCRITE   *see also* HYPOCRISY
the misery of the

245.   Let it never be forgotten that a hypocrite is a very unhappy man; he is a man who has devoted himself to a most deli-

cate and arduous intellectual art in which he may achieve master-
pieces which he must keep secret, fight thrilling battles and win
hairbreadth victories for which he cannot have a whisper of
praise. A really accomplished imposter is the most wretched of
geniuses: he is a Napoleon on a desert island.

G. K. Chesterton, *Robert Browning*

IDLENESS   *see also* WORK

246.   Idleness never can secure tranquility; the call of reason and
of conscience will pierce the closest pavilion of the sluggard, and
will be loud enough to hinder him from sleep. Those moments
which he cannot resolve to make useful by devoting them to the
great business of his being, will be usurped by powers that will not
leave them to his disposal; remorse and vexation will seize upon
them, and forbid him to enjoy what he is so desirous to appropri-
ate. . . .

The certainty that life cannot be long, and the probability that
it will be much shorter than nature allows, ought to awaken every
man to the active prosecution of whatever he is desirous to perform.
It is true that no diligence can ascertain success; death may inter-
cept the swiftest career; but he who is cut off in the execution of
an honest undertaking, has at least the honor of falling in his rank,
and has fought the battle though he missed the victory.

Samuel Johnson, *The Rambler*, No. 134

IMMORTALITY   *see also* DEATH, FUTURE LIFE
assurance of

247.   It must be so—Plato, thou reasonest well—
Else whence this pleasing hope, this fond desire,
This longing after immortality?
Or whence this secret dread, and inward horror
Of falling into naught? Why shrinks the soul
Back on herself, and startles at destruction?
'Tis heaven itself that points out an hereafter,
And intimates eternity to man.

Addison, *Cato*, Act V, Sc. 1 (Cato's soliloquy)

intimations of

248.   What shall we be like when
          We cast this earthly body and attain
          To immortality?
          What shall we be like then?
          Ah, who shall say
          What vast expansions shall be ours that day?
          What transformations of this house of clay
          To fit the heavenly mansions and the light of day?
          Ah, who shall say?

          But this we know . . .
          We drop a seed into the ground,
          A tiny shapeless thing, shrivelled and dry,
          And, in the fullness of its time, is seen
          A form of peerless beauty, robed and crowned
          Beyond the pride of any earthly queen,
          Instinct with loveliness, and sweet and rare
          The perfect emblem of its Maker's care.

          This from a shrivelled seed? . . .
          Then may man hope indeed!
                            John Oxenham, "Seeds"

249.   *(It was the poet's faith that the child presages immortality:)*
          Thou, whose exterior semblance doth belie
               Thy Soul's immensity;
          Thou best Philosopher, who dost yet keep
          Thy heritage, thou Eye among the blind,
          Haunted for ever by the eternal mind.
                    ❈   ❈   ❈

     (Immortality is in the child's instincts:)
          Those obstinate questionings
          Of sense and outward things,
          Fallings from us, vanishings;
          Blank misgivings of a Creature
          Moving about in worlds not realized,

High instincts before which our mortal nature
Did tremble like a guilty thing surprised:
*(Those shadowy recollections from childhood are a guiding light
to our vision, giving eternal meaning to our lives:)*
Are yet the fountain light of all our day,
Are yet a master light of all our seeing;
Uphold us, cherish, and have power to make
Our noisy years seem moments in the being
Of the eternal Silence: truths that wake,
To perish never.

❋　❋　❋

Hence in a season of calm weather
Though inland far we be,
Our souls have sight of that immortal sea. . . .
Wordsworth, "Ode on Intimations of Immortality"

man's longing for

250.　The aged Lama is searching for the healing River of the
Arrow—the stream of immortality. As the story goes: at the spot
where Buddha shot an arrow, there sprang up a river "whose nature,
by our Lords beneficence, is that whoso bathes in it washes away
all taint and speckle of sin." By it, moreover, one attains freedom
from "the Wheel of Things." Through cities, over hills, and across
plains, the old man wanders, ever asking the eternal question, "The
River,—the River of the Arrow?"—a heart-cry as old as man.

Rudyard Kipling, *Kim* (adapted)

INDECISION　　　*see also* CHOICE, PROCRASTINATION, WILL

251.　Irresolution is a worse vice than rashness. He that shoots
best may sometimes miss the mark; but he that shoots not at all
can never hit it. Irresolution loosens all the points of a state; like
an ague it shakes not this nor that limb, but all the body is at once
in a fit. The irresolute man is lifted from one place to another; so
hatcheth nothing, but addles all his actions.

Owen Feltham

INDIFFERENCE   *see also* APATHY, CHRISTIAN LIFE, CHRIS-
                                                    TIANS

to Christ

252.   And dars't thou venture still to live in sin,
           And crucify thy dying Lord again?
           Were not his pangs sufficient? Must he bleed
           Yet more? O, must our sinful pleasures feed
           Upon his torments, and augment the story
           Of the sad passion of the Lord of glory!
           Is there no pity? Is there no remorse
           In human breasts? Is there a firm divorce
           Betwixt all mercy and the hearts of men?
                              *   *   *

           We are cruel, Lord, to thee, and ourselves too;
           Jesu forgive us; we know not what we do.
                              Francis Quarles, "The Cruelty of Man"

253.   Am I a stone, and not a sheep,
             That I can stand, O Christ, beneath Thy Cross,
             To number drop by drop Thy Blood's slow loss,
           And yet not weep?

           Not so those women loved
             Who with exceeding grief lamented Thee;
             Not so fallen Peter weeping bitterly;
           Not so the thief was moved;

           Not so the Sun and Moon
             Which hid their faces in a starless sky.
             A horror of great darkness at broad noon—
           I, only I.
                              Christina Rossetti, "Good Friday"

254.   When Jesus came to Golgotha they hanged Him
             on a tree,
           They drave great nails through hands and feet,
             and made a Calvary;

They crowned Him with a crown of thorns, red
    were His wounds and deep,
For those were crude and cruel days, and human
    flesh was cheap.

When Jesus came to Birmingham, they simply
    passed Him by,
They never hurt a hair of Him, they only let Him
    die;
For men had grown more tender, and they would
    not give Him pain,
They only just passed down the street, and left
    Him in the rain.

Still Jesus cried, "Forgive them, for they know not
    what they do,"
And still it rained the winter rain that drenched
    Him through and through;
The crowds went home and left the streets with-
    out a soul to see,
And Jesus crouched against a wall and cried for
    Calvary.

           G. A. Studdert-Kennedy, "Indifference"

to the Church

255.   Mr. Arthur Clennam sat in the window of the coffee-house
on Ludgate Hill counting the chimes of a neighboring church
bell. As the hour of worship approached, its changes of measures
made it more and more exasperating. At the quarter, it went off
into a deadly-lively importunity, urging the populace in a voluble
manner to Come to church, Come to church, Come to church! At
the ten minutes it became aware that the congregation would be
scanty, and slowly hammered out in low spirits, They *won't* come,
They *won't* come, They *won't* come! At the five minutes it abandoned hope, and shook every house in the neighborhood for three
hundred seconds with one dismal swing per second, as a groan of
despair.

           Dickens, *Little Dorrit*

temptation to   *see also* TEMPTATION

256.   "You are very hot after mercy, but I will cool you; this
frame shall not last always; many have been as hot as you for a
spurt, but I have quenched their zeal. I will cool you insensibly by
degrees. What care I though I be seven years in chilling your
heart if I can do it at last? Continual rocking will lull a crying
child to sleep. Though you be burning hot at present, yet I can
pull you from this fire; I shall have you cold before long."

Bunyan, *Grace Abounding* (The Tempter)

INFLUENCE   *see also* GREATNESS—in obscurity
concern for one's own

257.   Johnson told me that he went up thither (to his library in
the garret story) without mentioning it to his servant when he
wanted to study secure from interruption; for he would not allow
his servant to say he was not at home when he really was. "A
servant's strict regard for truth (said he) must be weakened by such
a practice. A philosopher may know that it is merely a form of
denial; but few servants are such nice distinguishers. If I accustom
a servant to tell a lie for *me,* have I not reason to apprehend that
he will tell many lies for *himself?*"

Boswell, *Life of Johnson*

an ennobling

258.   *(The allusion is to Mr. Gladstone, the Prime Minister.)*
He had an exceedingly high sense of the duty of purity of life
and of the sanctity of domestic relations, and his rigid ideas of
decorum inspired so much awe that it used to be said to a person
who had told an anecdote with ever so slight a tinge of impro-
priety, "How many thousands of pounds would you take to tell
that to Gladstone?"

James Bryce, *Studies in Contemporary Biography*

259.   He had so much celestial light in his eyes that he assigned
to everyone whom he addressed a standing ground in some degree
equal to his own. He addressed ordinary individuals as if they
were heroes and princes; charged a candidate for the ministry to

be at once an apostle, a gentleman, and a scholar; made poor astonished women in tiny London apartments feel themselves ladies in the light of his courtesy; and unconsciously elevated every man he talked with into the ideal man he ought to have been.

Mrs. Oliphant, *The Life of Edward Irving*

260.   Wherever, in those vast wards, suffering was at its worst and the need for help was greatest, there, as if by magic, was Miss Nightingale. Her superhuman equanimity would, at the moment of some ghastly operation, nerve the victim to endure and almost to hope. Her sympathy would assuage the pangs of dying, and bring back to those still living something of the forgotten charm of life. Over and over again her untiring efforts rescued those whom the surgeons had abandoned as beyond the possibility of cure. Her mere presence brought with it a strange influence. A passionate idolatry spread among the men: they kissed her shadow as it passed. They did more. "Before she came," said a soldier, "there was cussin' and swearin', but after that it was 'oly as a church." The most cherished privilege of the fighting man was abandoned for the sake of Miss Nightingale. In those "lowest sinks of human misery," as she herself put it, she never heard the use of one expression "which could distress a gentlewoman."

G. Lytton Strachey, *Eminent Victorians*

of a good life lived in obscurity

261.   [Dorothea's] full nature spent itself in channels which had no great name on earth. But the effect of her being on those around her was incalculably diffusive; for the growing good of the world is partly dependent on unhistoric acts; and that things are not so ill with you and me as they might have been, is half owing to the number who lived faithfully a hidden life, and rest in unvisited tombs.

George Eliot, *Middlemarch*

unconscious

262.   Pippa, the little Italian girl, has a holiday on New Year's Day—her one day off in all the year from the silk factory in Asola. For sheer joy she goes out singing a song—a song of faith and

love, "God's in His heaven." As she passes through the narrow
streets, conscious only of her gratitude to God, her song arrests
the attention of individuals during moments of crisis in their lives.
A couple living in shame, on hearing the child's melody, are
awakened to a hunger for the good life. An artist on the verge of
yielding to an angry passion is restrained and set free. An anarchist
bent on assassinating the Emperor of Austria is roused to ardent
patriotism. An ecclesiastic, plotting a child's end for the sake of
financial gain, is smitten with remorse. And Pippa at last goes
home to rest—all unconscious of the fact that her innocent song
was God's arrow to sinful souls.

Browning, "Pippa Passes" (adapted)

INGRATITUDE   *see also* THANKSGIVING

263.   I hate ingratitude more in a man
          Than lying, vainness, babbling, drunkenness,
          Or any taint of vice whose strong corruption
          Inhabits our frail blood.
Shakespeare, *Twelfth Night,* Act III, Sc. 4 (Viola)

264.   Ingratitude, thou marble-hearted fiend,
          More hideous when thou show'st thee in a child
          Than the sea-monster!

✻   ✻   ✻

          How sharper than a serpent's tooth, it is
          To have a thankless child!
Shakespeare, *King Lear,* Act I, Sc. 4 (Lear)

INSINCERITY   *see also* HYPOCRISY
of conventional politeness

265.   I would rather see the feelings of our common nature expressed in the most naked and unqualified way than see every feeling of our nature suppressed, stifled, hermetically-sealed under
the smooth, cold glittering varnish of pretended refinement and
conventional politeness. The one may be corrected by being better
informed, the other is incorrigible, wilful, heartless depravity.
Hazlitt, *Table Talk,* "On Vulgarity and Affectation"

man's

266.   The play is done; the curtain drops,
                Slow falling to the prompter's bell:
              A moment yet the actor stops,
                And looks around to say farewell.
              It is an irksome word and task:
                And, when he's laughed and said his say,
              He shows, as he removes the mask,
                A face that's anything but gay.

                          Thackeray, "The End of the Play"

among nations

267.   Who can reflect, unmoved, upon the round
              Of smooth and solemnized complacencies
              By which, in Christian lands, from age to age,
              Profession mocks performance. Earth is sick
              And Heaven is weary of the hollow words
              Which States and Kingdoms utter when they talk
              Of truth and justice.

                          Wordsworth, *The Excursion*, Bk. V

INSPIRATION   *see also* WORK
the elusiveness of

268.   We cannot kindle when we will
              The fire which in the heart resides;
              The spirit bloweth and is still,
              In mystery our soul abides.
                But tasks in hours of insight willed,
                Can be through hours of gloom fulfilled.

              With aching hands and bleeding feet
              We dig and heap, lay stone on stone;
              We bear the burden and the heat
              Of the long day, and wish 't were done.
                Not till the hours of light return,
                All we have built do we discern.

                          Matthew Arnold, "Morality"

JEALOUSY *see also* ENVY
the subtlety of

269. *(Pope's attack on Addison was the result of a difference of political opinion as well as Pope's resentment of Addison's enmity toward him. If the poet's description of the essayist is unwarranted, it is, nevertheless, a shrewd exposition of the subtle workings of jealousy.)*

> Should such a man, too fond to rule alone,
> Bear, like a Turk, no brother near the throne,
> View him with scornful, yet with jealous eyes,
> And hate for arts that caused himself to rise;
> Damn with faint praise, assent with civil leer,
> And without sneering teach the rest to sneer;
> Willing to wound, and yet afraid to strike,
> Just hint a fault, and hesitate dislike;
> Alike reserved to blame, or to commend,
> A tim'rous foe, and a suspicious friend.
>
> Alexander Pope, "Epistle to Dr. Arbuthnot"

JUDGMENT *see also* MORAL LAW, RETRIBUTION, SIN—finds you out

the Day of

270. *(This hymn, a free translation from the Latin "Dies Irae," ends the poet's "Lay of the Last Minstrel.")*

> That day of wrath, that dreadful day,
> When heaven and earth shall pass away,
> What power shall be the sinner's stay?
> How shall he meet that dreadful day?
>
> When, shriveling like a parched scroll,
> The flaming heavens together roll;
> When louder yet, and yet more dread,
> Swells the loud trump that wakes the dead:
>
> Oh, on that day, that wrathful day,
> When man to judgment wakes from clay,

> Be Thou the trembling sinner's stay,
> Tho' heaven and earth shall pass away.
>
> Sir Walter Scott, "Dies Irae"

memory, the book of

271. That memory is the book of judgment I can well believe. I am convinced that the dread book of account which the Scriptures speak of is, in fact, the mind itself of each individual. Of this, at least, I feel assured—that there is no such thing as forgetting possible to the mind; a thousand accidents may and will interpose a veil between our present consciousness and the secret inscriptions on the mind; accidents of the same sort will also rend away this veil; but whether veiled or unveiled, the inscription remains for ever; just as the stars seem to withdraw before the common light of day; whereas, in fact, we all know that it is the light which is drawn over them as a veil, and that they are waiting to be revealed when the obscuring daylight shall have withdrawn.

De Quincey, *Confessions of an English Opium Eater*

and the memory of sin

272. The terror of being judged sharpens the memory: it sends an inevitable glare over that long-unvisited past which has been habitually recalled only in general phrases. With memory set smarting like a reopened wound, a man's past is not simply a dead history, an outworn preparation of the present: it is not a repented error shaken loose from the life: it is still a quivering part of himself, bringing shudders and bitter flavors and the tinglings of a merited shame.

George Eliot, *Middlemarch*

JUSTICE   see also MORAL LAW, RETRIBUTION, SOCIAL CONCERN

the Christian concept of

273. Most conceptions of justice, when set in the light of Christ's revelation of God, turn out to be wickeder than most crimes. To deal with a man according to his deserts is to repudiate the Gospel from beginning to end; the Gospel would have us deal with men according to their needs. What were our deserts when Christ died for us? He did not die for us because we were so good; He died for us because we were so bad. Yet we, who call ourselves His disciples, are content to cut off from ordinary fellowship the men who most need help. Our zeal for righteousness must work through mercy; "Blessed are the merciful." We must deal with men according to their needs; if they need the restraining or the bracing influence of punishment we shall not withhold it; but such punishment will always be a means, not in any conceivable circumstance an end in itself.

William Temple,
Studies in the Spirit and Truth of Christianity

the implacability of

274.   Though justice be thy plea, consider this,
That in the course of justice, none of us
Should see salvation: we do pray for mercy;
And that same prayer doth teach us all to render
The deeds of mercy.

Shakespeare, *The Merchant of Venice*,
Act IV, Sc. 1 (Portia)

no ultimate escape from

275.   In the corrupted currents of this world,
Offence's gilded hand may shove by justice;
And oft 'tis seen the wicked prize itself
Buys out the law: but 'tis not so above;
There is no shuffling, *there* the action lies
In his true nature; and we ourselves compelled,
Even to the teeth and forehead of our faults,
To give in evidence.

Shakespeare, *Hamlet,* Act III, Sc. 3 (King Claudius)

KINDNESS
in conversation

276.   There is nothing so brutally shocking, nor so little forgiven, as a seeming inattention to the person who is speaking to you. I have seen many people who, while you are speaking to them, instead of looking at and attending to you, fix their eyes upon the ceiling

or some other part of the room. Nothing discovers a little, futile
frivolous mind more than this: and nothing is so offensively ill-
bred.

Lord Chesterfield, *Advice to His Son*

magnanimous   *see also* HOSPITALITY

277.   Milner was the most selfless man I have ever known. He
thought of his work and his cause, much of his colleagues, never
of himself. He simply was not interested in what attracts common
ambition. He could not be bribed, for there was nothing on the
globe wherewith to bribe him; or deterred by personal criticism,
for he cared not at all for fame; and it would have been as easy
to bully the solar system, since he did not know the meaning of
fear. He was a solitary man; but his loneliness never made him
aloof and chilly, and in his manner there was always a gentle,
considerate courtesy. I have worked with him often when he was
desperately tired, but I never remember an impatient or querulous
word. He was a stern judge of himself, but lenient to other
people. . . . For the humble and unfortunate he had infinite
charity, and out of small resources he was always helping lame
dogs. Often he got little gratitude, and when I would remonstrate
he had the same answer, "The man's miserable, and misery has no
manners."

John Buchan, *Pilgrim's Way*

278.   *(The open-handed hospitality of Charles and Mary Lamb
was not infrequently taken advantage of by "the great race of
borrowers." De Quincey speaks of Lamb's generosity:)*
    Princely—nothing short of that in his beneficence. . . . Never
any one have I known in this world upon whom for bounty, for
indulgence and forgiveness, for charitable construction of doubtful
or mixed actions, and for regal munificence, you might have thrown
yourself with so much reliance as upon this comparatively poor
Charles Lamb.

Quoted in Anne Gilchrist, *Mary Lamb*

taken for granted

279.   It was Lady Castlewood's disposition to think kindnesses
and devise silent bounties, and to scheme benevolences for those

about her. We take such goodness for the most part as if it were
our due; the Marys who bring ointment for our feet get but little
thanks. Some of us never feel this devotion at all; others recall it
years after, when the days are past in which those sweet kindnesses were spent on us. Then forgotten tones of love recur to us,
and kind glances shine out of the past—oh, so bright and clear!—
oh, so longed after!—because they are out of reach; as sunshine
through bars—more prized because unattainable.

                                    Thackeray, *Henry Esmond*

KNOWLEDGE
and wisdom

280.   Knowledge and wisdom, far from being one,
            Have oft times no connection. Knowledge dwells
            In heads replete with thoughts of other men:
            Wisdom in minds attentive to their own.
            Knowledge is proud that he has learn'd so much;
            Wisdom is humble that he knows no more.

                                    William Cowper, *The Task*, Bk. VI

without imagination   *see also* SCIENCE

281.   We have more moral, political, and historical wisdom than
we know how to reduce into practice; we have more scientific and
economical knowledge than can be accommodated to the just
distribution of the produce which it multiplies. . . . We want the
creative faculty to imagine that which we know; we want the
generous impulse to act that which we imagine; we want the poetry
of life: our calculations have outrun our conception; we have eaten
more than we can digest. The cultivation of those sciences which
have enlarged the limits of the empire of man over the external
world, has, for want of the poetical faculty, proportionately cir-
cumscribed those of the external world; and man, having enslaved
the elements, remains himself a slave.

                                    Shelley, "A Defence of Poetry"

LEGALISM   *see also* SABBATH DAY—perversion of
in religion

282.   *(Edmund Gosse recalls that as a boy he once watched in
silent fascination a beetle crawl across his bed. When it drew un-*

comfortably near he screamed, "Papa! Papa!" His father, who was at his devotions, felt himself needlessly interrupted:)

"You, the child of a naturalist," he remarked in awesome tones, "*you* to pretend to feel terror at the advance of an insect? If your heart were fixed, if it panted after the Lord, it would take more than the movements of a beetle to make you disturb oral supplication at His footstool. Beware! for God is a jealous God and He consumes them in wrath who make a noise like a dog."

The theory of extreme Puritanism [adds Gosse] can surely offer no quainter example of its fallacy than this idea that the omnipotent Jehovah could be seriously offended, and could stoop to revenge, because a little, nervous child of nine had disturbed a prayer by being frightened at an insect.

Edmund Gosse, *Father and Son*

283. The bishop's gall rises at a new church with a high-pitched roof; a full-breasted black-silk waistcoat is with him a symbol of Satan; and a profane jest book would not, in his view, more fully desecrate the church seat of a Christian than a book of prayer printed with red letters, and ornamented with a cross on the back. Most active clergymen have their hobby, and Sunday observances are his. Sunday, however, is a word which never pollutes his mouth—it is always "the Sabbath." "The desecration of the Sabbath," as he delights to call it, is to him meat and drink—he thrives upon it. It is the loved subject of all his evening discourses, the source of all his eloquence, the secret of all his power over the female heart. To him the revelation of God appears only in that one law given for Jewish observance. To him the mercies of our Saviour speak in vain."

Anthony Trollope, *Barchester Towers*

LENT

284.
Is this a Fast, to keep
The larder lean,
And clean
From fat of veals and sheep?

Is it to quit the dish
Of flesh, yet still
To fill
The platter high with fish?

Is it to fast an hour,
Or ragg'd to go,
Or show
A downcast look and sour?

No: 'tis a Fast to dole
Thy sheaf of wheat
And meat,
Unto the hungry soul.

It is to fast from strife,
From old debate
And hate;
To circumcise thy life.

To show a heart grief-rent;
To starve thy sin,
Not bin:
And that's to keep thy Lent.
Robert Herrick, "To Keep a True Lent"

LIFE
a constricted view of   *see also* SELF-CENTEREDNESS, VISION

285.   I built my soul a lordly pleasure-house
Wherein at ease for aye to dwell.
I said, "O Soul, make merry and carouse,
Dear Soul, for all is well."

* * *

Four courts I made East, West, and South, and North
In each a squared lawn, wherefrom
The golden gorge of dragons spouted forth
A flood of fountain-foam.

And round the cool green courts there ran a row
   Of cloisters, branch'd like mighty woods,
Echoing all night to that sonorous flow
   Of spouted fountain-floods.
(But the life that withdraws itself from mankind to live in artistic and intellectual seclusion can end only in disillusionment. Such a life atrophies the higher instincts of the soul. Hence, the sequel:)
           I am on fire within.
Make me a cottage in the vale . . .
   Where I may mourn and pray.
               Tennyson, "The Palace of Art"

a fatalistic philosophy of

286.   Our revels now are ended. These our actors,
As I foretold you, were all spirits and
Are melted into air, into thin air;
And, like the baseless fabric of this vision,
The cloud-capped towers, the gorgeous palaces,
The solemn temples, the great globe itself,
Yes, all which it inherit, shall dissolve
And, like this unsubstantial pageant faded,
Leave not a rack behind. We are such stuff
As dreams are made on, and our little life
Is rounded with a sleep.
       Shakespeare, *The Tempest*, Act IV, Sc. 1 (Prospero)

the meaninglessness of   *see also* DOUBT, FAITH—consequence of loss of

287.   Yonder see the morning blink:
   The sun is up, and up must I,
To wash and dress and eat and drink
And look at things and talk and think
   And work, and God knows why.

Oh, often have I washed and dressed
   And what's to show for all my pain?
Let me lie abed and rest:

> Ten thousand times I've done my best
> And all's to do again.
>
> A. E. Housman, *Collected Poems*

288. To-morrow, and to-morrow, and to-morrow,
Creeps in this petty pace from day to day
To the last syllable of recorded time;
And all our yesterdays have lighted fools
The way to dusty death. Out, out, brief candle!
Life's but a walking shadow; a poor player
That struts and frets his hour upon the stage
And then is heard no more. It is a tale
Told by an idiot, full of sound and fury,
Signifying nothing.

> Shakespeare, *Macbeth*, Act V, Sc. 5 (Macbeth)

the measure of a man's

289. We live in deeds, not years; in thoughts, not breaths;
In feelings, not in figures on a dial.
We should count time by heart-throbs. He most lives
Who thinks most, feels the noblest, acts the best.
And he whose heart beats quickest lives the longest.
Life's but a means unto an end; that end—God.

> Philip James Bailey, *Festus*

290.   It is not growing like a tree
            In bulk, doth make Man better be;
        Or standing long an oak, three hundred year,
        To fall a log at last, dry, bald, and sere;
            A lily of a day
            Is fairer far in May,
        Although it fall and die that night—
        It was the plant and flower of Light.
    In small proportions we just beauty see;
    And in short measures life may perfect be.

> Ben Jonson, "A Pindaric Ode"

a mixture of joy and woe

291.   Joy and woe are woven fine,
            A clothing for the soul divine.

Under every grief and pine
Runs a joy with silken twine.
It is right it should be so;
Man was made for joy and woe;
And when this we rightly know,
Safely through the world we go.

William Blake, "Proverbs"

a mystery

292.   Flower in the crannied wall,
I pluck you out of the crannies,
I hold you here, root and all, in my hand,
Little flower—but if I could understand
What you are, root and all, and all in all,
I should know what God and man is.

Tennyson, "Flower in the Crannied Wall"

the paradox called

293.   It was the best of times, it was the worst of times, it was
the age of wisdom, it was the age of foolishness, it was the epoch
of belief, it was the epoch of incredulity, it was the season of Light,
it was the season of Darkness, it was the spring of hope, it was the
winter of despair.

Dickens, *A Tale of Two Cities* (opening lines)

a sacred trust

294.   To them life was not a thing to be idled away; it was a
sacred trust that implied true and laudable service to God and
man. . . . To both of them religion was the master-key of life. Mr.
Gladstone never thought of the Church but as the soul of the State.
In every act the religious motive was predominant. In everything
he thought, said, and did, he took for granted that right and wrong
depended on the same principles in public as in private life. It has
been truly said, "He lived and wrought in the sunlight."

Mrs. Gladstone used her gifts and graces in strengthening and
sweetening and purifying the sad, the lonely, the sinful, the suffering, whether poor or rich, weak or powerful; with both hands she
gave her love, her strength, her pity, her succor, to those who

needed them. In truth, the secret lay in their devotion to Him, "whose service is perfect freedom."

Mary Drew, *Mrs. Gladstone*

unbearable without faith in God   *see also* ADVERSITY—without God

295.   "I think if this should be the end of all; and if all I have been born for is just to work my heart and life away in this dull place, with those mill-stones in my ears for ever, until I could scream out for them to stop and let me have a little quiet; with my mother gone, and I never able to tell her again how I loved her, and of all my troubles—I think, if this life is the end and there is no God to wipe away all tears from all eyes, I could go mad."

Mrs. Elizabeth Gaskell, *Mary Barton*
(a Lancashire factory girl)

the uncertainty of   *see also* DEATH—man's indifference to the imminence of

296.   The period was the beginning of the Christian era. Pompeii, nestled almost within the shadow of Vesuvius, was a careless, dreaming city, devoted to luxurious living. Life was centered in the amphitheater and the forum, the shops and the baths, the lavishly-ornate palaces and the gladiatorial combats; it was one long round of pleasure. But one day Vesuvius erupted. Pompeii was attending the circus at the time. The terror-stricken people saw "a fire that shifted and wavered in its hues with every moment, now fiercely luminous, now of a dull and dying red that blazed forth terrifically with intolerable glare. Then there arose on high the universal shrieks of women. The men stared at one another, but were dumb. They felt the earth shake beneath their feet, the crash of falling roofs; an instant more and the mountain-cloud seemed to roll toward them, dark and rapid, like a torrent; it cast forth from its bosom a shower of ashes mixed with vast fragments of burning stone! Over the crushing vines, over the desolate streets, over the amphitheater itself, far and wide with many a mighty splash in the agitated sea, fell that shower. . . . Each turned to flee—dashing, pressing, crushing against the other. It was save himself who could in that night of horrors."

Bulwer-Lytton, *The Last Days of Pompeii* (adapted)

297. *(The reference is to Xerxes, king of Persia, whose fleet was defeated by the Greeks at Salamis, 480 B.C.)*

> A king sat on the rocky brow
> Which looks o'er sea-born Salamis;
> And ships, by thousands, lay below,
> And men in nations;—all were his!
> He counted them at break of day—
> And when the sun set where were they?

Byron, Don Juan

298. On that day, on that lovely 6th of April, such as I have described it,—that 6th of April, about nine o'clock in the morning, —we were seated at breakfast near the open window—we, that is, Agnes, myself, and little Francis. The freshness of morning spirits rested upon us; the golden light of the morning sun illuminated the rooms; incense was floating through the air from the gorgeous flowers within and without the house. There in youthful happiness we sat together, a family of love, and there we never sat again. Never again were we three gathered together, nor ever shall be, so long as the sun and its golden light, the morning and the evening, the earth and its flowers, endure.

De Quincey, The Household Wreck

the vanity of   *see also* PRIDE

299. When I look upon the tombs of the great, every emotion of envy dies within me. . . . When I see kings lying by those who deposed them, or holy men who divided the world with their disputes, I reflect with sorrow on the little competitions and factions of mankind. When I read the several dates of the tombs, of some that died yesterday and some six hundred years ago, I consider that Great Day when we shall all of us be contemporaries, and make our appearance together.

Addison, The Spectator, No. 26

without aim   *see also* VISION

300.
> What is the course of the life
> Of mortal men on the earth?
> Most men eddy about
> Here and there—eat and drink,

> Chatter and love and hate,
> Gather and squander, are raised
> Aloft, are hurl'd in the dust,
> Striving blindly, achieving
> Nothing; and then they die—
> Perish;—and no one asks
> Who or what have they been,
> More than he asks what waves,
> In the moonlit solitudes mild
> Of the midmost ocean, have swelled,
> Foam'd for a moment, and gone.
>
> Matthew Arnold, "Rugby Chapel"

301. "I think of too many things—sow all sorts of seeds, and get no great harvest from any one of them. I'm cursed with suscepti- bility in every direction, and effective faculty in none. I care for painting and music; I care for classic literature, and medieval litera- ture, and modern literature; I flutter all ways, and fly in none."

George Eliot, *The Mill on the Floss* (Philip Wakem)

LOGIC
and the old lady

302. The old lady in the anecdote was accused by her nieces of being illogical. For some time she could not be brought to under- stand what logic was, and when she grasped its true nature she was not so much angry as contemptuous. "Logic! Good gracious! What rubbish!" she exclaimed. "How can I tell what I think till I see what I say?"

E. M. Forster

LOVE   *see also* Forgiveness, God Seeking Man, Mercy,
Mother, Social Concern
cannot be chained

303.   Stone walls do not a prison make
>   Nor iron bars a cage;
>   Minds innocent and quiet take
>   That for an hermitage;
>   If I have freedom in my love
>   And in my love am free,

> Angels alone, that soar above,
>   Enjoy such liberty.
>   Richard Lovelace, "To Althea from Prison"

the courage of   *see also* COURAGE

304.   Scott tells the story, with some basis in fact, of a Scottish
lassie, Jeanie Deans, who heroically saved her younger sister Effie
from the gallows. Scarce eighteen, Effie lay in the Tolbooth charged
with child murder. It seems that she had earlier disappeared from
her shop work in Edinburgh and had shown up at her native village
in a distressed state of mind. It did not take the shrewd, tender
Jeanie long to discover the misfortune that had overtaken her
younger sister, who in spite of the pleadings of love refused to
admit her guilt, remaining as mute as the grave. Had she only con-
fided in Jeanie, Effie would not have come under the letter of the
cruel Scots law.

At the trial Jeanie could have saved her sister's life by deviating
a little from the truth. All she had to do was to say that Effie had
disclosed her condition. But Jeanie could not satisfy her conscience
by bearing false witness. Tortured as she was with grief, she felt
that she must rise above lesser considerations to yield obedience to
a Higher Power. When admonished "the truth to tell, and no truth
to conceal, as far as she knew or was asked in the name of God,
and as the witness should answer God at the great Day of Judgment," Jeanie owned that her sister, in reply to her questionings,
had insisted that there was nothing the matter with her. Whereupon
the sentence of doom was pronounced upon Effie.

It was then that Jeanie Deans set out alone and on foot on the
long, dangerous road that led from Edinburgh to London to "see
the Queen's face that gives grace" and beg pardon for her sister.
Scott tells with pathos the story of her obstinate courage and endurance. Against tremendous odds she at last won from Queen
Caroline the petition she sought. Even Scott can hardly do justice
to the happiness and gratitude that were hers when she started back
to Scotland. The One whom she honored and whom she refused to
betray had not failed her.

                    Scott, *The Heart of Midlothian* (adapted)

knows no barriers

305.   In the stupendous roar and light-blast of the final barrage
that broke the Hindenburg Line I see only one thing, which grows
radiant before my eyes until it fills all my world: the sight of a Saxon
boy half-crushed under a shattered tank, moaning, "Mutter, Mutter,
Mutter," out of ghastly gray lips. A British soldier, wounded in the
leg, and sitting near by, hears the words, and dragging himself to
the dying boy, takes his cold hand and says, "All right, son, it's all
right. Mother's here with you."

Henry Williamson, The Wet Flanders Plain

life without

306.   *(Paracelsus has pursued knowledge to the exclusion of love.
Now that he is dying he sees his mistake. For all his learning he has
failed to sympathize with mankind, failed to be appreciative—)*

>   Of their half-reasons, faint aspirings, dim
>   Struggles for truth; their poorest fallacies,
>   Their prejudice and fears and cares and doubts;
>   All with a touch of nobleness, upward tending.

Browning, "Paracelsus"

a man in

307.   When a man is in love with one woman in a family, it is
astonishing how fond he becomes of every person connected with
it. He ingratiates himself with the maids; he is bland with the
butler; he interests himself in the footman; he runs errands for
the daughters; he gives advice and lends money to the young son
at college; he pats little dogs which he would otherwise kick; he
smiles at old stories which would make him break out in yawns,
were they uttered by any one but papa. He beats time when darling
little Fanny performs her piece on the piano; and smiles when
wicked little Bobby upsets the coffee over his shirt.

Thackeray, The Virginians

never faileth

308.   *(When little Emily suddenly disappears with the handsome
young Steerforth, her old uncle Peggoty, his heart torn with grief,
starts out to search for her. But before doing so, he repeats to David*

Copperfield the instructions he has just given Mrs. Gummidge, his housekeeper:)

"My wishes is, sir, as it shall look, day and night, winter and summer, as it has always looked, since she fust know'd it. If ever she should come a wandering back, I wouldn't have the old place seem to cast her off, you understand; but seem to tempt her to draw nigher to 't, and to peep in, maybe, like a ghost, out of wind and rain, through the old winder, at the old seat by the fire. Then, maybe, Mas'r Davy, seein' none but Mrs. Gummidge there, she might take heart to creep in, trembling; and might come to lay down in her old bed, and rest her weary head where it was once so gay. . . ." "Every night," said Mr. Peggoty, "as reglar as the night comes, the candle must be stood in its old pane of glass, that if ever she should see it, it may seem to say, 'Come back, my child, come back.' "

Dickens, *David Copperfield*

the sacrifice of

309. In that night of horrors when Vesuvius erupted, Nydia the blind girl seemed the only person in Pompeii who felt at home in the darkness. As the molten lava was pouring like a torrent upon that vast human sea she remained unafraid. In the confusion of a terrified populace rushing wildly about in hope of reaching a place of safety, she threaded her way through the streets in search of Glaucus, the one man she loved in all the world. But Glaucus loved another, Ione. The sightless girl sought till she found first Glaucus and then her successful rival. Through the narrow, winding streets she guided them till they reached the water's edge, where lay a boat that was to take them all to safety. That night, on going out to sea, everyone on board fell asleep from exhaustion. As the darkness wore on, "a sailor, half-dozing on the deck, heard a slight splash on the waters. Drowsily he looked up, and behind, as the vessel merrily bounded on, he fancied he saw something white above the waves; but it vanished in an instant."

Bulwer-Lytton, *The Last Days of Pompeii* (adapted)

310. *(Father Damien, the poor Belgian priest who gave his life to the lepers on the island of Molokai, himself died of the disease.)*
Crowded with abominable deformities of our common manhood,

a population such as surrounds us in the horror of a nightmare, every fourth face a blot on the landscape, the [stumps] of human beings lying there almost unrecognizable, but still breathing, still thinking, still remembering. . . .

Damien went there, and shut to with his own hand the door of his own sepulcher, and made his great renunciation, and slept that first night under a tree with his rotting brethren, alone with pestilence, and looking forward with what courage (with what pitiful shrinkings of dread God only knows) to a lifetime of dressing sores and stumps.

R. L. Stevenson, "The Life of Father Damien"

the sensitivity of

311.   Where is the poem that surpasses the "Task" in the genuine love it breathes, at once toward inanimate and animate existence. . . . How Cowper's exquisite mind falls with the mild warmth of morning sunlight on the commonest objects, at once disclosing every detail and investing every detail with beauty! No object is too small to prompt his song; and yet his song is never trivial, for he is alive to small objects, not because his mind is narrow, but because his glance is clear and his heart is large.

George Eliot, *Miscellaneous Essays*

untempered by justice

312.   In truth, there was in his character much to love but very little to respect. His heart was soft even to weakness; he was so generous that he quite forgot to be just; he forgave injuries so readily that he might be said to invite them; and he was so liberal to beggars that he had nothing left for his tailor and his butcher.

Macaulay, "Oliver Goldsmith"

LYING   *see also* HYPOCRISY, HYPOCRITE
the sin of

313.   There is no vice that doth so cover a man with shame as to be found false and perfidious; and therefore Montaigne saith prettily . . . "If it be well weighed, to say that a man lieth, is as much as to say that he is brave towards God, and a coward towards man." For a lie faces God, and shrinks from man.

Bacon, *Essays*, "Of Truth"

314.   Lie not: but let thy heart be true to God,
         Cowards tell lies, and those that fear the rod;
         The stormy-working soul spits lies and froth.
         Dare to be true. Nothing can need a lie:
         A fault which needs it most, grows two thereby.

George Herbert, "The Church Porch"

MAN   *see also* HUMAN NATURE, SELF
created a free agent

315.   I made him just and right,
     Sufficient to have stood, though free to fall.

❖   ❖   ❖

     Freely they stood who stood, and fell who fell.
     Not free, what proof could they have given sincere
     Of true allegiance, constant faith or love?

❖   ❖   ❖

         They therefore as to right belonged,
     So were created, nor can justly accuse
     Their Maker, or their making, or their fate;
     As if predestination over-ruled
     Their will, dispos'd by absolute decree
     Or high foreknowledge. They themselves decreed
     Their own revolt, not I: if I foreknew,
     Foreknowledge had no influence on their fault,
     Which had no less prov'd certain unforeknown.

Milton, *Paradise Lost,* Bk. III

a creature of infinity

316.   Whether we be young or old,
         Our destiny, our being's heart and home,
         Is with infinitude, and only there;
         With hope it is, hope that can never die,
         Effort, and expectation, and desire,
         And something evermore about to be.

Wordsworth, *The Prelude,* Bk. VI

drifting further from God   *see also* WORLD

317.   The Eagle soars in the summit of Heaven,
         The Hunter with his dogs pursues his circuit.

O perpetual revolution of configured stars,
O perpetual recurrence of determined seasons,
O world of spring and autumn, birth and dying!
The endless cycle of idea and action,
Endless invention, endless experiment,
Brings knowledge of motion, but not of stillness;
Knowledge of speech, but not of silence;
Knowledge of words, and ignorance of the Word.
All our knowledge brings us nearer to our ignorance,
All our ignorance brings us nearer to death,
But nearness to death no nearer to God.
Where is the Life we have lost in the living?
Where is the wisdom we have lost in knowledge?
Where is the knowledge we have lost in information?
The cycles of Heaven in twenty centuries
Bring us further from God and nearer to the Dust.

T. S. Eliot, "The Rock"

an elusive creature to his fellows

318.   It is when we try to grapple with another man's infinite
need that we perceive how incomprehensible, wavering, and misty
are the beings that share with us the sight of the stars and the
warmth of the sun. It is as if loneliness were a hard and absolute
condition of existence; the envelope of flesh and blood on which
our eyes are fixed melts before the outstretched hand, and there
remains only the capricious, unconsolable, and elusive spirit that
no eye can follow, no hand can grasp.

Conrad, Lord Jim

319.   A wonderful fact to reflect upon, that every human creature
is constituted to be that profound secret and mystery to every
other. A solemn consideration, when I enter a great city by night,
that every one of those darkly-clustered houses encloses its own
secret; that every room in every one of them encloses its own
secret; that every breathing heart in the hundreds of thousands of
breasts there, is, in some of its imaginings, a secret to the heart
nearest it! . . . In any of the burial-places of this city through which
I pass, is there a sleeper more inscrutable than its busy inhabitants
are, in their innermost personality, to me, or than I am to them?

Dickens, A Tale of Two Cities

eulogy on

320.   What a piece of work is man! how noble in reason! how
infinite in faculty! in form and moving how express and admirable!
in action how like an angel! in apprehension how like a god! the
beauty of the world! the paragon of animals!

Shakespeare, Hamlet, Act II, Sc. 2 (Hamlet)

satire on

321.   (When Gulliver accidentally finds himself ashore on Brob-
dingnag, where the inhabitants are as tall as steeples, the king of
the land, after inquiring into the customs and government of
Europe, addresses Gulliver as follows:)

"By what I have gathered . . . I cannot but conclude the bulk
of your natives to be the most pernicious race of little odious vermin
that nature ever suffered to crawl upon the surface of the earth."

Swift, Gulliver's Travels

the seeker   see also HAPPINESS

322.   I see that all are wanderers, gone astray
          Each in his own delusions; they are lost
          In chase of fancied happiness, still wooed
          And never won. Dream after dream ensues,
          And still they dream that they shall still succeed,
          And still are disappointed. Rings the world
          With the vain stir. I sum up half mankind,
          And add two-thirds to the remaining half,
          And find the total hopes and fears
          Dreams, empty dreams.

Cowper, The Task, Bk. III

323.   We have never made a statue worthy of our dreams. And
where we have discovered a continent, or crossed a chain of mountains, it is only to find another ocean or another continent on the
farther side. . . .

O toiling hands of mortals! O unwearied feet! Soon, soon it
seems to you, you must come forth on some conspicuous hilltop,
and but a little way farther, against the setting sun, descry the
spires of El Dorado. Little do ye know your own blessedness; for

to travel hopefully is a better thing than to arrive, and the true
success is to labor.

> R. L. Stevenson, *Virginibus Puerisque,*
> "An Apology for Idlers"

seeking God *see also* GOD SEEKING MAN

324. "I tell you, Hapgood, that plumb down in the crypt and
abyss of every man's soul is a hunger, a craving for other food
than this earthy stuff. And the churches know it; and instead of
reaching down to him what he wants—light, light—they invite him
to dancing and picture shows, and you're a jolly good fellow, and
religion's a jolly fine thing and no spoilsport, and all that sort of
latter-day tendency. . . .

"I've got the secret. I've got the key to the riddle that's been
puzzling me all my life. I've got the new revelation in terms good
enough for me to understand. Here it is: God is *love*. Not this,
that, not the other thing that the intelligence revolts at, and puts
aside, and goes away, and goes on hungering, hungering and un-
satisfied; nothing like that: but just this; plain for a child, clear as
daylight for grown intelligence: *God is love.* 'He that dwelleth in
love dwelleth in God and God in him; for God is love.' "

> A. S. M. Hutchinson, *If Winter Comes*

MARRIAGE
a costly venture

325. "Wen you're a married man, Samivel, you'll understand a
good many things as you don't understand now; but vether it's
worth while goin' through so much to learn so little, as the charity
boy said ven he got to the end of the alphabet, is a matter of
taste."

> Dickens, *Pickwick Papers* (Sam Weller)

Dr. Johnson on

326. Boswell. "Pray, Sir, do you suppose that there are fifty
women in the world, with any one of whom a man may be as happy
as with any one woman in particular?" Johnson. "Ay, Sir, fifty thousand." Boswell. "Then, Sir, you are not of opinion with some who
imagine that certain men and certain women are made for each

other; and that they cannot be happy if they miss their counter-
parts." Johnson. "To be sure not, Sir. I believe marriages would in
general be as happy, and often more so, if they were all made by
the Lord Chancellor, upon a due consideration of characters and
circumstances, without the parties having any choice in the matter."

Boswell, Life of Johnson

MARTYRDOM
in fashion nowadays

327.   When stakes and faggots were in vogue, there were ob-
jections to the honor of becoming a martyr; but now it would be
hard to show a man a more delicate attention than to prosecute
him for heresy, whether theological, political, or even scientific;
for he is certain to become a "lion," and not improbably the pet of
some enthusiastic clique.

Sir Leslie Stephen, "A Cynic's Apology"

the spirit of

328.   Martyrdom . . . is often a battlefield where no clash of
earthly combatants is heard; it is often a theater no wider than a
nameless home. Sometimes it is passive endurance; sometimes it is
active opposition; sometimes it is the stout declaration of a truth;
but it is always a firm belief in the eternal distinctions between
right and wrong; . . .

To have the spirit of a martyr—and he who has it will be in the
highest sense a martyr—is to be true at all costs to the best and
highest things you know.

F. W. Faber, Treasure Thoughts of, ed. by Rose Porter

MENTALLY SICK
treatment of the

329.   (*In a letter to a friend whose mother was afflicted with insanity, Mary Lamb, who herself knew what it meant to be an in-
mate of a madhouse, discloses what she found to be the most
important thing in the management of the insane:*)
"Let your whole care be to be certain that she is treated with

tenderness. I lay a stress upon this because it is a thing of which people in her state are uncommonly susceptible, and which hardly any one is at all aware of; a hired nurse never, even though in all other respects they are good kind of people. I do not think your own presence necessary, unless she *takes to you very much,* except for the purpose of seeing with your own eyes that she is very kindly treated."

Anne Gilchrist, Mary Lamb

MERCY   *see also* LOVE
the quality of

330.   The quality of mercy is not strain'd,
           It droppeth as the gentle rain from heaven
           Upon the place beneath. It is twice-blest;
           It blesseth him that gives and him that takes.
           'Tis mightiest in the mightiest: it becomes
           The throned monarch better than his crown.

*   *   *

           And earthly power doth then show likest God's
           When mercy seasons justice. . . .
           Though justice be thy plea, consider this—
           That in the course of justice none of us
           Should see salvation. We do pray for mercy;
           And that same prayer doth teach us all to render
           The deeds of mercy.

Shakespeare, The Merchant of Venice,
Act IV, Sc. 1 (Portia)

MONEY   *see also* GREED, POSSESSIONS
the power of

331.   Sir, money, money, the most charming of all things—money, which will say more in one moment than the most eloquent lover can in years. Perhaps you will say a man is not young; I answer, he is rich; he is not genteel, handsome, witty, brave, good-humored, but he is rich, rich, rich, rich,—that one word contradicts everything you can say against him.

Henry Fielding, The Miser, Act III

the stewardship of

332.   "My other piece of advice, Copperfield," said Mr. Micawber, "you know. Annual income twenty pounds, annual expenditure nineteen, nineteen and sixpence, result happiness. Annual income twenty pounds, annual expenditure twenty pounds and sixpence, result misery."

Dickens, *David Copperfield*

MORAL LAW   *see also* JUDGMENT, JUSTICE, RETRIBUTION
implacability of the

333.   The Moving Finger writes; and, having writ,
            Moves on: nor all your Piety nor Wit
            Shall lure it back to cancel half a Line,
            Nor all your Tears wash out a Word of it.

Edward Fitzgerald,
"The Rubáiyát of Omar Khayyám"

written into history

334.   History is a voice for ever sounding across the centuries the laws of right and wrong. Opinions alter, manners change, creeds rise and fall; but the moral law is written on the tablets of eternity. For every false word or unrighteous deed, for cruelty and oppression, for lust and vanity, the price has to be paid at last. . . . Justice and truth alone endure and live. Injustice and falsehood may be long-lived, but doomsday comes to them at last.

J. A. Froude, *The Science of History*

MOTHER   *see also* REMORSE—a son's
the influence of a good

335.   *(Carlyle made this entry in his diary after his mother's death:)*

O pious mother! kind, brave, and truthful soul as I have ever found, and more than I have ever elsewhere found in this world, your poor Tom, long out of his school-days now, has fallen very lonely, very lame and broken in this pilgrimage of his; and you cannot help him or cheer him by a kind word any more. From your

grave in Ecclefechen kirkyard yonder you bid him trust in God;
and that also he will try if he can understand and do.

D. A. Wilson, *Carlyle to Threescore-and-Ten*

the love of a

336.   If I were hanged on the highest hill,
          Mother o' mine, O mother o' mine!
      I know whose love would follow me still,
          Mother o' mine, O mother o' mine!
      If I were drowned in the deepest sea,
          Mother o' mine, O mother o' mine!
      I know whose tears would come down to me,
          Mother o' mine, O mother o' mine!
      If I were damned o' body and soul,
      I know whose prayers would make me whole,
          Mother o' mine, O mother o' mine.

Rudyard Kipling, "Mother O' Mine"

337.   I love my little son, and yet when he was ill
      I could not confine myself to his bedside.
      I was impatient of his squalid little needs,
      His labored breathing, and the fretful way he cried,
      And longed for my wide range of interests again;
      Whereas his mother sank without another care
      To that dread level of nothing but life itself
      And stayed, day and night, till he was better, there.

      Women may pretend, yet they always dismiss
      Everything but mere being just like this.

Hugh MacDiarmid, "The Two Parents"

MYSTERY OF BEING
man's longing to inquire into the

338.   I feel a nameless sadness o'er me roll.

*   *   *

      But often in the world's most crowded streets,
      But often in the din of strife,
      There rises an unspeakable desire
      After the knowledge of the buried life;

A thirst to spend our fire and restless force
In tracking out our true original course;
A longing to inquire
Into the mystery of this heart that beats
So wild, so deep in us—to know
Whence our lives come and where they go.

* * *

From the soul's subterranean depth upborne
As from an infinitely distant land,
Come airs, and floating echoes, and convey
A melancholy into all our day.

Matthew Arnold, "The Buried Life"

NATIONALISM   see also PATRIOTISM
undue pride of

339. *(Written on the occasion of the Jubilee celebration of the
sixtieth year of Queen Victoria's reign, when the British Empire
had reached a pinnacle of world power.)*

God of our fathers, known of old,
    Lord of our far-flung battle line,
Beneath whose awful hand we hold
    Dominion over palm and pine—
Lord God of Hosts, be with us yet,
Lest we forget—lest we forget!

The tumult and the shouting dies;
    The Captains and the Kings depart:
Still stands Thine ancient sacrifice,
    An humble and a contrite heart.
Lord God of Hosts, be with us yet,
Lest we forget—lest we forget!

Far-called, our navies melt away;
    On dune and headland sinks the fire:
Lo, all our pomp of yesterday
    Is one with Nineveh and Tyre!
Judge of the Nations, spare us yet,
Lest we forget—lest we forget!

If, drunk with sight of power, we loose
　　Wild tongues that have not Thee in awe,
Such boasting as the Gentiles use,
　　Or lesser breeds without the Law—
Lord God of Hosts, be with us yet,
Lest we forget—lest we forget!

For heathen heart that puts her trust
　　In reeking tube and iron shard,
All valiant dust that builds on dust,
　　And guarding, calls not Thee to guard,
For frantic boast and foolish word—
Thy mercy on Thy People, Lord!

Amen.
Rudyard Kipling, "Recessional"

NATURE
created for man's perpetual pleasure

340.　　There is not a moment of any day of our lives when nature is not producing scene after scene, picture after picture, glory after glory, and working still upon such exquisite and constant principles of the most perfect beauty, that it is quite certain it is all done for us, and intended for our perpetual pleasure. And every man, wherever placed, however far from other sources of interest or of beauty, has this doing for him constantly.

Ruskin, Modern Painters

esteemed by Christ

341.　　Jesus made plain in his life how dear to him was the beauty of the world. He loved to wander by the lake, among the corn, and on the grassy hills. He marked the aspects of the beauty of flowers. He loved animals, and drew some of his loveliest teaching from their ways. When weary, he sought the hilltop by night; when uplifted by strong communion, the higher ridges of Hermon; when exceeding sorrowful, the lonely olive grove.

Stopford Brooke, Theology in the English Poets

an expression of God's will

342. What we see here of this world is but an expression of God's will, so to speak—a beautiful earth and sky and sea—beautiful affections and sorrows, wonderful changes and developments of creation, suns rising, stars shining, birds singing, clouds and shadows changing and fading, people loving each other, smiling and crying, the multiplied phenomena of Nature. . . . And who is to say that we are to ignore all this, or not value them and love them, because there is another unknown world yet to come? . . . An angel glorified or a sparrow on a gutter are equally part of His creation.

Thackeray, *Microcosmographie*

God revealed in   *see also* GOD—the evidence for

343.   A garden is a lovesome thing, God wot!
                Rose plot,
                Fring'd pool,
            Fern'd grot—
                The veriest school
                Of peace; and yet the fool
            Contends that God is not—
            Not God! in gardens! when eve is cool?
                Nay, but I have a sign;
                'Tis very sure God walks in mine.

Thomas Edward Brown, "My Garden"

344. You may find God everywhere. The Most High dwelleth not in temples made with hands. The great glorious world is His, the sky is His with its driving clouds, with its sunset colorings, with its overarching canopy of stainless blue. The trees of the forest are His, with every moss and lichen that inlay their gnarled boughs with silver and emerald, and the flowers that nestle at their feet, and the birds that sing among their branches. The long summer, and the autumn with its raiment of gold and purple—and the sea is His, and He made it, and all that moveth therein.

F. W. Faber, *Treasure Thoughts of*, ed. by Rose Porter

345.   He came and took me by the hand
                Up to a red rose tree,

He kept His meaning to Himself
    But gave the rose to me.

I did not pray Him to lay bare
    The mystery to me,
Enough the rose was Heaven to smell,
    And His own face to see.

                Ralph Hodgson, "The Mystery"

346.   Study Nature. Do not study matter for its own sake, but as
the countenance of God. Try to extract every line of beauty, every
association, every moral reflection, every inexpressible feeling, from
it. Study the forms and colors of leaves and flowers, and the growth
and habits of plants, not to classify them, but to admire them and
adore God.

             Charles Kingsley, *Letters and Memories*

ministers to the child

347.   *(On a winter's night, after the rest of the household have
retired, the poet lingered by the cradle of his infant son, musing
thus:)*

                            I was reared
In the great city, pent mid cloisters dim,
And saw nought lovely but the sky and stars.
But thou, my babe! shalt wander like a breeze
By lakes and sandy shores, beneath the crags
Of ancient mountain, and beneath the clouds,
Which image in their bulk both lakes and shores
And mountain crags: so shalt thou see and hear
The lovely shapes and sounds intelligible
Of that eternal language, which thy God
Utters, who from eternity doth teach
Himself in all, and all things in himself.
Great universal Teacher! he shall mould
Thy spirit, and by giving make it ask.

Therefore all seasons shall be sweet to thee.

             Coleridge, "Frost at Midnight"

NEW YEAR

348.   And I said to the man who stood at the gate of the
year:
"Give me a light, that I may tread safely into the
unknown!"
And He replied:
"Go out into the darkness and put your hand into
the Hand of God.
That shall be to you better than a light and safer
than a known way."
So I went forth, and finding the Hand of God,
trod gladly into the night.
And He led me towards the hills and the breaking
of day in the lone East.

M. Louise Haskins, "The Gate of the Year"

OLD AGE   *see also* COURAGE
the courage of

349.   *(After his long years of fighting and wandering, Ulysses
returns home to Ithaca; but he cannot rest. Though now an old man
he resolves to set forth again, with a handful of comrades, in
search of new knowledge and adventure.)*

Death closes all: but something e'er the end,
Some work of noble note may yet be done.

*   *   *

Tho' much is taken, much abides: and tho'
We are not now that strength which in old days
Moved earth and heaven, that which we are, we are;
One equal temper of heroic hearts,
Made weak by time and fate, but strong in will
To strive, to seek, to find, and not to yield.

Tennyson, "Ulysses"

the trials of

350.   There is a wicked inclination in most people to suppose an
old man decayed in his intellect. If a young or middle-aged man,
when leaving a company, does not recollect where he laid his hat,

it is nothing; but if the same inattention is discovered in an old man, people shrug their shoulders, and say, "His memory is going."

Boswell, *Life of Johnson* (Dr. Johnson)

the vanity of

351.   Enlarge my life with multitude of days!
         In health, in sickness, thus the suppliant prays:
         Hides from himself his state, and shuns to know
         That life protracted is protracted woe.
         Time hovers o'er, impatient to destroy,
         And shuts up all the passages of joy:
         In vain their gifts the bounteous seasons pour,
         The fruit autumnal, and the vernal flower;
         With listless eyes the dotard views the store,
         He views, and wonders that they please no more.
         Now pall the tasteless meats and joyless wines,
         And Luxury with sighs her slave resigns.
                    *   *   *

         Unnumbered maladies his joints invade,
         Lay siege to life, and press the dire blockade;
         But unextinguished Av'rice still remains,
         And dreaded losses aggravate his pains;
         He turns, with anxious heart and crippled hands,
         His bonds of debt, and mortgages of land;
         Or views his coffers with suspicious eyes,
         Unlocks his gold, and counts it till he dies.
                    Samuel Johnson, "The Vanity of Human Wishes"

when one's work is done

352.   Lord, when Thou seest that my work is
             done,
         Let me not linger on,
         With failing powers,
         Adown the weary hours,—
         A workless worker in a world of work.
         But, with a word,
         Just bid me home,
         And I will come

Right gladly,—
Yea, right gladly
Will I come.

John Oxenham, "After Work"

worldliness in

353. *(The allusion is to Beatrix Esmond.)*
Here was old age, I fear, without reverence. Here were gray
hairs that were hidden or painted. The world was still here, and she
tottering on it with her crutch. For fourscore years she had moved
on it, and eaten of the tree, forbidden and permitted. She had had
beauty, pleasure, flattery: but what secret rages, disappointments,
defeats, humiliations! what thorns under the roses! what stinging
bees in the fruit!

Thackeray, *Henry Esmond*

OPPORTUNITY   *see also* CHOICE, INDECISION, PROCRASTINA-
TION, REMORSE, REPENTANCE

354.   But once I pass this way,
And then—no more.
But once—and then, the Silent Door
Swings on its hinges—
Opens . . . Closes—
And no more
I pass this way.
So while I may,
With all my might,
I will assay
Sweet comfort and delight,
To all I meet upon the Pilgrim Way.
For no man travels twice
The Great Highway
That climbs through Darkness up to Light—
Throught Night
To Day.

John Oxenham, "The Pilgrim Way"

355.   There is a tide in the affairs of men,
Which, taken at the flood, leads on to fortune;

> Omitted, all the voyage of their life
> Is bound in shallows and in miseries;
> And we must take the current when it serves,
> Or lose our ventures.

Shakespeare, Julius Caesar, Act IV, Sc. 3 (Brutus)

PARASITE   *see also* DEBT, MONEY
a social

356.   Whoever was acquainted with him was certain to be solicited
for small sums, which the frequency of the request made in time
considerable, and he was therefore quickly shunned by those who
were become familiar enough to be trusted with his necessities . . .

It was observed that he always asked favors of this kind without the least submission or apparent consciousness of dependence,
and that he did not seem to look upon a compliance with his request
as an obligation that deserved any extraordinary acknowledgments;
but a refusal was resented by him as an affront, or complained of
as an injury; nor did he readily reconcile himself to those who
either denied to lend, or gave him afterwards any intimation that
they expected to be repaid.

Samuel Johnson, The Lives of the English Poets,
"Richard Savage"

PATRIOTISM   *see also* NATIONALISM

357.   Breathes there the man, with soul so dead,
> Who never to himself hath said,
>   This is my own, my native land!
> Whose heart hath ne'er within him burn'd
> As home his footsteps he hath turn'd
>   From wandering on a foreign Strand?
> If such there breathe, go, mark him well;
> For him no minstrel raptures swell;
> High though his titles, proud his name,
> Boundless his wealth as wish can claim,—
> Despite those titles, power, and pelf,
> The wretch, concentered all in self,
> Living, shall forfeit fair renown,
> And doubly dying shall go down

To the vile dust, from whence he sprung,
Unwept, unhonor'd, and unsung.
> Scott, *The Lay of the Last Minstrel*, Canto VI

PEACE
man's longing for spiritual

358.   Calm soul of all things! make it mine
To feel, amid the city's jar,
That there abides a peace of thine,
Man did not make, and cannot mar!

The will to neither strive nor cry,
The power to feel with others give!
Calm, calm me more! nor let me die
Before I have begun to live.
> Matthew Arnold, "Lines in Kensington Gardens"

peace-of-mind cults

359.   *(Newman was skeptical of the peace-of-mind cults of his day.)*

Doubtless, peace of mind, a quiet conscience, and a cheerful countenance are the gift of the Gospel, and the sign of the Christian; but the same effects (or rather, what appears to be the same) may arise from very different causes. Jonah slept in the storm; so did our blessed Lord. The one slept in an evil security; the Other in the "peace of God which passeth all understanding." The two states cannot be confounded together, they are perfectly distinct; and as distinct is the calm of the man of the world from the calm of the Christian.
> John Henry Newman, "The Religion of the Day" (sermon)

PERFECTION
without soul

360.   *(Andrea del Sarto, the faultless painter, knew that his work was technically superior to that of his colleagues, that he could sketch more accurately than Raphael. He could do with ease that which others toiled to accomplish. Yet he knew, too, that Michelangelo and Raphael were the greater artists because their soul was in their work. He acknowledged that it was his stultifying infatua-*

tion for his soulless wife that caused him to prostitute his talent.
Lesser painters, he sighed, because—)

>There burns a truer light of God in them,

>   ❖   ❖   ❖

>Reach many a heaven that's shut to me;
>Enter and take their place there sure enough.

>   ❖   ❖   ❖

>Ah, but a man's reach should exceed his grasp,
>Or what's a heaven for? . . .

>   ❖   ❖   ❖

>And yet how profitless to know, to sigh
>"Had I been two, another and myself,
>Our head would have o'erlooked the world!"
>>Browning, "Andrea del Sarto"

PIETY
lack of

361.   If you will here stop and ask yourselves, why you are not as pious as the primitive Christians were, your own heart will tell you, that it is neither through ignorance nor inability, but purely because you never thoroughly intended it.
>William Law, *Serious Call*

and practicality

362.   I've nothing to say again' her piety, my dear; but I know very well I shouldn't like her to cook my victuals. When a man comes in hungry an' tired, piety won't feed him, I reckon. Hard carrots 'ull lie heavy on his stomach, piety or no piety. It's right enough to be speritial—I'm no enemy to that; but I like my potatoes mealy."
>George Eliot, *Janet's Repentance* (Mrs. Linnet)

PLEASURE

363.   But pleasures are like poppies spread,
>You seize the flower, its bloom is shed;
>Or like the snow falls in the river,
>A moment white—then melts forever;
>Or like the borealis race,

> That flit e'er you can point their place,
> Or like the rainbow's lovely form
> Evanishing amid the storm.
>
> Burns, "Tam o' Shanter"

POSSESSIONS   *see also* GREED, MONEY
the emptiness of material

364.
> I'll give my jewels for a set of beads,
> My gorgeous palace for a hermitage,
> My gay apparel for an almsman's gown,
> My figur'd goblets for a dish of wood,
> My scepter for a palmer's walking staff,
> My subjects for a pair of carved saints,
> And my large kingdom for a little grave.
>
> Shakespeare, *King Richard II*,
> Act III, Sc. 3 (King Richard)

multiply sorrows

365.
> A time there was, ere England's griefs began,
> When every rood of ground maintained its man;
> For him light labor spread her wholesome store,
> Just gave what life requir'd but gave no more:
> His best companions, innocence and health;
> And his best riches, ignorance of wealth.
>
> Goldsmith, "The Deserted Village"

PRACTICALITY   *see also* ZEAL—a misplaced

366. It was clear that in the state of disorganization into which the hospitals at Scutari had fallen the most pressing, the really vital, need was for something more than nursing; it was for the necessary elements of civilized life—the commonest material objects, the most ordinary cleanliness, the rudimentary habits of order and authority. "Oh, dear Miss Nightingale," said one of her party as they were approaching Constantinople, "when we land, let there be no delays, let us get straight to nursing the poor fellows!" "The strongest will be needed at the wash-tub," was Miss Nightingale's answer. And it was upon the wash-tub, and all that the wash-tub stood for, that she expended her greatest energies.

> G. Lytton Strachey, *Eminent Victorians*

PRAISE   *see also* THANKSGIVING
scrupulosity in bestowing

367. Among the smaller duties of life, I hardly know any one
more important than that of not praising where praise is not due.
Reputation is one of the prizes for which men contend: it produces more labor and more talent than twice the wealth of a country
could ever rear up. It is the coin of genius, and it is the imperious
duty of every man to bestow it with the most scrupulous justice
and the wisest economy.

Sydney Smith, Sketches on Moral Philosophy

seeking

368. *(The reference is to Browning's "Bishop Blougram's
Apology.")*

Blougram tells of Verdi conducting his worst opera in Florence.
At the close of the performance (Verdi knowing all the time that
it was a poor thing) the audience rose in a body and applauded,
throwing roses at the composer. There he stood drinking in the
praise, acknowledging it, until—he looked around to where sat
Rossini, patient in his stall! Rossini, a master, looking at him, saying
in effect, "Oh, Verdi, Verdi!" Such is the lot of a man who chooses
the praise of men, and suddenly catches the eye of some sincere
artist or catches the eye of God.

John Hutton, The Dark Mile

PRAYER
a classic

369. O Lord, support us all the day long of our troublous life,
until the shadows lengthen and the evening comes, and the busy
world is hushed, and the fever of life is over, and our work is done.
Then in thy mercy grant us a safe lodging and a holy rest, and
peace at the last; through Jesus Christ our Lord. Amen.

John Henry Newman, "Wisdom and Innocence"
(sermon, 1834)

before death

370. *(Dr. Johnson, before receiving the Holy Sacrament for the
last time, composed and fervently uttered this prayer:)*

"Almighty and most merciful Father, I am now, as to human eyes it seems, about to commemorate, for the last time, the death of thy Son Jesus Christ, our Saviour and Redeemer. Grant, O Lord, that my whole hope and confidence may be in His merits, and Thy mercy; enforce and accept my imperfect repentance; make this commemoration available to the confirmation of my faith, the establishment of my hope, and the enlargement of my charity; and make the death of Thy Son Jesus Christ effectual to my redemption. Have mercy upon me, and pardon the multitude of my offences. Bless my friends; have mercy upon all men. Support me, by Thy Holy Spirit, in the days of my weakness, and at the hour of death; and receive me, at my death, to everlasting happiness, for the sake of Jesus Christ. Amen."

Boswell, *Life of Johnson*

courage in

371.   The new boy dropped on his knees by his bed as he had done since childhood. Two or three of the boys laughed or sneered, and a big brutal fellow picked up a slipper and shied it at the kneeling boy. It was then that Tom saw the whole, and the next moment the boot he had just pulled off flew in the direction of the bully, who roared in pain. But Tom was miserable. He recalled promising his mother that he would never forget to kneel to pray at bed-time. The fourteen-year-old lad cried as if his heart would break. On first coming to school he himself had waited till the candle was extinguished before stealing out of bed to say his prayers. A little later he began to think that he might just as well say his prayers in bed. Finally, he got out of the habit altogether. And now, feeling keenly his cowardice, he resolved to bear testimony. Next morning, after washing and dressing, he knelt by his bed in the face of the whole room. Not five words could he say; he was listening for every whisper in the room. When he arose it was to find that at least two others had followed his example. On the way down to breakfast he knew that he who has conquered his own coward spirit has conquered the whole world. For a few nights there was a sneer and a laugh when he knelt down, but one by one all the other boys but three or four followed his lead.

Thomas Hughes, *Tom Brown's Schooldays* (adapted)

and early rising

372.   If you were to rise early every morning, as an instance of
self-denial, as a method of renouncing indulgence, as a means of
redeeming your time, and fitting your spirit for prayer, you would
find mighty advantages from it. This method, though it seems
such a small circumstance of life, would in all probability be a
means of great piety. It would keep it constantly in your head,
that softness and idleness were to be avoided, that self-denial was
a part of Christianity. It would teach you to exercise power over
yourself; and make you able by degrees to renounce other pleasures and tempers that war against the soul.

William Law, Serious Call

family

373.   (*The poet faithfully describes a phase of domestic life in
eighteenth century Scotland. The evening meal ended, the humble
cotter gathers his family around the hearth. A psalm is sung and
the Word is read:*)
>   Then kneeling down to Heaven's Eternal King
>   The saint, the father, and the husband prays:
>   Hope "springs exulting on triumphant wing"
>   That thus they all shall meet in future days.

*   *   *

>   From scenes like these old Scotia's grandeur springs,
>   That makes her loved at home, revered abroad:
>   Princes and lords are but the breath of kings,
>   "An honest man's the noblest work of God."

Burns, "The Cotter's Saturday Night"

a futile

374.   (*King Claudius, with the guilt of a brother's blood on his
hands, would seek relief in prayer:*)
>   Pray can I not,
>   Though inclination be as sharp as will:
>   My stronger guilt defeats my strong intent;
>   And, like a man to double business bound,

I stand in pause where I will first begin,
And both neglect.

* * *

　　　　　　　　But, O, what form of prayer
Can serve my term? "Forgive me my foul murder"?
That cannot be; since I am still possess'd
Of those effects for which I did the murder,
My crown, mine own ambition, and my queen.
May one be pardon'd and retain the offence?

* * *

Bow, stubborn knees; and, heart with strings of steel,
Be soft as sinews of the new-born babe!
All may be well.

* * *

My words fly up, my thoughts remain below:
Words without thoughts never to heaven go.
　　　　　　　　　　Shakespeare, *Hamlet,* Act III, Sc. 4

of the House of Commons

375.　Almighty God, by whom alone kings reign and princes decree justice, and from whom alone cometh all counsel, wisdom, and understanding,

We, thine unworthy servants, here gathered together in Thy name, do most humbly beseech Thee to send down the heavenly wisdom from above, to direct and guide us in all our consultations:

And grant that, we having Thy fear always before our eyes, and laying aside all private interests, prejudices, and partial affections, the result of all our counsels may be the glory of Thy blessed name, the maintenance of true religion and justice, and the safety, honor, and happiness of the King, the public welfare, peace and tranquility of the realm, and the uniting and knitting together of the hearts of all persons and estates within the same in true Christian love and charity towards one another,

Through Jesus Christ our Lord and Saviour.

　　(Composed about 1578 by Sir Christopher Yelverton, M.P.)

man's imperfections in

376.　But when we consider with a religious seriousness the manifold weaknesses of the strongest devotions in time of Prayer, it is a sad consideration. I throw my selfe downe in my Chamber, and I call in, and invite God and his Angels thither, and when they are there I neglect God and his Angels for the noise of a Flie, for the rattling of a Coach, for the whining of a doore; I talke on, in the same posture of praying; eyes lifted up; knees bowed downe; as though I prayed to God; and, if God or his Angels should aske me, when I thought last of God in that prayer, I cannot tell: Sometimes I finde that I had forgot what I was about, but when I began to forget it I cannot tell. A memory of yesterday's pleasures, a feare of tomorrow's dangers, a straw under my knee, a noise in mine ears, a light in mine eye, an any thing, a nothing, a fancy, a Chimera in my brain, troubles me in my prayer. So certainly is there nothing, nothing in spiritual things, perfect in this world.

John Donne, Sermons

for the nation

377.   Almighty God, who has given us this good land for our heritage; We humbly beseech thee that we may always prove ourselves a people mindful of thy favor and glad to do thy will. Bless our land with honorable industry, sound learning, and pure manners. Save us from violence, discord, and confusion; from pride and arrogancy, and from every evil way. Defend our liberties, and fashion into one united people the multitudes brought hither out of many kindreds and tongues. Endue with the spirit of wisdom those to whom in thy Name we entrust the authority of government, that there may be justice and peace at home, and that, through obedience to thy law, we may show forth thy praise among the nations of the earth. In the time of prosperity, fill our hearts with thankfulness, and in the day of trouble, suffer not our trust in thee to fail; all which we ask through Jesus Christ our Lord. Amen.

The Book of Common Prayer

perseverance in

378.   Often when I had been making to the promise, I have seen as if the Lord would refuse my soul for ever. Then I would think of Esther, who went to petition the king contrary to the law. I thought of Benhadad's servants, who went with ropes upon their heads to their enemies for mercy. The woman of Canaan, that

would not be daunted, though called "dog" by Christ; and that man that went to borrow bread at midnight, were also great encouragements to me.

Bunyan, *Grace Abounding*

the place of

379.   If you were to use yourself (as far as you can) to pray always in the same place; if you were to reserve that place always for devotion, and not allow yourself to do anything common in it; if you were never to be there yourself but in times of devotion; if any little room, or if any particular part of a room was thus used, this kind of consecration of it as a place holy unto God, would very much assist your devotion. This would dispose you to be always in the spirit of religion, when you were there; and fill you with wise and holy thoughts when you were by yourself.

William Law, *Serious Call*

380.   A pious Frenchman visiting Westminster Abbey knelt down to pray. The verger, who had never seen such a thing before, promptly handed him over to the police and charged him with brawling. Fortunately the magistrate had compassion on the foreigner's ignorance and even went to the length of asking why he should not be allowed to pray in church. The reply of the verger was simple. "If we allowed that," he said, "we should have people praying all over the place."

George Bernard Shaw

the power of

381.   Prayer can put a holy restraint upon God, and detain an angel till he leave a blessing; it can open the treasures of rain and soften the iron ribs of rocks till they melt into tears and a flowing river; prayer can unclasp the girdles of the north, saying to a mountain of ice, "Be thou removed hence and cast into the bottom of the sea;"—it can arrest the sun in the midst of his course and send the swift-winged winds upon our errand. And all those strange things and unrevealed transactions which are above the clouds and far beyond the regions of the stars shall combine in ministry for the praying man. . . .

Jeremy Taylor, *The Worthy Communicant*

382.   More things are wrought by prayer
              Than this world dreams of. Wherefore, let thy voice
              Rise like a fountain for me night and day.
              For what are men better than sheep or goats
              That nourish a blind life within the brain,
              If knowing God, they lift not hands of prayer
              Both for themselves and those who call them friend?
              For so the whole earth is every way
              Bound by gold chains about the feet of God.
                                    Tennyson, "Morte d'Arthur"

the primacy of

383.   Lord, I confess, this morning I remembered my breakfast,
but forgot my prayers. And as I have returned no praise, so thou
mightest justly have afforded me no protection. Yet thou hast care-
fully kept me to the middle of this day. It is now noon, too late for
a morning, too soon for an evening sacrifice. Be pleased, therefore,
now to accept them. See how I am ashamed the sun should shine
on me, who now newly start in the race of my devotions, when
he like a giant hath run more than half his course in the heavens.
                                    Thomas Fuller, *Personal Meditations*

a romantic attitude toward

384.   *(The archbishop had been so busy encouraging others to
"try prayer" and all other respectable means of help that he himself
had almost forgotten how to pray. Life had treated him well. In
fact, he had never really felt the need of prayer in his own life.
The day came, however, when the good man found himself in
desperate circumstances. He knew that he must have help from a
source greater than man. It occurred to him to try prayer for himself. After all, it could do no harm.)*
      Yes, he would pray.
      Slowly he sank to his knees and put his hands together. He was
touched by a sort of childish trustfulness in his own attitude. "O
God," he began, and paused.
      He paused, and a sense of awful immanence, a monstrous awe
gripped him. And then he heard a voice.
      It was not a harsh voice, but it was a clear, strong voice. There

was nothing about it still or small. It was neither friendly nor hostile; it was brisk.

"Yes," said the voice. "What is it?"

They found His Grace in the morning. He had slipped off the steps on which he had been kneeling, and lay sprawling on the crimson carpet. Plainly his death had been instantaneous.

But instead of the serenity, the almost fatuous serenity, that was his habitual expression, his countenance, by some strange freak of nature, displayed an extremity of terror and dismay.

H. G. Wells,
"Answer to Prayer," in *The New Yorker*, May 1, 1937

and social relationships

385.   There is nothing that makes us love a man so much as praying for him; and when you can once do this sincerely for any man, you have fitted your soul for the performance of everything that is kind and civil towards him. This will fill your heart with a generosity and tenderness that will give you a better and sweeter behaviour than anything that is called fine breeding or good manners. By considering yourself as an advocate with God for your neighbors and acquaintance, you would never find it hard to be at peace with them yourself. It would be easy for you to bear with and forgive those for whom you particularly implored the divine mercy and forgiveness.

William Law, *Serious Call*

in time of trial

386.   O Lamb of God, that takest away the sins of the world.
Give me peace, give me peace!
The mists are round me, rolled and curled,
The dark and dangers of the way increase.
I cannot pray,
Pray as of old.
My thoughts are like a flock astray,
Wilt Thou not call them back,
Back to the heavenly track,
Unto the trodden pathway of Thy fold?
Bid these strange tumults cease!

Thyself upon my heart enthrone!
Make me Thine own, Thine own!
Give me peace, give me peace!

Alfred Austin,
"Agnus Dei, Qui Tollis Peccata Mundi"

an unavailing

387. *(When Michael comes to dispossess Adam and Eve of Paradise, Adam reasons thus with himself:)*

If by prayer
Incessant I could hope to change the will
Of him who all things can, I would not cease
To weary him with my assiduous cries;
But prayer against his absolute decree
No more avails than breath against the wind
Blown stifling back on him that breathes it forth:
Therefore to his great bidding I submit.

Milton, *Paradise Lost*, Bk. XI

without ceasing

388. I have resolved to pray more, and to pray always; to pray in all places where quietness inviteth, in the house, on the highway, and on the street. I purpose to take occasion of praying upon the sight of any church which I may pass, that God may be worshipped there in spirit, and that souls may be saved there; to pray for my sick patients and for the patients of other physicians; at my entrance into any home to say, "May the peace of God abide here"; after hearing a sermon, to pray for a blessing upon God's truth and upon the messenger; upon the sight of a beautiful person to bless God for His creatures, to pray for the beauty of such a person's soul; upon the sight of a deformed person, to pray God to give him wholeness of soul, and by and by to give him beauty of the resurrection.

Sir Thomas Browne, *Private Journal*

PREACHERS AND PREACHING
apathetic preaching

389. The Rev. Samuel H. represented a class who understand by religion a respectable code of ethics—leaning for support upon some

great mysteries dimly traced in the background, and commemorated in certain great church festivals. . . . As a preacher, Mr. H. was sincere, but not earnest. He was a good and conscientious man; and he made a high valuation of the pulpit as an organ of civilization for cooperation with books; but it was impossible for any man, starting from the low ground of themes so unimpassioned and so desultory as the benefits of industry, the danger from bad companions, the importance of setting a good example, or the value of perseverance—to pump up any persistent stream of earnestness either in himself or in his auditors.

De Quincey, *Confessions of an English Opium Eater*

Christ lifted up

390.   (*John, just out of the theological college and settled in his Highland parish, was getting ready for his first sermon when he remembered the words of his dying mother, five years earlier:*)

"Ye'll follow Christ, and gin He offers ye his Cross, ye'll no refuse it, for He aye carries the heavy end Himsel'. He's guided your mother a' these years, and been as guid as a husband since your father's death, and He'll hold me fast tae the end. He'll keep ye too; and John, I'll be watchin' for ye. Ye'll no fail me," and her poor cold hand that had tended him all his days tightened on his head. But he could not speak, and her voice was failing fast.

"I canna see ye noo, John, but I know you're there, and I've just one other wish. If God calls ye to the ministry, ye'll no refuse; an' the first day ye preach in your ain kirk speak a guid word for Jesus Christ; an', John, I'll hear ye that day, though ye'll no see me; and I'll be satisfied."

Ian Maclaren, *Beside the Bonnie Briar Bush*

clerical verbosity

391.   "My friends," says the Reverend Mr. Chadband, "what is this which we now behold as being spread before us? Refreshment. Do we need refreshment, my friends? We do. And why do we need refreshment, my friends? Because we are but mortal, because we are but sinful, because we are but of the earth, because we are not of the air. Can we fly, my friends? We cannot. Why cannot we fly, my friends?"

Mr. Snagsby ventures to suggest in a cheerful and knowing tone, "No wings." But is immediately frowned down by Mrs. Snagsby.

"I say, my friends," pursues Mr. Chadband, utterly rejecting and obliterating Mr. Snagsby's suggestion, "why can we not fly? Is it because we are calculated to walk? It is. Could we walk, my friends, without strength? We could not. What should we do without strength, my friends? Our legs would refuse to bear us, our knees would double up, our ankles would turn over, and we should come to the ground. Then from whence, my friends, in a human point of view, do we derive the strength that is necessary to our limbs? Is it," says Mr. Chadband, glancing over the table, "from bread in various forms, from butter which is churned from the milk which is yielded unto us by the cow, from the eggs which are laid by the fowl, from ham, from tongue, from sausage, and from such like? Then let us partake of the good things which are set before us!"

Dickens, Bleak House

concern for souls

392.   When at midnight I hear a bell toll from this steeple, must not I say to myself, what have I done at any time for the instructing or rectifying of that man's conscience, who lieth there now ready to deliver up his own account to Almighty God? If he be not able to make a good account, he and I are in danger, because I have not enabled him; and though he be for himself able, that delivers me not if I have been no instrument for the doing of it.

John Donne, Sermons

courage in speaking the truth

393.   *(The priest, Clement Blair, is cautioned by the good Simon Glover against giving voice to his doctrines: if he does so, it will inevitably cost him his life. Clement's reply is:)*

"Heaven be my witness, that I would comply in all lawful things to conciliate the love and sympathy of my fellow-creatures! It is no light thing to be shunned by the worthy as an infected patient; to be persecuted by the Pharisees of the day as an unbelieving heretic; to be regarded with horror and contempt by the multitude, who consider me as a madman. But were all those evils multiplied an hundredfold, the fire within must not be stifled, the voice which says within me—speak, must receive obedience. Woe unto me if I preach not the Gospel, even should I at length preach it from amidst the pile of flames!"

Scott, *The Fair Maid of Perth*

394.   *(When Baron Avenal, the cruel border chieftain, seized the maid Catherine, Warden, the Protestant preacher, confronted the tyrant in his stronghold.)*

"Sit down," said Avenal fiercely, "else by my father's crest and my mother's honor . . ." But Warden remained standing. "Lord Baron," he said, "thou hast placed me in extremity. But if the question be, whether I am to hide the light which I am commanded to show forth, or to lose the light of this world, my choice is made. I say to thee, like the Holy Baptist to Herod, it is not lawful for thee to have this woman; and I say it though bonds and death be the consequence, counting my life as nothing in comparison with the ministry to which I am called."

Scott, *The Monastery*

criticized

395.   The things that mount the rostrum with a skip,
       And then skip down again; pronounce a text,
       Cry "Hem," and reading what they never wrote,
       Just fifteen minutes, huddle up their work,
       And with a well-bred whisper close the scene.

Cowper, *The Task*, Bk. II

396.   One curious omission will be noted in the sermons of Jeremy Taylor—the absence of almost all allusion to the life of the poor. The teaching of Taylor is in the main aristocratic; it is delivered from a seraphic height, and addressed to all classes of men, but particularly to those who are influential and well-to-do. No temptation, no frailty of the rich is allowed to pass unreproved. The preacher is speaking in the private chapel of a great house, and mainly to those who are responsible from their wealth, their intellect, or their influence. Outside are the hordes of the wild Welsh, but of them the preacher never speaks. We cannot help wishing

that the democratic element in society had also had an opportunity
to attract him.

Edmund Gosse, Jeremy Taylor

the Devil, the most diligent preacher

397.   Who is the most diligent bishop and prelate in all England,
that passeth all the rest in doing his office? It is the Devil. He is
the most diligent preacher of all others, he is never out of his diocese,
ye shall never find him unoccupied. . . . He is no lordly loiterer, but
a busy ploughman. . . . Therefore, ye prelates, learn of the Devil
to be diligent in doing of your office. If you will not learn of God
or good men, for shame learn of the Devil.

Bishop Latimer, Sermon on the Ploughers (1549)

emotional and intellectual appeal in preaching

398.   (*Archbishop Temple draws a comparison:*)
When I hear the Bishop of London, I get very much excited—
and feel ready to do anything: all of which is done away by the
next excitement, a concert or reading "The Critic": and when I come
on his text in the Bible, I remember that I was excited, and have a
vague sort of conception why. But when I hear the Bishop of
Stepney I am not moved at all: I have to listen for fear of losing
the inevitable connection of his points, and the pleasure is intellectual and not emotional: but when I come on his text afterwards I
can remember all his points, just because their connection is inevitable, and can then see whether I am following the precepts so
obviously implied in the text. And for me there is no doubt that
this is more edifying by far.

F. A. Iremonger,
William Temple, His Life and Letters

an exemplary pastor

399.   The word of Christ most truly did he preach,
And his parishioners devoutly teach.
Benign was he, in labors diligent,
And in adversity was still content—
As proved full oft. . . .
Wide was his parish, scattered far asunder,

Yet none did he neglect, in rain, or thunder.
Sorrow and sickness won his kindly care;
With staff in hand he travelled everywhere.
This good example to his sheep he brought
That first he wrought, and afterwards he taught.
This parable he joined the Word unto—
That, "If gold rust, what shall iron do?"
For if a priest be foul in whom we trust,
No wonder if a common man should rust!

       ❖   ❖   ❖

Though holy in himself and virtuous
He still to sinful men was piteous,
Not sparing of his speech, in vain conceit,
But in his teaching kindly and discreet.
To draw his flock to heaven with noble art,
By good example, was his holy art.
No less did he rebuke the obstinate,
Whether they were of high or low estate.
For pomp and worldly show he did not care;
No morbid conscience made his rule severe.
The lore of Christ and his apostles twelve
He taught, but first he followed it himself.

Chaucer, The Canterbury Tales,
Prologue (tr. by H. C. Leonard)

400.   Unpractised he to fawn, or seek for power,
By doctrines fashioned to the varying hour;
Far other aims his heart had learned to prize,
More skilled to raise the wretched than to rise.
His house was known to all the vagrant train;
He chid their wanderings, but relieved their pain;

       ❖   ❖   ❖

Pleased with his guests, the good man learned to glow,
And quite forgot their vices in their woe;
Careless their merits or their faults to scan,
His pity gave e'er charity began.
   Thus to relieve the wretched was his pride.
And e'en his failings lean'd to Virtue's side;

But in his duty prompt at every call,
He watched and wept, he prayed and felt for all;
And as a bird each fond endearment tries,
To tempt each new-fledged offspring to the skies,
He tried each art, reprov'd each dull delay,
Allur'd to brighter worlds, and led the way.

Goldsmith, "The Deserted Village"

forthrightness in preaching

401. I met the society [at Norwich] at seven, and told them in plain terms that they were the most ignorant, self-conceited, self-willed, fickle, intractable, disorderly, disjointed society that I knew in the three kingdoms. And God applied it to their hearts: so that many were profited; but I do not find that one was offended.

John Wesley, *Journal* (Sept. 9, 1759)

lightness in the pulpit

402.   He who negotiates between God and man,
As God's ambassador, the grand concerns
Of judgment and of mercy, should beware
Of lightness in his speech. 'Tis pitiful
To court a grin, when you should woo a soul.

Cowper, *The Task*, Bk. II

the man himself

403. Wesley's great missionary tours in Devon and Cornwall, and the wild, remote parts of Lancashire, lack no single element of sublimity. To this day the memories of those apostolic journeys are green and precious, and a source of strength and joy: the portrait of the eager preacher hangs up in almost every miner's cottage, whilst his name is pronounced with reverence by a hundred thousand lips. "You seem a very temperate people here," once observed a thirsty pedestrian (who was, indeed, none other than the present writer) to a Cornish miner; "how did it happen?" He replied solemnly, raising his cap, "There came a man amongst us once, and his name was John Wesley."

Augustine Birrell, *Collected Essays and Addresses*, Vol. II

404.   It is said of John Welsh, minister of Ayr, that he used to sleep with a plaid upon his bed that he might wrap it around him when he arose in the night to pray. He used to spend whole nights in wrestling with God for Zion, and for the purity of the Church of Scotland; and he wondered how Christians could lie all night in bed without rising to pray. Oh! we have few Welshes now; therefore our church is so dim, and our land a barren wilderness.

McCheyne, *Memoirs of*, ed. by Andrew Bonar

405.   My brother might have spoken like an angel for hours without anything like the effect that Saint Francis had with a few sentences. *It is the man that does it.* His figure has such a power about it, and such a past behind it, that people listen not so much to what his voice says as to his presence. You want the individual with his heart on fire.

John Buchan, *A Lodge in the Wilderness*

406.   What gave him his extraordinary personal power was this: that from the Pope to the beggar, from the Sultan of Syria in his pavilion to the ragged robbers crawling out of the wood, there was never a man looked into those brown, burning eyes without being certain that Francis Bernardone was really interested in him; in his own inner individual life from the cradle to the grave; that he himself was being valued and taken seriously, and not merely added to the spoils of some social policy or to the names in some clerical document.

G. K. Chesterton, *St. Francis of Assisi*

mediating God to men

407.   "I think, sir, when God makes his presence felt through us, we are like the burning bush: Moses never took any heed what sort of bush it was—he saw only the brightness of the Lord."

George Eliot, *Adam Bede* (Dinah Morris)

mediating the Presence of Christ

408.   *(Ian Maclaren describes John Carmichael's first sermon at Drumtochty:)*

I have been in Mr. Spurgeon's Tabernacle, where the people wept one minute and laughed the next; have heard Canon Liddon

in St. Paul's, and the sound of that high, clear voice is still with
me, "Awake, awake, put on thy strength, O Zion"; have stood in
the dusk of the Duomo at Florence when Padre Agostino thundered
against the evils of the day. But I never realized the unseen world
as I did that day in the Free Kirk of Drumtochty. . . . The subject
was Jesus Christ, and before he had spoken five minutes I was convinced that Jesus was present. The preacher faded from before
one's eyes, and there rose the figure of the Nazarene. . . . His voice
might be heard any moment, as I have imagined it in my lonely
hours by the winter fire or on the solitary hills . . . "Come unto
Me . . . and I will give you rest."

Ian Maclaren, *Beside the Bonnie Briar Bush*

ministerial blindness

409.   *(Donald Menzies, an elder in the Free Kirk at Drumtochty,
tells of an experience he had while he was seeking God, in the days
before his conversion.)*

"But sore sickness came upon me, and I was nigh unto death,
and my soul awoke within me and began to cry like a child for its
mother. All my days I had lived on Loch Tay; and now I thought
of the other country into which I would have to be going, where I
had no rest. And my soul would be driven to and fro in the darkness
as a bird on the moor of Rannoch.

"Janet sent for the minister, and he was very kind, and spoke
about my sickness and my farm, and I said nothing. For I was
hoping he would tell me what I was to do for my soul. But he began
upon the sheep market at Amulree, and I knew he was also in the
dark. After he left I turned my face to the wall and wept."

Ian Maclaren, *Beside the Bonnie Briar Bush*

ministerial consistency

410.   In one of his walks to Salisbury he saw a poor man with a
poorer horse that was fallen under his load. They were both in
distress and needed present help. Mr. Herbert perceiving this put
off his canonical coat and helped the man unload and load again
his horse. The poor man blessed him for it; and he blessed the
poor man, and was so like the Good Samaritan in that he gave
the man money to refresh both himself and his horse. At Mr.

Herbert's coming to his musical friends at Salisbury they began to wonder that he, who used to be so trim and clean, should come into their company so soiled and discomposed; but he told them the occasion. And when one of the company told him he had disparaged himself by so dirty an employment, his answer was that the thought of what he had done would prove music to him at midnight; and that the omission of it would have upbraided and made discord in his conscience whenever he should pass that place: "for if I be bound to pray for all that be in distress, I am sure that I am bound, so far as it is in my power, to practise what I pray for."

Izaak Walton, Life of Mr. George Herbert

ministerial inconsistency

411.   But, good my brother,
    Do not, as some ungracious pastors do,
    Show me the steep and thorny way to heaven,
    Whilst, like a puffed and reckless libertine,
    Himself the primrose path of dalliance treads.

Shakespeare, Hamlet, Act I, Sc. 3 (Ophelia)

ministerial self-centeredness   *see also* SELF-CENTEREDNESS

412.   (*Dr. Tusher, the parson, has mentioned to Lady Castlewood the danger of a smallpox epidemic in the village. If his assistant has been foolish enough to expose himself to it, the good doctor vows he will not tolerate the fellow near him.*)

"If a parishioner dying of the smallpox sent for you, would you not go?" asked my Lady.

"We are not in a popish country; and a sick man doth not absolutely need absolution and confession," said the Doctor. "'Tis true they are a comfort and a help to him when attainable. . . . But in a case where the life of a parish priest in the midst of his flock is highly valuable to them, he is not called upon to risk it (and therewith the lives, future prospects, and temporal, even spiritual welfare of his own family) for the sake of a single person, who is not very likely in a condition even to understand the religious message whereof the priest is the bringer—being uneducated, and likely stupefied or delirious by disease. If your Ladyship or his Lordship,

my excellent good friend and patron, were to take it . . . I would
lay my life down."

Thackeray, Henry Esmond

motive in entering the ministry

413.   *(Alton is urged by his worldly-minded cousin George to be-*
come a minister if he would better his personal interests:)

"If you are once a parson all is safe. Be you who you may before, from that moment you are a gentleman. No one will offer you
an insult. You are good enough for any man's society. You can dine
at any nobleman's table. You can be friend, confidant, father-con-
fessor if you like, to the highest women in the land; and if you
have person, manner, and common sense, marry one of them into
the bargain, Alton, my boy."

Charles Kingsley, Alton Locke

the preacher's task

414.   *(The author, discussing the function of the poet, might well*
be setting forth the function of the preacher:)

He must shake people out of their indifference, and force them
to make some election in this world, instead of sliding dully forward
in a dream. Life is a business we are all apt to mismanage; either
living recklessly from day to day, or suffering ourselves to be gulled
out of our moments by the inanities of custom. . . . There is something stupefying in the recurrence of unimportant things. And it is
only on rare provocations that we can rise to take an outlook
beyond daily concerns, and comprehend the narrow limits and great
possibilities of our existence. It is the duty of the poet to induce
such moments of clear insight. He is the declared enemy of all
living by reflex action. . . . He has to electrify his readers into an
instant unflagging activity.

R. L. Stevenson, Familiar Studies of Men and Books

preaching without aim

415.   *(When Lauchlan Campbell is asked his opinion concerning*
a rhetorical young preacher, he replies:)

"A very nice speaker, and well pleased with himself. But I would
be thinking when he would be giving his images. Oh, yes, I would

be thinking. There was a laddie fishing in the burn [creek] before
my house, and a very pretty laddie he was. He had a rod and a
string, and he threw his line beautifully. It was a great pity he had
no hook."

Ian Maclaren, *Beside the Bonnie Briar Bush*

preaching of a high order

416.   *(The preacher referred to is the famous headmaster of
Rugby, Dr. Arnold.)*

We listened, as all boys in their better moods will listen, to a
man who we felt was with all his heart and soul and strength striving against whatever was mean and unmanly and unrighteous in our
little world. It was not the cold clear voice of one giving advice
and warning from serene heights to those who were struggling and
sinning below, but the warm living voice of one who was fighting
for us and by our sides, and calling on us to help him and ourselves
and one another. . . . And so was brought home to the young boy
the meaning of his life: that it was no fool's or sluggard's paradise,
but a battle-field where there are no spectators, and where the
stakes are life and death.

Thomas Hughes, *Tom Brown's Schooldays*

417.   *(John Donne, Dean of St. Paul's Cathedral, was the greatest
English pulpiteer of his day.)*

A preacher in earnest: weeping sometimes for his hearers, sometimes with them; always preaching to himself, like an Angel from
a cloud, but in none; carrying some, as St. Paul was, to Heaven
in holy raptures, and enticing others by a sacred art and courtship
to amend their lives; here picturing a vice so as to make it ugly
to those that practised it; and a virtue so as to make it be beloved
even by those that loved it not; and all this with a most particular
grace and an unexpressible addition of comeliness.

Izaak Walton, *Life of Dr. John Donne*

preaching, a kind of spiritual wrestling

418.   To a great extent Scottish sermons were delivered without
book, having been committed to memory. When notes were used
they were sometimes concealed on a small shelf beneath the pulpit;

for the people had a prejudice, almost a superstition, against "the papers," and could not reconcile them with the action of the Holy Ghost in the preaching of the Gospel. Reading, pure and simple, was very rare. There was a traditional and almost universal idea of preaching as a kind of spiritual wrestling with a congregation; and the better professors of the art entered into it as athletes, and strove habitually and throughout to get a good "grip" of the hearer, as truly and as much as the Cumbrian wrestler struggles with persistent and varied movements to get a good grip of his antagonist.

Gladstone, *The Might of Right*

preaching that misrepresents God

419. I believe that the root of almost every schism and heresy from which the Christian church has ever suffered, has been the effort of men to earn, rather than to receive their salvation; and that the reason preaching is so commonly ineffectual is, that it calls on men oftener to work for God than to behold God working for them. If, for every rebuke that we utter of men's vices, we put forth a claim upon their hearts; if for every assertion of God's demands from them, we could substitute a display of his kindness to them; if side by side with every warning of death, we could exhibit proofs and promises of immortality; if, in fine, instead of assuming the being of an awful Deity, which men, though they cannot and dare not deny, are always unwilling, sometimes unable, to conceive, we were to show them a near, visible, inevitable, but all-beneficent Deity, whose presence makes the earth itself a heaven, I think there would be fewer deaf children in the market-place.

Ruskin, *Modern Painters*, Vol. II

preaching partial truths

420. The teaching of half-truths is indefensible and mischievous when they are taught as whole truths. But there is an order and succession in the progress of instruction; and that which is not good as a resting-place may be most excellent and most necessary as a stage in an onward journey. It was not at the commencement of his career, but it was on the very evening of his passion that our Lord himself was pleased to say to his disciples, "I have many things to say unto you, but ye cannot bear them now." Indeed, the negation of this principle would throw every established method of acquiring knowledge into confusion; and, if enforced and persevered in, would condemn the human understanding to a hopeless and imbecile sterility.

Gladstone, *The Might of Right*

need of preaching practical morality

421.   We have had thirty years of unexampled clerical activity among us. Churches have been doubled; theological books, magazines, reviews, newspapers have been passed out by the hundreds of thousands; while by the side of it there has sprung up an equally astonishing development of moral dishonesty. We have false weights, false measures, cheating and shoddy everywhere. Yet the clergy have seen all this grow up in absolute indifference; and the great question which at the moment is agitating the Church of England is the color of the ecclesiastical petticoats. Many a hundred sermons have I heard in England, many a dissertation on the mysteries of the faith, on the divine mission of the clergy, on apostolical succession, on bishops, and justification, and the theory of good works, and verbal inspiration, and the efficacy of the sacrament; but never, during these thirty years, never one that I can recollect on common honesty, or these primitive commandments, Thou shalt not lie, and Thou shalt not steal.

J. A. Froude, "Inaugural Address, St. Andrews University," 1869

need of sermon criticism

422.   A little supply of cynicism should be kept on hand to test the genuine nature of the article. Let us only reflect, to use one obvious illustration, how much good would be done if in every church there came in at sermon time the cynic who is so often denounced in his absence; if he was accommodated with a seat, and allowed to put the clergyman a few questions afterwards in private: would not the logic to which we are treated be generally sounder, the eloquence more severe, and a little more care be shown not to shelter sheer nonsense under the respect due to sacred things? We should, I fancy, more frequently enjoy what, in spite of all that is said against sermons, is really one of the most elevating of all

possible influences, the eloquence of a man who has put the whole
powers of his mind to enforce doctrines of whose truth and vital
importance he is even passionately convinced, and who further
remembers that he is talking to men as well as to children.

Sir Leslie Stephen, "A Cynic's Apology"

sermon delivery

423.   No doubt preaching, in the proper sense of the word, is
more effective than reading. But as things now are, I am quite
sure I prefer going to church to a pastor who reads his discourse;
for I never yet heard more than one preacher without book, who
did not forget his argument in three minutes' time, and fall into
vague and unprofitable declamation. These preachers never progress; they eddy round and round. Sterility of mind follows their
ministry.

Coleridge, Table Talk

the significance of the pulpit

424.   The pulpit
> Must stand acknowledged while the world
>   shall stand,
> The most important and effectual guard,
> Support, and ornament of Virtue's cause.
> There stands the messenger of truth: there
>   stands
> The legate of the skies!—His theme divine,
> His office sacred, his credentials clear.
> By him the violated law speaks out
> Its thunders; and by him, in strains as sweet
>   as angels use, the Gospel whispers peace.

Cowper, The Task, Bk. II

style in preaching

425.   *(The author, speaking of style in men of letters, might well
be alluding to style in preaching.)*
And yet we know how fatal the pursuit of liveliness may be:
it may result in the tiresome acrobatics of Meredith. Macaulay and
Carlyle were in their different ways arresting; but at the heavy cost

of naturalness. Their flashy effects destroy their persuasiveness; you would not believe a man was very intent on ploughing a furrow if he carried a hoop with him and jumped through it at every other step. A good style should show no sign of effort.

W. Somerset Maugham, *Mr. Maugham Himself*

the testimony of the preacher's life in the home

426. Pastor Irwine was one of those men, and they are not the commonest, of whom we can know the best only by following them away from the market-place, the platform, and the pulpit, entering with them into their own homes, hearing the voice with which they speak to the young and aged about their own hearthstone, and witnessing their thoughtful care for the every-day wants of every-day companions, who take all their kindness as a matter of course, and not as a subject for panegyric.

George Eliot, *Adam Bede*

PREJUDICE *see also* SECTARIANISM, SOCIAL CASTE, SOCIAL JUSTICE

the force of

427. Seek roses in December—ice in June;
Hope constancy in wind, or corn in chaff;
Believe a woman or an epitaph,
Or any other thing that's false, before
You trust in critics who themselves are sore.

Byron, *English Bards and Scotch Reviewers*

national

428. *(North, in humorous vein, is speaking to the shepherd:)*
"Minds like ours, my dear James, must be above national prejudices; and in all companies it gives me true pleasure to declare that, as a people, the English are indeed very little inferior to the Scotch."

Christopher North, *Noctes Ambrosianae*, Vol. II

PRIDE
of ancestry

429. Lady Clara Vere de Vere,
There stands a specter in your hall:

The guilt of blood is at your door:
 You changed a wholesome heart to gall.
You held your course without remorse,
 To make him trust his modest worth;
And last, you fix'd a vacant stare
 And slew him with your noble birth.

Trust me, Clare Vere de Vere,
 From yon blue heavens above us bent
The gardener Adam and his wife
 Smile at the claims of long descent.
Howe'er it be, it seems to me,
 'Tis only noble to be good;
Kind hearts are more than coronets,
 And simple faith than Norman blood.
      Tennyson, "Lady Clara Vere de Vere"

an antidote to   *see also* AMBITION

430. *(In church the poet saw a louse on the bonnet of a fashionably dressed lady.)*

  O wad some Pow'r the giftie gie us
  To see oursels as others see us!
  It wad frae monie a blunder free us,
     An' foolish notion.
  What airs in dress an' gait wad lea'e us,
     An' ev'n devotion!
        Burns, "To a Louse"

the costliness of

431. *(Satan, nearing Paradise and Adam, falls into many doubts with himself; but at length he confirms himself in evil.)*

        Is there no place
Left for repentance, none for pardon left?
None left but by submission; and that word
Disdain forbids me, and my dread of shame
Among the Spirits beneath, whom I seduced
With other promises and other vaunts
Than to submit, boasting I could subdue
The Omnipotent. Ay me! they little know

How dearly I abide that boast so vain,
Under what torments inwardly I groan.

* * *

So farewell hope, and, with hope, farewell fear,
Farewell remorse! All good to me is lost;
Evil, be thou my Good.

Milton, *Paradise Lost*, Bk. IV

the hollowness of

432.   Dust are our frames; and, gilded
                dust, our pride
            Looks only for a moment whole and
                sound;
            Like that long-buried body of the king,
            Found lying with his urns and orna-
                ments,
            Which at a touch of light, an air of
                Heaven,
            Slipt into ashes and was found no more.

Tennyson, "Aylmer's Field" (opening lines)

intellectual

433.   To be vague may be a short cut to a certain kind of popularity. It provides a debating point, and man is an argumentative
animal. To write a poem, a play or a book which will become a
dinner-table topic may be a profitable occupation. It is jam for the
intellectual snobs who relish telling you what the author was really
getting at. Because you do not know, and do not pretend to know,
you are supposed to be a crude simpleton. The history of the Snob
Value of the Obscure deserves a book in itself. When Browning remarked that only the author knew the meaning of his "Sordello"
and that he had forgotten it, he gave enormous joy to the Browning
Societies of his day, who then got to work on unravelment and so
displayed their own surpassing acumen and ingenuity.

Ivor Brown, "In Praise of Clarity"

a sinister

434.   The one kind of pride which is wholly damnable is the
pride of the man who has something to be proud of. The pride
which, proportionately speaking does not hurt the character, is the

pride in things which reflect no credit on the person at all. Thus
it does a man no harm to be proud of his country, and comparatively
little harm to be proud of his remote ancestors. It does him more
harm to be proud of having made money, because in that he has a
little more reason for pride. It does him more harm still to be proud
of what is nobler than money—intellect. And it does him most
harm of all to value himself for the most valuable thing on earth—
goodness.

                                        G. K. Chesterton, *Heretics*

spiritual

435.   *(The subject of the poem is a Syrian anchorite who, to
mortify the flesh, lived thirty years on top of a column successively
raised from a height of nine to sixty feet.)*
    Let this avail, just, dreadful, mighty God,
This not be all in vain, that thrice ten years,
Thrice multiplied by superhuman pangs,
In hungers and in thirsts, fevers and cold,
Patient on this tall pillar I have borne
Rain, wind, frost, heat, hail, damp, and sleet, and snow.
           ❖   ❖   ❖

O Jesus, if thou wilt not save my soul,
Who may be saved? who is it may be saved?
Who may be made a saint, if I fail here?
Show me the man hath suffer'd more than I.
           ❖   ❖   ❖

Bethink thee, Lord, while thou and all the saints
Enjoy themselves in heaven, and men on earth
House in the shade of comfortable roofs,
      . . . and even beasts have stalls,
I, 'tween the spring and downfall of the light,
Bow down one thousand and two hundred times
To Christ, the Virgin Mother, and the Saints.
                              Tennyson, "St. Simeon Stylites"

PROCRASTINATION

436.   Late, late, so late! and dark the night and chill!
    Late, late, so late! but we can enter still.
      Too late, too late! ye cannot enter now.

No light had we; for this we do repent,
And learning this, the bridegroom will relent.
Too late, too late! ye cannot enter now.

No light! so late! and dark and chill the night!
O, let us in, that we may find the light!
Too late, too late! ye cannot enter now.

Have we not heard the bridegroom is so sweet?
O, let us in, tho' late, to kiss his feet!
No, no, too late! ye cannot enter now.

Tennyson, "Guinevere"

437.   Procrastination is the thief of time; year after year it steals, till all are fled, and to the mercies of a moment leaves the vast concerns of an eternal state. At thirty, man suspects himself a fool; knows it at forty; and reforms his plan; at fifty chides his infamous delay, pushes his prudent purpose to resolve; in all the magnanimity of thought, resolves, and re-resolves, then dies the same.

Edward Young, *Night Thoughts*, Vol. I

PROGRESS
not a law of human nature

438.   Men wiser and more learned than I, have discerned in history a plot, a rhythm, a predetermined pattern. These harmonies are concealed from me. I can see only one emergency following another as wave follows upon wave, only one great fact with respect to which there can be no generalizations, only one safe rule for the historian: that he should recognize in the diversity of human destinies the play of the contingent and the unforeseen. This is not a doctrine of cynicism or despair. The fact of progress is written plain and large on the page of history; but progress is not a law of nature. The ground gained by one generation may be lost by another. The thoughts of men may flow into channels which lead to disaster and barbarism.

H. A. L. Fisher, *History of Europe*, Preface

Victorian doctrine of the inevitability of human progress

439.   For I dipped into the future, far as human eye could see,
Saw the Vision of the world, and all the wonder that would be;

Saw the heavens fill with commerce, argosies of magic sails,
Pilots of the purple twilight, dropping down with costly bales;

Heard the heavens fill with shouting, and there rain'd a ghastly dew
From the nations' airy navies grappling in the central blue;

Far along the world-wide whisper of the south-wind rushing warm,
With the standards of the peoples plunging thro' the thunder-storm;

Till the war-drum throbbed no longer, and the battle-flags were
    furled
In the Parliament of man, the Federation of the world.

There the common sense of most shall hold a fretful realm in awe
And the kindly earth shall slumber, lapped in universal law.

*   *   *

Yet I doubt not thro' the ages one increasing purpose runs,
And the thoughts of men are widen'd with the process of the suns.

Tennyson, "Locksley Hall"

PROSPERITY
the danger of national

440.   *(The poet, returned from scenes of desolation in the France
of the Revolution, was struck with the vanity and parade of the
large English towns and cities. The sonnet is a protest against "the
mischief engendered and fostered among us by undisturbed
wealth.")*

O Friend! I know not which way I must look
For comfort, being, as I am, opprest
To think that now our life is only drest
For show; mean handy-work of craftsman, cook,
Or groom!—We must run glittering like a brook
In the open sunshine, or we are unblest;
The wealthiest man among us is the best:
No grandeur now in nature or in book
Delights us. Rapine, avarice, expense,
This is idolatry; and these we adore:
Plain living and high thinking are no more:
The homely beauty of the good old cause

> Is gone; our peace, our fearful innocence,
> And pure religion breathing household laws.
>
> Wordsworth, "In London, 1802"

the illusion of worldly

441.   The hidden and awful Wisdom which apportions the destinies of mankind is pleased so to humiliate and cast down the
tender, good, and wise; and to set up the selfish, the foolish, or the
wicked. Oh, be humble, my brother, in your prosperity! Be gentle
with those who are less lucky, if not more deserving. Think, what
right have you to be scornful, whose virtue is a deficiency of temptation, whose success may be a chance, whose rank may be an an-
cestor's accident, whose prosperity is very likely a satire.

Thackeray, *Vanity Fair*

PROVIDENCE   *see also* GOD, GUIDANCE
an intervening

442.   *(The author, aboard a ship that was fast driven toward the
dangerous coast of Cape Finisterre, tells of a miraculous deliverance:)*

We were now close to the rocks when a horrid convulsion of
the elements took place. The lightning enveloped us as with a
mantle; thunders were louder than the roar of a million cannon;
the dregs of the ocean seemed to be cast up, and in the midst of
all this turmoil, the wind, without the slightest intimation, veered
right about and pushed us from the horrible coast faster than it had
previously driven us to it. The oldest sailors on board acknowledged
that they had never witnessed so providential an escape. I said
from the bottom of my heart, "Our Father, Hallowed by Thy name."

George Borrow, *The Bible in Spain*

an overruling

443.   *(Edward Wilson, doctor and zoologist, accompanied Robert
Scott on his last Antarctic expedition.)*

It was his steadfast and unalterable conviction that for a man
who has wrapped his will in God's will, put his life consciously in
the stream of the divine life, freed his soul from all personal ambitions, taken his life on trust as a divine gift, that for such a man
there is an over-ruling Providence which guards and guides him

in every incident of his life, from the greatest to the least. He held that all annoyances, frustrations, disappointments, mishaps, discomforts, hardships, sorrows, pains, and even final disaster itself, are simply God's ways of teaching us lessons that we could never else learn. That circumstances do not matter, are nothing; but that the response of the spirit that meets them is everything; that there is no situation in human life, however apparently adverse, nor any human relationship, however apparently uncongenial, that cannot be made, if God is in the heart, a thing of perfect joy; . . . that the worth of life is not to be measured by its results in achievement or success, but solely by the motive of one's heart and the effort of one's will.

George Seaver, The Faith of Edward Wilson

RELIGION   *see also* CHRISTIAN LIFE
of expediency

444.   Religion more or less in every country is for the most part a wise prudential feeling, grounded on mere calculation; a matter, as all others now are, of expediency and utility; whereby some smaller quantum of earthly enjoyment may be exchanged for a far larger quantum of celestial enjoyment. Thus religion, too, is profit, a working for wages.

Carlyle, Signs of the Times

of morality

445.   *(The allusion is to George Eliot.)*
The external aspects of religion, and even more the moral effects of religious belief, were intensely interesting to her mind. We remember hearing it said by one who had the best right to speak on the subject that her interest in any manifestation of the religious sentiment was such that she would willingly sit for hours in a poor little chapel watching Italian peasants praying to a winking Madonna. But her concern in religion seems to have invariably ceased with its effects on conduct. Of any interest in truth for its own sake we find no trace except in *Janet's Repentance*. Even the wonderful description of the change wrought in Maggie Tulliver (no doubt drawn from her own experience) is only a study of its effects on the development of her character; it is the moral result,

the lesson of self-sacrifice, that she dwells upon, not the object of belief. . . .

To Romola, as to Maggie, religion is presented as the force of self-sacrifice, not as the revelation of an overmastering truth before which the soul must bow; and that is a human and moral force, not supernatural or, in the truest sense of the word, religious.

Arthur T. Lyttelton,
Modern Poets of Faith, Doubt, and Paganism

REMORSE   *see also* CONSCIENCE, CONVICTION, REPENTANCE
Lord Byron's

446.   *(Written the year of the poet's death.)*
> My days are in the yellow leaf;
>   The flowers and fruits of love are gone;
> The worm, the canker, and the grief,
>   Are mine alone!
>
> The fire that in my bosom preys
>   Is like to some volcanic isle;
> No torch is kindled at its blaze,—
>   A funeral pile.

Byron, "On This Day I Complete
My Thirty-sixth Year"

for lost opportunity

447.   There were many things he had neglected. Little matters while he was at home and surrounded by them, but things of mighty moment when he was at an immeasurable distance. There were many, many blessings that he had inadequately felt, there were many trivial injuries that he had not forgiven, there was love that he had but poorly returned, there was friendship that he had too lightly prized, there were a million words that he might have spoken, a million kind looks that he might have given, unaccountable slight easy deeds in which he might have been most truly great and good. O for a day, for one day to make amends! But the sun never shone upon that happy day, and out of his remote captivity he never came.

Dickens, *Reprinted Pieces*, "The Long Voyage"

448.   O the anguish of that thought that we can never atone to
our dead for the stinted affection we gave them, for the light
answers we returned to their plaints or their pleadings, for the little
reverence we showed to that sacred human soul that lived so close
to us, and was the divinest thing God had given us to know.

George Eliot, Amos Barton

449.   The lost days of my life until today,
             What were they, could I see them on the street
             Lie as they fell?

✻   ✻   ✻

             I do not see them here: but after death
             God knows I know the faces I shall see,
             Each one a murdered self, with low last breath.
             "I am thyself,—what hast thou done for me?"
             "And I—and I—thyself," (lo, each one saith,)
             "And thou thyself to all eternity!"

Dante Gabriel Rossetti, "Lost Days"

man slow to feel

450.   For my part I believe that remorse is the least active of all
a man's moral senses—the very easiest to be deadened when
wakened; and in some never wakened at all. We grieve at being
found out, and at the idea of shame or punishment. But the mere
sense of wrong makes very few people unhappy in Vanity Fair.

Thackeray, Vanity Fair

for marital infidelity

451.   *(Queen Guinevere was the fairest flower in Arthur's court,
pure as she was beautiful, the pride and joy of Arthur's heart. Yet
in an evil hour she sinned. Later, when the king stands before her,
she realizes afresh something of the moral stature of this man
against whom she has sinned. Falling before him, the wretched
queen cries in anguish:)*

                    I cannot kill my sin,
             If soul be soul; nor can I kill my shame;
             No, nor by living can I live it down.
             The days will grow to weeks, the weeks to months,

The months will add themselves and make the years,
The years will roll into the centuries,
And mine will ever be a name of scorn.

❉   ❉   ❉

                                        Ah, my God,
What might I not have made of thy fair world,
Had I but loved thy highest creature here?

Tennyson, "Guinevere"

for neglect   *see also* HUMAN NATURE—the self-centeredness of

452.   There broke upon him in his late years, like a flash of
lightning from heaven, the terrible revelation that he had sacrificed
his wife's health and happiness in his absorption in his work; that
he had been oblivious of his most obvious obligations, and had been
negligent, inconsiderate, selfish. The fault was grave and the remorse agonizing. For many years after she had left him, when we
passed the spot in our walks where she was last seen alive, he
would bare his gray head in the wind and rain—his features wrung
with unavailing sorrow.

J. A. Froude, *Thomas Carlyle, 1795-1835*, Vol. II

Peter's

453.   The Saviour looked on Peter. Ay, no word,
No gesture of reproach; the Heavens serene
Though heavy with armed justice, did not lean
Their thunders that way: the forsaken Lord
Looked only, on the traitor. . . .
And Peter, from the height of blasphemy—
"I never knew this man"—did quail and fall
As knowing straight THAT GOD; and turnèd free
And went out speechless from the face of all,
And filled the silence, weeping bitterly.

Elizabeth Barrett Browning, "The Look"

a son's

454.   I think sometimes, could I recall the days that are past,
which among them should I choose? not those "merrier days," not
the "pleasant days of hope," not "those wanderings with a fair-hair'd
maid." But the days, Coleridge, of a mother's *fondness* for her

schoolboy. What would I give to call her back to earth for *one* day!
—on my knees to ask her pardon for all those little asperities of
temper which, from time to time, have given her gentle spirit pain!
                    Charles Lamb, in a letter to Coleridge, Nov. 14, 1796

two kinds of

455.   Remorse is as the heart in which it grows:
           If that be gentle, it drops balmy dews
           Of true repentance; but if proud and gloomy,
           It is the poison tree that, pierced to the inmost,
           Weeps only tears of poison.
                              Coleridge, *Remorse*, Act I, Sc. 1

REPENTANCE   *see also* CONVICTION, REMORSE
a difficult matter

456.   The world will not believe a man repents;
           And this wise world is mainly right.
           Full seldom does a man repent, or use
           Both grace and will to pick the vicious quitch
           Of blood and custom wholly out of him,
           And make all clean, and plant himself afresh.
                              Tennyson, "Geraint and Enid"

an inadequate

457.   There are men guilty of very great sins which they have
lived in for many years, who are very sensible of their past wickedness and heartily sorry for their sins, and seriously resolved by the
grace of God to forsake them; yet they are not satisfied of the
sincerity of their repentance, because they have not (with all their
sorrows and resolutions) conquered their inclinations to sin, but
are guilty of frequent relapses. As time wears off their sorrow for
their last offence, their old inclinations revive, and a new temptation conquers them again. Now such men's consciences cannot
speak peace to them. Since, however, they are not perfect slaves
to sin, their consciences do not absolutely condemn them; but as
they prevail or yield, so their hopes or fears increase.
                              William Sherlock,
                "A Practical Discourse Concerning a Future Judgment"

a matter of expediency

458. I expected every wave would have swallowed us up and that every time the ship fell down in the hollow of the sea, we should never rise more; and in this agony of mind I made vows and resolutions, that if it would please God here to spare my life this one voyage, if ever I got once my foot upon dry land again, I would go directly home to my father and never set it in a ship again while I lived. . . . But the next day the wind was abated and the sea calmer, and I began to be a little inured to it. . . . In a word, as the sea returned to its smoothness of surface and settled calmness, so my fears and apprehensions of being swallowed up by the sea being forgotten, I entirely forgot the vows and promises that I made in my distress.

Defoe, *Robinson Crusoe*

459. Pepys had not used his wife well: he had wearied her with his jealousies, even while himself unfaithful; he had grudged her clothes and pleasures while lavishing both upon himself; he had abused her in words; he had bent his fist at her in anger; he had once blackened her eye; . . . But now, when he is in the wrong, nothing can exceed the long-suffering affection of this impatient husband. While he was still sinning and still undiscovered, he seems not to have known a touch of penitence stronger than what might lead him to take his wife to the theater, or for an airing, or to give her a new dress, by way of compensation. Once found out, however, and he seems to have lost to himself all claim to decent usage. It is perhaps the strongest instance of his externality.

R. L. Stevenson, *Familiar Studies of Men and Books*

possibility of a late

460. *(For Guido, Browning's arch-villain, the Pope sees small prospect of redemption. Yet, recalling an experience he once had, the churchman hopes against hope that even Guido will repent at the eleventh hour:)*

I stood at Naples once, a night so dark
I could have scarce conjectured there was earth
Anywhere, sky or sea or world at all:

But the night's black was burst through with a blaze—
Thunder struck blow on blow, earth groaned and bore,
Through her whole length to mountain visible:
There lay the city thick and plain with spires,
And like a ghost disshrouded, white the sea.
So may the truth be flashed out by one blow,
As Guido see, one instant, and be saved.

Browning, The Ring and the Book

too late

461.   (*Faustus, in medieval legend, the learned doctor who sold
his soul to the Devil in exchange for youth, knowledge, and magical
power. In Marlowe's version Faustus, now facing the end, his mind
filled with anguish, seeks in vain a place of repentance:*)

Now thou hast but one bare hour to live,
And then thou must be damned perpetually!
Stand still, you ever-moving spheres of heaven,
That time may cease, and midnight never come;
Fair Nature's eye, rise, rise again, and make
Perpetual day; or let this hour be but
A year, a month, a week, a natural day,
That Faustus may repent and save his soul!

*   *   *

Oh, I'll leap up to God!—Who pulls me down?
See, see where Christ's blood streams in the firmament!
One drop would save my soul, half a drop!

*   *   *

Mountains and hills, come, come, and fall on me,
And hide me from the heavy wrath of God!
No, no!
Then will I headlong run into the earth:
Earth, gape! O, no, it will not harbor me!

*   *   *

Let Faustus live in hell a thousand years,
A hundred thousand and at last be saved;
Oh, no end is limited to damnéd souls!

Marlowe, The Tragical History of Doctor Faustus

REPRESSION
the danger of

462.   When I was at Naples I went with Signor Manso to see the burning mountain Vesuvius. I wondered how the peasants could venture to dwell so fearlessly and cheerfully on its sides, when the lava was flowing from its summit; but Manso smiled, and told me that when the fire descends freely they retreat before it without haste or fear. They can tell how fast it will move, and how far; and they know, moreover, that though it may work some little damage it will soon cover the fields, over which it has passed, with rich vineyards and sweet flowers. But when the flames are pent up in the mountain, then it is that they have reason to fear; then it is that the earth sinks and the sea swells; then cities are swallowed up, and the place knoweth them no more.

Milton

RESENTMENT see also FORGIVENESS, RETALIATION
must vanish in His Presence

463.   "Do you remember how we both hated Flashman?" said Tom eagerly.

"Of course I do," said East.

"Well, when I came to take the Sacrament, I had a great struggle about that. I tried to put him out of my head; and when I couldn't do that, I tried to think of him as evil, as something that the Lord who was loving me hated, and which I might hate too. But it wouldn't do. I broke down; I believe Christ Himself broke me down; and when the Doctor gave me the bread and wine, and leant over me praying, I prayed for poor Flashman as if it had been you."

Thomas Hughes, Tom Brown's Schooldays

REST see also PEACE, SILENCE
an element in great works of art

464.   I say fearlessly respecting repose, that no work of art can be great without it, and that all art is great in proportion to the appearance of it. It is the most unfailing test of beauty, whether of matter or motion; nothing can be ignoble that possesses it, nothing right that has it not, and in strict proportion to its appearance in the work is the majesty of mind to be inferred to the artificer.

Ruskin, Modern Painters, Part III

RETALIATION   *see also* FORGIVENESS, RESENTMENT
freedom from

465.   *(The allusion is to Gladstone, the Prime Minister.)*

Of how few who have lived for more than sixty years in the full sight of their countrymen, and have as party leaders been exposed to angry and sometimes spiteful criticism, can it be said that there stands against them no malignant word and no vindictive act! This was due not perhaps entirely to natural sweetness of disposition, but rather to self-control and to a certain largeness of soul which would not condescend to anything mean or petty.

James Bryce, Studies in Contemporary Biography

466.   The highest proof of virtue is to possess boundless power without abusing it. No kind of power is more formidable than the power of making men ridiculous; and that power Addison possessed in boundless measure. How grossly that power was abused by Swift and by Voltaire is well known. But of Addison it may be confidently affirmed that he has blackened no man's character; nay, that it would be difficult, if not impossible, to find in all the volumes which he has left us a single taunt which can be called ungenerous or unkind. Yet he had detractors, whose malignity might have seemed to justify a terrible revenge. He was a politician; he was the best writer of his party; he lived in times of fierce excitement, in times when persons of high character and station stooped to scurrility such as is now practised only by the basest of mankind. Yet no provocation and no example could induce him to return railing for railing.

Macaulay, "Essay on Addison"

467.   He was an absolute sepulcher in swallowing oppression and ill-usage. It vanished in him. There was no echo of complaint, no murmur of resentment from the hollows of that soul. The blows that fell on him resounded not, and no one but God remembered them.

George MacDonald, Robert Falconer

468.   *(A tribute to Archbishop Cranmer.)*

    To do him wrong was to beget
    A kindness from him; for his heart was rich—

Of such fine mould that if you sow'd therein
The seed of Hate, it blossom'd Charity.

Tennyson, *Queen Mary*, Act IV, Sc. 1 (Thirlby)

RETRIBUTION *see also* JUDGMENT, JUSTICE, MORAL LAW,
the fact of SIN

469.   Retribution, which often travels slowly—especially when
heaviest—had tracked his footsteps with a sure and certain scent,
and was gaining on him fast. Unmindful of her stealthy tread,
her victim holds his course in fancied triumph. Still at his heels
she comes, and, once afoot, is never turned aside!

Dickens, *The Old Curiosity Shop*

slow but sure

470.   (*Defarge is impatient for the revolution that is to engulf
France.*)

"It *is* a long time," repeated his wife; "and when is it not a long
time? Vengeance and retribution require a long time; it is the rule."

"It does not take a long time to strike a man with lightning,"
said Defarge.

"How long," demanded madame, composedly, "does it take to
make the lightning? Tell me."

Defarge raised his head thoughtfully, as if there was something
in that too.

"It does not take a long time," said madame, "for an earthquake
to swallow a town. Eh well! Tell me how long it takes to prepare the
earthquake?"

"A long time, I suppose," said Defarge.

"But when it is ready, it takes place, and grinds to pieces everything before it. In the meantime, it is always preparing, though
it is not seen or heard. That is your consolation. Keep it."

Dickens, *A Tale of Two Cities*

REVERENCE *see also* WORSHIP
for God's name

471.   (*Dolly Winthrop, the wheelwright's wife, encourages Silas
to go to church regularly. Her use of the plural pronoun is her way
of avoiding a presumptuous familiarity with the Deity.*)

"When a bit o' trouble comes I feel as I can put up wi' it, For
I've looked for help i' the right quarter, and give myself up to Them
as we must all give ourselves up to at the last; and if we've done
our part, it isn't to be believed as Them as are above us 'ud be
worse nor we are, and come short o' Theirn."

George Eliot, *Silas Marner*

472.   Now when Father Malachy pronounced the Sacred Name
he did not, like many priests, articulate It as though it were
"Ramsay Macdonald"; but he spoke It slowly and reverently, so that
the syllables seemed to be printed before the eyes in scarlet and
gold, as indeed they are in illuminated mediaeval missals. And
Canon Geoghegan and the Reverend Humphrey Hamilton, hearing
him, knew, each in his own way, that there was a man to whom the
practice of religion was as important as the theory.

Bruce Marshall, *Father Malachy's Miracle*

social implications of

473.   Reverence towards God makes men natural and simple to
each other. There is a modest yet unabashed naturalness of manner
which occasionally distinguishes spiritual persons, into whatever
company they are come. A man will hardly ever be awkward in
public, who in secret pays habitual reverent court to God. Habitual
reverence is the high breeding of the spiritual life.

F. W. Faber, *Passages from the Spiritual Life*

SABBATH DAY
the blessing of the

474.   There was a time when it delighted me to flash my satire
on the English Sunday; I could see nothing but antiquated foolishness and modern hypocrisy in this weekly pause from labor and from
bustle. Now I prize it as an inestimable boon, and dread every
encroachment upon its stillness. . . . The idea is surely as good a
one as ever came to heavy-laden mortals; let one whole day in every
week be removed from the common life of the world. . . . Sunday
has always brought large good to the generality, and to a chosen
number has been the very life of the soul. . . . If its ancient use
perish from among us, so much the worse for our country.

George Gissing, *The Private Papers of Henry Ryecroft*

keeping the

475.   *(Boswell tells us that Dr. Johnson, in his forty-sixth year, wrote in his Journal this scheme of life for the Lord's day:)*

"Having lived not without an habitual reverence for the Sabbath, yet without that attention to its religious duties which Christianity requires, I resolve herewith—(1) To rise early, and in order to do so, to go to sleep early on Saturday. (2) To use some extraordinary devotion in the morning. (3) To examine the tenor of my life, and particularly the last week; and to mark my advances in religion, or recession from it. (4) To read the Scriptures methodically with such helps as are at hand. (5) To go to Church twice. (6) To read books of divinity, either speculative or practical. (7) To instruct my family. (8) To wear off by meditation any worldly soil contracted during the week."

Boswell, *Life of Johnson*

perversion of the   *see also* LEGALISM

476.   "Heaven forgive me," said Clennam, "how I hated this day."

There was the dreary Sunday of his childhood, when he sat with his hands before him, scared out of his senses by a horrible tract which commenced business with the poor child by asking him in its title why he was going to Perdition. There was the sleepy Sunday of his boyhood when, like a military deserter, he was marched to chapel by a picket of teachers three times a day morally handcuffed to another boy, and when he would willingly have bartered two meals of indigestible sermon for another ounce or two of inferior mutton at his scanty dinner. There was the interminable Sunday of his non-age, when his mother, stern of face and unrelenting of heart, would sit all day behind a Bible—bound, like her own construction of it, in the hardest, barest, and straightest boards. There was the resentful Sunday of a little later, when he sat glowering and gloomy through the tardy length of the day, with a sullen sense of injury in his heart, and no more real knowledge of the beneficent history of the New Testament than if he had been bred among idolaters. There was a legion of Sundays, all days of unserviceable bitterness and mortification, slowly passing before him.

Dickens, *Little Dorrit*

SACRIFICE   *see also* COURAGE, MARTYRDOM, SUFFERING
the call to

477. *(Fighting for the unification of Italy, Garibaldi for a time suffered defeat in Rome. On quitting the city [July 2, 1849], he challenged his followers thus:)*

"I am going out of Rome. Let those who wish to continue the war against the stranger come with me. I offer neither pay, nor quarters, nor provisions; I offer hunger, thirst, forced marches, battles, and death. Let him who loves his country in his heart, and not with his lips only, follow me."

G. M. Trevelyan, *Garibaldi's Defence of the Roman Republic*

a courageous

478. *(When the French scholar Salmasius was commissioned by Charles II to prepare an indictment against the English people for the beheading of Charles I, Milton, in spite of great personal afflictions, rose to the defense of the regicide government.)*

When I was publicly solicited to write a reply to the Defense of the royal cause, when I had to contend with the pressure of sickness, and when my medical attendants clearly announced that if I did engage in the work, [the sight of my remaining eye] would be irreparably lost, their premonitions caused no hesitancy and inspired no dismay. I would not have listened to the voice of Aesculapius himself in preference to the suggestions of the heavenly monitor within my breast. I resolved to make the short interval of sight, which was left me to enjoy, as beneficial as possible to the public interest.

John Milton, "Defensio Secunda pro Populo Anglicano"

SALVATION
in facing the storm   *see also* ESCAPISM

479. Mr. Gladstone once paid a visit to a Tweedside country, and in the afternoon went out for a walk and came to a gate which gave upon a glen. It was late in November, a snowstorm was threatening; and the sheep, as is their custom, were drawing out from the burnside to the barer hill where drifts could not lie. An old shepherd was leaning on the gate, and to him Mr. Gladstone spoke in his high manner. "Are not sheep the most foolish of all animals? Here is a storm pending, and instead of remaining in shelter they are courting the fury of the blast. If I were a sheep I should remain in the hollows." To which the shepherd replied, "Sir, if ye were a sheep ye'd have mair sense."

John Buchan, *Pilgrim's Way*

in facing that which we most dread

480.   For twelve years Robinson Crusoe lived a solitary existence on his unknown island off the coast of South America. Then one day he discovered, to his consternation, the print of a man's naked foot in the sands.

"I stood like one thunderstruck, I listened, I looked. I went up the shore, down the shore, but it was all one. Terrified to the last degree, looking behind me at every two or three steps I came to my habitation like one pursued, and for three days and nights thereafter I did not stir out."

Yet the footprints were to bring into his life his man Friday, the best friend he ever had.

How frequently, adds Defoe, the evil which we seek most to shun turns out to be the door of deliverance by which alone we can be raised again from the affliction that has overtaken us.

Defoe, *Robinson Crusoe* (adapted)

in this life, not in the hour and article of death   *see also*
CHRIST—salvation in

481.   If thou art not in heaven in this life, thou wilt never be in heaven in the life to come. At death, says the wise man, each thing returns into its own element, into the ground of its life; the light into the light, and the darkness into the darkness. As the tree falls, so it lies. My friends, you who call yourselves enlightened Christian folk, do you suppose that you can lead a mean, worldly, covetous, spiteful life here, and then, the moment your soul leaves the body, that you are to be changed into the very opposite character, into angels and saints. . . . A sinful, worldly man enjoy being in heaven? Does a fish enjoy being on dry land?

Charles Kingsley, *Village Sermons*

by works

482.   "As for being saved without works, there's a many, I dare-
say, can do without that doctrine; but I thank the Lord I never
needed to put *my*self on a level with the thief on the cross. I've
done *my* duty, and more, if it comes to that; for I've gone without
my bit of meat to make broth for a sick neighbor. And if there's
any of the church-members say they've done the same, I'd ask them
if they had the sinking at the stomach as I have."

George Eliot, *Felix Holt* (Mrs. Holt)

not of works

483.   *(No man was more beloved than old Dr. MacLure. He was
the Good Samaritan of the Glen. Never a snowdrift too deep or a
night too dark to keep him from answering a call, let it come from
rich or poor. His fees were whatever his patients could afford.
He kept no account books. And now as he lies a-dying his old
friend Drumsheugh is by his bedside.)*

"Ma mither aye wantit this read tae her when she was sick," says
Drumsheugh. And he begins to read, "In my Father's house are
many mansions . . ."

But the old doctor interrupts him, "It's a bonnie word, an' yir
mither was a saint; but it's no for the like o' me." And he has him
read the parable of the pharisee and the publican till they come to
the words, "God be merciful to me a sinner. . . ."

"That micht hae been written for me," said the dying man, "or
ony ither auld sinner that has feenished his life, an' has naething
tae say for himself."

Ian Maclaren, *Beside the Bonnie Briar Bush*

SCIENCE   *see also* KNOWLEDGE
consequences of undue devotion to

484.   "Up to the age of thirty, poetry gave me great pleasure; and
even as a schoolboy I took great delight in Shakespeare. Pictures
gave me considerable, and music very great, delight. But now I
cannot endure to read a line of poetry. I have lost all my taste for
pictures and music. My mind seems to have become a kind of machine for grinding laws out of a large collection of facts. If I had

to live my life again, I would make it a rule to read some poetry
and listen to some music at least once every week. The loss of
these tastes is a loss of happiness, and may possibly be injurious
to the intellect and more probably to the moral character by en-
feebling the emotional part of our nature."

Charles Darwin, *Life and Letters of*, ed. by Francis Darwin

taken as an absolute

485. *(The poet sees modern science, taken as an absolute, as an
enemy of the spirit, reducing everything to rational knowledge.)*
God is a proposition,
   And we that prove him are his priests, his chosen.
From that bare hypothesis
Of strata and wind, of stars and tides, watch me
Construct his universe,
A working model of my majestic notions,
A sum done in my head.
Last week I measured the light, his little finger;
The rest is a matter of time.

C. Day Lewis, *The Magnetic Mountain*, Pt. III

SECTARIANISM   *see also* PREJUDICE, SOCIAL CASTE

486. "When I mention religion I mean the Christian religion and
not only the Christian religion but the Protestant religion, and not
only the Protestant religion but the Church of England."

Henry Fielding, *Tom Jones* (Pastor Thwackum)

487.   We are God's chosen few,
All others will be damned;
There is no place in heaven for you,
We can't have heaven crammed!

Jonathan Swift

SELF
man's greatest enemy

488. *(Sidney Carton, the gifted lawyer who ended his life nobly
by taking the place of Charles Darnay at the guillotine, had wasted
the substance of his life in drink. Dickens relates Carton's returning*

home one morning at break of day, after a night of hard drinking:)

Waste forces within him, and a desert all around, this man stood still in his way across a silent terrace, and saw for a moment, lying in the wilderness before him, a mirage of honorable ambition, self-denial, and perseverance. In the fair city of this vision there were airy galleries from which the loves and graces looked upon him, gardens in which the fruits of life hung ripening, waters of Hope that sparkled in his sight. A moment, and it was gone. Climbing to a high chamber, in a well of houses, he threw himself down in his clothes on a neglected bed, and its pillow was wet with wasted tears.

Sadly, sadly, the sun rose; it rose upon no sadder sight than the man of good abilities and good emotions, incapable of their directed exercise, incapable of his own help and his own happiness, sensible of the blight on him, and resigning himself to let it eat him away.

Dickens, *A Tale of Two Cities*

489.   God strengthen me to bear myself;
            That heaviest weight of all to bear,
            Inalienable weight of care.

                    *   *   *

            God harden me against myself,
            This coward with pathetic voice
            Who craves for ease, and rest, and joys.

            Myself, arch-traitor to myself;
            My hollowest friend, my deadliest foe,
            My clog whatever road I go.

            Yet One there is can curb myself,
            Can roll the strangling load from me,
            Break off the yoke and set me free.
                    Christina Rossetti, "Who Shall Deliver Me?"

490.   Meanwhile, whether as a man, a husband, or a poet, his steps led downward. He knew, knew bitterly, that the best was out of him. The battle of his life was lost; in forlorn efforts to do well, in desperate submissions to evil the last years flew by. It is the fashion to say he died of drink; many a man has drunk more and yet lived

with reputation, and reached a good age. That drink and de-
bauchery helped to destroy his constitution, and were the means of
his unconscious suicide, is doubtless true; but he had failed in life
and had lost the power of work. . . . He had trifled with life, and
must pay the penalty. He had chosen to be Don Juan, he had
grasped at temporary pleasures; and substantial happiness and
solid industry had passed him by. He died of being Robert Burns.

R. L. Stevenson, *Familiar Studies of Men and Books*

SELF-CENTEREDNESS   *see also* HUMAN NATURE, SOCIAL
CONCERN, VISION

491.   *(On their way to the vicarage to fulfill a social obligation the
Knightleys encounter disagreeable weather. All the way there Mr.
Knightley expresses his discontent:)*

"A man," said he, "must have a very good opinion of himself
when he asks people to leave their own fireside and encounter such
a day as this for the sake of coming to see him. He must think himself a most agreeable fellow. I could do no such thing. It is the
greatest absurdity—actually snowing at this moment! The folly
of not allowing people to be comfortable at home—and the folly
of people's not staying comfortably at home when they can! If we
were obliged to go out on such an evening as this, by any call of
duty or business, what a hardship we should deem it; and here we
are, probably with rather thinner clothing than usual, setting forth
voluntarily, without excuse, in defiance of the voice of nature, which
tells man to stay at home himself, and keep all under shelter that
he can;—here we are setting forward to spend five dull hours in
another man's house, with nothing to say or to hear that was not
heard or said yesterday, and may not be said or heard again to-
morrow. Going in dismal weather, to return probably in worse;—
four horses and four servants taken out for nothing but to convey
five idle shivering creatures into colder rooms and worse company
than they might have at home."

Jane Austen, *Emma*

492.   One reason why we meet so few people who are reasonable
and agreeable in conversation is that there is scarcely anybody who
does not think more of what he has to say than of answering what

is said to him. Even those who have the most address and politeness
think they do enough if they only seem to be attentive; at the same
time their eyes and their minds betray a distraction as to what is
addressed to them, and an impatience to return to what they themselves were saying; not reflecting, that to be thus studious of pleasing themselves is but a poor way of pleasing or convincing others;
and that to hear patiently and answer precisely are the perfections
of conversation.

Lord Chesterfield, *Advice to His Son*

493.   Dombey and Son . . . Those three words conveyed the one
idea of Mr. Dombey's life. The earth was made for Dombey and
Son to trade in, and the sun and moon were made to give them
light. Rivers and seas were formed to float their ships; rainbows
gave them promise of fair weather; winds blew for or against their
enterprises; stars and planets circled in their orbits to preserve
inviolate a system of which they were the center . . . A.D. had no
concern with Anno Domini, but stood for Anno Dombey—and Son.

Dickens, *Dombey and Son*

494.   There is a disease called "touchiness"—a disease which, in
spite of its innocent name, is one of the gravest sources of restlessness in the world. Touchiness, when it becomes chronic, is a morbid
condition of an inward disposition. It is self-love inflamed to the
acute point.

Henry Drummond, *Pax Vobiscum*

495.   *(The noble Romola, toward the end of the novel bearing her
name, makes an incisive comment on the character of Tito, the man
she married:)*
"There was a man to whom I was very near, so that I could see
a great deal of his life; who made almost everyone fond of him for
he was young, clever, and beautiful, and his manners to all were
gentle and kind. I believe, when I first knew him, he never thought
of anything cruel or base. But because he tried to slip away from
everything that was unpleasant, and cared for nothing else so much
as his own safety, he came at last to commit some of the basest
deeds, such as make men infamous. He denied his father, and left
him to misery; he betrayed every trust that was reposed in him,

that he might keep himself safe and get rich and prosperous. Yet calamity overtook him."

George Eliot, Romola

496. *(Mr. Barrett refused to entertain the idea of the marriage of any of his children. He particularly resented Elizabeth's marriage to Robert Browning.)*

The reasons for his feeling, it is probable he could not have explained to himself. He was fond of his family after his own fashion —proud, too, of his daughter's genius; but he could not, it would seem, regard them in any other light than as belonging to himself. The wish to leave his roof and to enter into new relations was looked upon as unfilial treachery; and no argument or persuasion could shake him from his fixed idea. So long as this disposition could be regarded as the result of a devoted love of his children it could be accepted with respect, if not with full acquiescence; but circumstances brought the proof that this was not the case, and thereby ultimately paved the way to Elizabeth's marriage.

Sir Frederic G. Kenyon,
Letters of Elizabeth Barrett Browning

497. *(The doctor is congratulating himself and his wife that their marital bliss has not been marred by the presence of children:)*

"I think of it more and more as the years go on, and with more and more gratitude toward the Powers that dispense such afflictions. Your health, my darling, my studious quiet, our little kitchen delicacies, how they would all have been sacrificed! And for what? Children are the last word of human imperfection. Health flees before their face. They cry, my dear; they put vexatious questions; they demand to be fed, to be washed, to be educated; and then, when the time comes, they break our hearts, as I break this piece of sugar. A pair of professed egoists like you and me should avoid offspring like an infidelity."

R. L. Stevenson, The Treasure of Franchard

498.   I would buy me a perfect island home,
                Sweet set in a southern sea,
        And there would I build me a paradise
                For the heart of my Love and me.

> I would plant me a perfect garden there,
>   The one that my dream soul knows,
> And the years would flow as the petals grow
>   That flame to a perfect rose.
>
> I would build me a perfect temple there,
>   A shrine where my Christ might dwell,
> And then I would wake to behold my soul
>   Damned deep in a perfect Hell.
>   G. Studdert-Kennedy, "If I Had a Million Pounds"

SELF-EXAMINATION
the fear of

499.   The most frequent impediment to men's turning the mind
inward upon themselves is that they are afraid of what they shall
find there. There is an aching hollowness in the bosom, a dark cold
speck at the heart, an obscure and boding sense of something that
must be kept *out of sight* of the conscience; some secret lodger,
whom they can neither resolve to reject nor retain.

Coleridge, *Aids to Reflection*

man's need of

500.   Find out what you are. Do not think vaguely about it: take
pen and paper and write down as accurate a description of yourself as you can, with the date to it. If you dare not do so, find out
why you dare not, and try to get strength of heart enough to look
yourself fairly in the face, in mind as well as body. I do not doubt
but that the mind is a less pleasant thing to look at than the face,
and for that very reason it needs more looking at.

Ruskin, *Sesame and Lilies*

SELF-ILLUSION
the blessing of

501.   Thank heaven, then, that a little illusion is left to us, to
enable us to be useful and agreeable—that we don't know exactly
what our friends think of us—that the world is not made of looking-
glass, to show us just the figure we are making, and just what is

going on behind our backs! By the help of our dear friendly
illusion, we are able to dream that we are charming—and our faces
wear a becoming air of self-possession; we are able to dream that
other men admire our talents—and our benignity is undisturbed;
we are able to dream that we are doing much good—and we do a
little.

George Eliot, *Amos Barton*

SELF-RIGHTEOUSNESS
the blindness of

502.   *(Maggie Tulliver to her brother Tom:)*
"You have always enjoyed punishing me. You have always been
hard and cruel to me. Even when I was a little girl, and always
loved you better than anyone else in the world, you would let me
go crying to bed without forgiving me. You have no pity: you
have no sense of your own imperfection and your own sins. It is
a sin to be hard: it is not fitting for a mortal—for a Christian. You
are nothing but a Pharisee. You thank God for nothing but your
own virtues—you think they are great enough to win you everything
else. You have not even a vision of feelings by the side of which
your shining virtues are mere darkness."

George Eliot, *The Mill on the Floss*

SENTIMENT
a worthy

503.   Few sailors can behold the ship in which they have sailed
sinking before their eyes without the same emotion of distress and
pity almost which the spectacle of a drowning man excites in them.
She has grown a familiar name, a familiar object; thus far she has
borne them in safety; she has been rudely beaten, and yet has done
her duty. But the tempest has broken her down at last; all the
beauty is shorn from her; she is weary with the long and dreadful
struggle with the vast forces that Nature arrayed against her; she
sinks, a desolate, abandoned thing in mid-ocean, carrying with her
a thousand memories which surge up in the heart with the pain of
a strong man's tears.

William Clark Russell, *The Wreck of the Grosvenor*

SERVICE   *see also* GREATNESS—in obscurity, SOCIAL CON-
                                            CERN, WORK

encouragement for

504.   Think not the good,
        The gentle deeds of mercy thou hast done,
        Shall die forgotten all; the poor, the prisoner,
        The fatherless, the friendless, and the widow,
        Who daily owe the bounty of thy hand,
        Shall cry to Heaven, and pull a blessing on thee.
                            Nicholas Rowe, *Jane Shore*, Act I, Sc. 2

a life of social

505.   I have attained my ideal: I am a roadmender . . .

My road has been lonely to-day. A parson came by in the afternoon, a stranger in the neighbourhood, for he asked his way. He
talked awhile, and with kindly rebuke said it was sad to see a man
of my education brought so low, which shows how the outside
appearance may mislead the prejudiced observer. "Was it misfortune?" "Nay, the best of good luck," I answered, gaily.

The good man with beautiful readiness sat down on a heap of
stones and bade me say on. "Read me a sermon in stone," he said,
simply; and I stayed my hand to read.

He listened with courteous intelligence.

"You hold a roadmender has a vocation?" he asked.

"As the monk or the artist, for, like both, he is universal. The
world is his home; he serves all men alike, ay, and for him the
beasts have equal honour with the men. His soul is 'bound up in
the bundle of life' with all other souls, he sees his father, his mother,
his brethren in the children of the road. For him there is nothing
unclean, nothing common; the very stones cry out that they serve."

Parson nodded his head.

"It is all true," he said; "beautifully true. But need such a view
of life necessitate the work of roadmending? Surely all men should
be roadmenders."

O wise parson, so to read the lesson of the road!

"It is true," I answered; "but some of us find our salvation in the actual work, and earn our bread better in this than in any other way. No man is dependent on our earning, all men on our work. We are 'rich beyond the dreams of avarice' because we have all that we need, and yet we taste the life and poverty of the very poor. We are, if you will, uncloistered monks, preaching friars who speak not with the tongue, disciples who hear the wise words of a silent master."

"Robert Louis Stevenson was a roadmender," said the wise parson.

"Ay, and with more than his pen," I answered. "I wonder was he ever so truly great, so entirely the man we know and love, as when he inspired the chiefs to make a highway in the wilderness. Surely no more fitting monument could exist to his memory than the Road of Gratitude, cut, laid, and kept by the pure-blooded tribe kings of Samoa."

Parson nodded.

He knew that the people who make no roads are ruled out from intelligent participation in the world's brotherhood. . . .

He rose to go.

"I wish I could come and break stones," he said, a little wistfully.

"Nay," said I, "few men have such weary roadmending as yours, and perhaps you need my road less than most men, and less than most parsons."

We shook hands, and he went down the road and out of my life.

Michael Fairless, The Roadmender

506.   As the funeral cortege passed into Parliament Street a sight was seen which will never be forgotten while this generation lasts. Grouped on the east side of the street were deputations from the Homes, and Refugees, and Training Ships; from the Costermongers' Society, from Missions, and Charities, each with their craped banners emblazoned with such words as these: "Naked and ye clothed Me." "A stranger and ye took me in."

Rarely, if ever, had there been such a company assembled in Westminster Abbey as on that day. Royalty, the Church, both Houses of Parliament, diplomacy, municipal power, society, were represented; but the real significance of that enormous gathering,

filling every inch of space, lay in the spontaneous homage of thousands of men and women representing all that was powerful for
good in the land. The Abbey was full of mourners. Never before in
the memory of living men had there been brought together at one
time in one place so many workers for the common good. For no
other man in England could such an assemblage have been gathered
together.

Edwin Hodder,
Life and Work of the Seventh Earl of Shaftesbury

507.   *(Florence Nightingale, of a well-to-do family, was in her
twenties when she announced, to her mother's horror, her intention
of taking up nursing as a career. The difficulties in her path were
great, says her biographer.)*

For not only was it an almost unimaginable thing in those days
for a woman of means to make her own way in the world and to
live in independence, but the particular profession for which Florence was clearly marked out both by her instincts and her capacities
was at that time a peculiarly disreputable one. A "nurse" meant then
a coarse old woman, always ignorant, usually dirty, often brutal, a
Mrs. Gamp, in bunched-up sordid garments, tippling at the brandy-
bottle or indulging in worse irregularities. The nurses in the hospitals were especially notorious for immoral conduct; sobriety was
almost unknown among them; and they could hardly be trusted to
carry out the simplest medical duties.

With an amazing persistency she struggled and worked and
planned. While superficially she was carrying on the life of a brilliant girl in high society she yet possessed the energy to collect the
knowledge and to undergo the experience which alone would enable her to do what she had determined she would do in the end.
In secret she devoured the reports of medical commissions, the
pamphlets of sanitary authorities, the histories of hospitals and
homes. She spent the intervals of the London season in ragged
schools and workhouses. When she went abroad with her family,
she used her spare time so well that there was hardly a great
hospital in Europe with which she was not acquainted, hardly a
great city whose slums she had not passed through. . . .

But one other trial awaited her. The allurements of the world she had brushed aside with disdain and loathing; she had resisted the subtler temptation which, in her weariness, had sometimes come upon her, of devoting her baffled energies to art or literature; the last ordeal appeared in the shape of a desirable young man. . . . For a moment she wavered. . . . The most powerful and the profoundest of all the instincts of humanity laid claim upon her. . . . And she had the strength to stamp it underfoot.

G. Lytton Strachey, *Eminent Victorians*

in little things

508. How often do we sigh for opportunities of doing good, whilst we neglect the openings of Providence in little things, which would frequently lead to the accomplishment of most important usefulness! Dr. Johnson used to say, "He who waits to do a great deal of good at once will never do any." Good is done by degrees. However small in proportion the benefits which follow *individual attempts* to do good, a great deal may thus be accomplished by perseverance, even in the midst of discouragements and disappointments.

George Crabbe

509. There is a greatness in unknown names, there is an immortality of quiet duties, attainable by the meanest of human kind; and when the Judge shall reverse the tables many of these last shall be first. . . .

To fill a little space because God wills it; to go on cheerfully with a petty round of little duties, little avocations; to accept unmurmuringly a low position; to be misunderstood, misrepresented, maligned, without complaint; to smile for the joys of others when the heart is aching; to banish all ambition, all pride, and all restlessness, in a single regard to our Saviour's work;—he who does this is a greater hero than he who for one hour storms a breach, or for one day rushes onward undaunted in the flaming front of shot and shell. His works will follow him. He may be no hero to the world, but he is one of God's heroes.

F. W. Faber, *Treasure Thoughts of,* ed. by Rose Porter

in merely waiting

510. *(Milton was totally blind at forty-four.)*
When I consider how my light is spent,

E'er half my days, in this dark world and wide,
And that one talent which is death to hide,
Lodged with me useless, though my Soul more bent
To serve therewith my Maker, and present
My true account, lest he returning chide,
Doth God exact day-labor, light denied,
I fondly ask; but Patience, to prevent
That murmur, soon replies, God doth not need
Either man's work or his own gifts. Who best
Bear his mild yoke, they serve him best. His state
Is kingly: thousands at his bidding speed,
And post o'er land and ocean without rest;
They also serve who only stand and wait.

Milton, "On His Blindness"

SILENCE
not always a mark of wisdom

511.　Silence does not always mark wisdom. I was at dinner some
time ago, in company with a man who listened to me and said
nothing for a long time; but he nodded his head, and I thought
him intelligent. At length, towards the end of the dinner
some apple dumplings were placed on the table, and my man
had no sooner seen them than he burst forth with—"Them's the
jockies for me!" I wish Spurzheim could have examined the fellow's head.

Coleridge, Table Talk

SIMPLICITY
in religion

512.　One came to me, by whom I used to profit much. But her
conversation was now too high for me: it was far above, out of my
sight. My soul is sick of this sublime divinity. Let me think and
speak as a little child! Let my religion be plain, artless, simple!
Meekness, temperance, patience, faith, and love, be these my highest
gifts; and let the highest words wherein I teach them be those I
learn from the Book of God!

John Wesley, Journal (Jan. 30, 1740)

SIN   *see also* CONVICTION, JUDGMENT, MORAL LAW, REMORSE,
                                      REPENTANCE, RETRIBUTION

the blindness of

513.   While I was thus afflicted with the fears of my own damna-
tion, there were two things would make me wonder. One was,
when I saw old people hunting after the things of this life, as if
they should live here always; the other was, when I found professors
much distressed and cast down when they met with outward losses.
Lord, thought I, what ado is here about such little things as these!

Bunyan, *Grace Abounding*

breaks a father's heart

514.   *(The story of "Michael" has some basis in fact. According to
the* Journal *of Dorothy Wordsworth most of the poem was written
in the unfinished sheepfold here mentioned.)*

Michael, an old shepherd of superior skill, and his wife Isabel,
twenty years younger, lived among the mountains of the English
Lake District with Luke their only child, born when the father was
sixty-six. Between father and son was a strong bond of affection.
Together they worked outdoors by day, and by the light of the fire
by night. The two were inseparable.

When Luke was in his teens, Michael found himself in straitened
circumstances. A nephew, for whom he had stood bond, failed in
a business venture, and the old man became liable to the extent
of half his property. To save his own land, it was decided that
Luke should find work in a distant city, in care of a prosperous
kinsman. Another local lad had grown rich by seeking his fortune
abroad. The day before Luke left home, Michael took him to a
heap of stones near the brook of Greenhead Ghyll, where he had
planned they should together build a sheepfold. He had the lad
lay the cornerstone. If the time ever came when Luke fell among
evil companions he was to remember this moment.

In the city Luke did well, and Michael worked on the sheepfold.
But the day came when the lad, finding himself in serious trouble,
fled impulsively beyond the seas. The blow to Michael was a hard
one. Luke was never heard of again. Wordsworth, in the poem, tells

of his having spoken with several who remembered Michael well;
and he adds:

                    'Tis not forgotten yet
        The pity which was then in every heart
        For the old man—and 'tis believed by all
        That many and many a day he thither went,
        And never lifted up a single stone.

                    *   *   *

        There by the sheepfold sometimes was he seen
        Sitting alone, or with his faithful dog,
        Then old, beside him, lying at his feet.
        The length of full seven years, from time to time,
        He at the building of this sheepfold wrought,
        And left the work unfinished when he died.
                            Wordsworth, "Michael" (adapted)

the contagion of

515. There is no sort of wrong deed of which a man can bear the
punishment alone; you can't isolate yourself, and say that the evil
which is in you shall not spread. Men's lives are as thoroughly
blended with each other as the air they breathe; evil spreads as
disease.

                            George Eliot, *Adam Bede*

516. *(Lancelot, "our mightiest," failed in his search for the Holy
Grail—the Cup, legend has it, which our Lord used at the Last
Supper. Only the pure in heart might discover it. Lancelot con-
fesses the reason for his failure:)*

                    "In me lived a sin
        So strange, of such a kind, that all of pure,
        Noble and knightly in me twined and clung
        Round that one sin, until the wholesome flower
        And poisonous grew together, each as each,
        Not to be plucked asunder."

                            Tennyson, "The Holy Grail"

defined   *see also* SELF-CENTEREDNESS

517. There is only one sin, and it is characteristic of the whole
world. It is the self-will which prefers "my" way to God's—which

puts me in the center where only God is in place. It pervades the universe. It accounts for the cruelty of the jungle, where each animal follows its own appetite, unheeding and unable to heed any general good. It becomes conscious, and thereby, tenfold more virulent in man. And no individual is "responsible" for it; but it sets us at enmity against God: it is the sin of the world.

William Temple, *Readings in John's Gospel*, Vol. I

deliverance from

518.   Now I saw in my dream that the highway up which Christian was to go was fenced on either side with a wall, and that wall was called Salvation. Up this way, therefore, did burdened Christian run, but not without great difficulty, because of the load on his back. He ran thus till he came to a place somewhat ascending; and upon that place stood a Cross, and a little below, in the bottom, a sepulcher. So I saw in my dream that just as Christian came up to the Cross, his burden loosed from off his shoulders and fell from his back and began to tumble, and so continued till it came to the mouth of the sepulcher, where it fell in, and I saw it no more.

Bunyan, *Pilgrim's Progress*

finds you out

519.   The rewards and penalties of heaven are inward, and move within the region of the soul. If Macbeth, winning his heart's desire, were left with a tranquil and expanded heart; if in outward triumph of his hopes he had the inward triumph of his spirit; then it would be reasonable to hold that heaven was indifferent and regardless.

But the horror of the tragedy is this, that in accomplishing the evil he was set on, all that makes life beautiful departs from him, and he moves down into the darkness of the night.

Be sure your sin will find you out, says the Scripture. It does not say your sin will be found out. It says that sooner or later it will find you out, in the deep and secret places of the soul. And the awfullest horror in "Macbeth" is not the murder of the helpless Duncan; it is the way in which Macbeth's sin found him out.

His soul sank and shrivelled; all that was sensitive in him turned

to stone; he became the prey of agonizing fears; he could not sleep
—"Macbeth hath murdered sleep."

G. H. Morrison, Christ in Shakespeare

the implacability of

520.   "What though the field be lost?
        All is not lost—the unconquerable will,
        And study of revenge, immortal hate,
        And courage never to submit or yield;

                        *   *   *

                    To bow and sue for grace
        With suppliant knee . . .
                    —that were low indeed;
        That were an ignominy and shame beneath
        This downfall."

                        *   *   *

        So spake the apostate Angel, though in pain,
        Vaunting aloud, but racked with deep despair.

Milton, Paradise Lost, Bk. I (Satan)

no justification for

521.   (*Godfrey Cass, under deep conviction, confesses to his wife
that six years before he married her he had fathered a child by
another, now dead. For a time Nancy is silent. When she does speak,
her concern is for the child, long neglected.*)

"But you wouldn't have married me then, Nancy, if I'd told you,"
said Godfrey, urged in the bitterness of self-respect to prove to himself that his conduct had not been utter folly.

"I can't say what I would have done about that, Godfrey. I
should never have married anybody else. But I wasn't worth doing
wrong for—nothing is, in the world."

George Eliot, Silas Marner

national

522.   Arnold saw the England of his day overpowered by such
unintelligent forces as prejudice, insularity, stupid individualism,
blind worship of liberty, faith in machinery whether governmental,
economic, or religious. Society he divides into three classes: the

Barbarians—the aristocracy, who have a superficial sweetness and light and who are primarily concerned with maintaining and enjoying their class privileges; the Philistines—the middle classes, whose chief interests in life are money-making and religion of a most provincial kind; and the Populace—the lowest part of the people, uninhibited in their prejudices and coarse in their pleasures. The chief end of all these classes, he says, is doing as one likes.

Matthew Arnold,
Culture and Anarchy, "Sweetness and Light"

need of urgency in dealing with

523.   You cannot run away from a weakness; you must some time fight it out or perish; and if that be so, why not now, and where you stand?

R. L. Stevenson, *The Amateur Immigrant*

in professed Christians

524.   This I well remember, that though I could myself sin with the greatest delight and ease, and also take pleasure in the vileness of my companions, yet even then if I saw at any time wicked things in those who professed goodness, it would make my spirit tremble. As once, when I was in the height of my vanity and heard one sware who was reckoned for a religious man, it had so great a stroke upon my spirit that it made my heart ache.

Bunyan, *Grace Abounding*

separates from God

525.   "God can't bless you while you have one falsehood in your soul; His pardoning mercy can't reach you until you open your heart to Him, and say, 'I have done this great wickedness; O God, save me, make me pure from sin.' While you cling to one sin and will not part with it, it must drag you down to misery after death. It is sin that brings dread and darkness and despair. There is light and blessedness for us as soon as we cast it off; God enters our souls then, and teaches us, and brings us strength and peace."

George Eliot, *Adam Bede*
(Dinah Morris, the Methodist preacher)

the sting of the memory of

526.   *(After his unhappy marriage, which ended within twelve months in a legal separation, Lord Byron left England in disgrace. He was never to return. It was during a tour in Switzerland that he wrote to a friend:)*

In the weather for this tour I have been fortunate—fortunate in a companion, fortunate in our prospects. I was disposed to be pleased. I am a lover of nature and an admirer of beauty. I can bear fatigue and welcome privation, and have seen some of the noblest views in the world. But in all this the recollection of bitterness, and more especially of recent and more home desolation which must accompany me through life, has preyed upon me here; and neither the music of the shepherd, the crashing of the avalanche, nor the torrent, the mountain, the glacier, the forest, nor the cloud, have for one moment lightened the weight upon my heart, nor enabled me to lose my own wretched identity in the majesty, and the power, and the glory, around, above, and beneath me.

Quoted in Lord Brougham,
Recollections of a Long Life, Vol. II

SOCIAL CASTE   *see also* SECTARIANISM
in America

527.   Of all the hokum with which this country [America] is filled the most odd is the common notion that it is free of class distinctions. I was asked one day out West to lunch with a woman who, I was told, had twenty millions. I have never seen a duke in Europe treated with such deference as she was. You might have thought that every word that fell from her opulent lips was a hundred dollar bill that the guests would be allowed to take away with them. It is true that there is a pretence that one man is as good as another but it is only a pretence. . . . I know of a mushroom city in the Far West which was built only a few years ago to house the employees of a great factory. White-collar workers and factory hands live in adjoining blocks in houses built on the same pattern and as like as peas; they eat the same canned goods, read the same papers, go to the same movies, drive the same automobiles; but the wives of the white-collar workers will not play bridge with the wives of the factory hands. It looks as though the existence of class distinctions is inseparable from life in the social state, and instead of denying its existence, it would be more honest to admit it.

W. Somerset Maugham, *A Writer's Notebook*

SOCIAL CONCERN   *see also* LOVE, SELF-CENTEREDNESS,
SERVICE
absence of

528.   In looking back, it sometimes appears to me as if I had in a manner slept out my life in a dream or shadow on the side of the hill of knowledge, where I have fed on books, on thoughts, on pictures, and only heard in half-murmurs the trampling of busy feet, or the noises of the throng below.

Hazlitt, *Table Talk,* "On the Fear of Death"

for the blind

529.   I seem to remember a poor old grateful kind of a creature, blinking, and looking up with his no-eyes in the sun. Is it possible I could have steeled my purse against him? Perhaps I had no small change. Reader, do not be frightened at the hard words, "imposition, imposture." Give, and ask no questions.

Charles Lamb, *Essays of Elia,* "On the Decay of Beggars"

the challenge to

530.   Is not our want the occasion of our brother's charity, and thus does not good come out of that evil? When the traveler (of whom the Master spoke) fell among thieves, his mishap was contrived to try many a heart besides his own—the knave's who robbed him, the Levite's and Priest's who passed him as he lay bleeding, the humble Samaritan's whose hand poured out oil into his wound and held out its pittance to relieve him.

Thackeray, *Philip*

for the fallen

531.   Into one pitiful field of work, the work of tenderness and compassion for the fallen, rescue and prevention work among women, Mr. and Mrs. Gladstone had thrown the full fervor of their hearts. . . . In the streets of London they worked with tireless

energy; she shrank from nothing. When walking home one night with a friend, Mr. Gladstone turned back to rescue a poor lost creature. "But what will Mrs. Gladstone say if you take this woman home?" Mr. Gladstone turned round in surprise, "Why, it is to Mrs. Gladstone I am taking her."

Mary Drew, Mrs. Gladstone

for genius unrewarded

532.   It is true that men of extraordinary abilities have spent the most useful and laborious lives without earning the barest competence, that many of the most splendid works of genius and many of the most fruitful and conscientious researches are due to men whose lives were spent between the garret and the spunging house, and who were reduced to penury sometimes verging upon starvation. Neither Bacon, Newton, Locke, Descartes, Gibbon, Coleridge, Milton, or Wordsworth, could have made a livelihood of their works; and the same may be said of the greatest majority of the writers in other fields. Very few of these men whose genius has irradiated nations, and whose writings have become the eternal heritage of mankind, obtained from their works the income of a successful village doctor or provincial attorney.

Lecky, History of England in the Eighteenth Century

for ill-usage of children

533.   (In nineteenth century England the gross ill-usage of little boys as chimneysweeps, by employers who found it cheaper to drop them down soot-choked chimneys than to use a long brush, had at different times been exposed to public indignation, but redress was slow. Notations like the following are frequent in the diary of the Earl of Shaftesbury, English statesman and philanthropist of the period.)

Great anxiety about bill for relief of Chimney Sweepers. Have suffered actual tortures through solicitude for prevention of these horrid cruelties. . . .

The Government in the House of Commons threw out the Chimney Sweepers Bill, and said not a word for the wretched children, nor of desire to amend the law.

Very sad and low about the loss of the Sweeps Bill. . . . I must persevere, and by God's help so I will; for however dark the view, however contrary to all argument the attempt, however painful and revolting the labor, I see no Scripture reason for desisting; and the issue of every toil is in the hands of the Almighty.

Edwin Hodder,
Life and Work of the Seventh Earl of Shaftesbury

for man's inhumanity to man

534.   Blow, blow, ye winds, with heavier gust!
    And freeze, thou bitter-biting frost!
    Descend, ye chilly, smothering snows!
    Not all your rage, as now united, shows
      More hard unkindness, unrelenting,
      Vengeful malice unrepenting,
    Than heaven-illumined man on brother man bestows.

Burns, "A Winter's Night"

for oppressed races

535.   *(Even as Jeremiah, groaning under the burden of the sins of Judah, was tempted to run away from it all [Jer. 9:2], so Cowper, depressed by his country's participation in the African slave trade, would also seek refuge in flight:)*

    Oh for a lodge in some vast wilderness,
    Some boundless contiguity of shade . . .

❋   ❋   ❋

                My ear is pained,
    My soul is sick with every day's report
    Of wrong and outrage with which earth is filled.
    There is no flesh in man's obdurate heart,
    It does not feel for man; the natural bond
    Of brotherhood is severed as the flax
    That falls asunder at the touch of fire.
    He finds his fellow guilty of a skin
    Not colored like his own, and having power
    To enforce the wrong . . .
    Dooms and devotes him as his lawful prey.

❋   ❋   ❋

And worse than all, and most to be deplored,
As human nature's broadest, foulest blot,
Canes him, and tasks him, and exacts his sweat
With stripes that Mercy, with a bleeding heart,
Weeps when she sees inflicted on a beast.

*   *   *

I would not have a slave to till my ground,
To carry me, to fan me while I sleep,
And tremble when I wake, for all the wealth
That sinews bought and sold have ever earned.
No: dear as freedom is . . .
I had much rather be myself the slave
And wear the bonds, than fasten them on him.

Cowper, The Task, Bk. II

for the poor

536.   At this season (New Year) we usually distribute coal and
bread among the poor of the Society. But I now considered, they
wanted clothes as well as food. So on this day and the four following days I walked through the town, and begged two hundred
pounds, in order to clothe them that needed it most. But it was
hard work as most of the streets were filled with melting snow,
which often lay ankle-deep; so that my feet were steeped in snow
water nearly from morning till evening. I held out pretty well till
Saturday evening; but I was laid up with a violent flux, which
increased every hour till, at six in the morning, Dr. Whitehead
called upon me.

John Wesley (at age eighty-two), Journal (Jan. 4, 1785)

for the salvation of others

537.   *(The poet is speaking of his father, the famous Dr. Thomas
Arnold, headmaster of Rugby:)*

But thou wouldst not *alone*
Be saved, my father, *alone*
Conquer and come to thy goal,
Leaving the rest in the wild.
We were weary, and we
Fearful, and we in our march

Fain to drop down and to die.
Still thou turnedst, and still
Gavest the weary thy hand.

Matthew Arnold, "Rugby Chapel"

for the underprivileged

538.   The ideal of service to man was the rule of Stevenson's life.
In all places he seems to have been impelled into some local
tussle or other, and impelled to champion the cause of the weak and
wronged. In the Samoan troubles he spent his last years in the
defense of the natives against the unsympathetic and blundering
governments of Europe. He wrote incessantly on their behalf—
letters, articles, and a book which cost him infinite labor. He fought
for them in meetings, to which he went through storm and rain
while sick with colic or in the intervals of hemorrhage. He did
this at the risk of trial, prison, and banishment. It is no wonder
that the natives loved him, and built "the road of gratitude" to
his house. For a man of his temperament and in his health to do
so much from pure love of helpless and half-savage fellow-men
is surely a very honorable record on the roll of heroic self-sacrifice
and service.

John Kelman, The Faith of Robert Louis Stevenson

for the weak

539.   "Alas!" cried poor Mr. Feeble-mind, "I want a suitable companion; you are all so lusty and strong; but I, as you see, am weak.
I choose, therefore, rather to come behind, lest by reason of my
many infirmities I should be both a burden to myself and to you.
I am a very ignorant Christian man. It is with me as it is with
a weak man among the strong, or as a sick man among the healthy.
"But, brother," said Mr. Greatheart, "I have it in my commission
to support the weak. You must needs go along with us; we will wait
for you, and we will lend you our help; we will deny ourselves of
some things, both opinionated and practical, for your sake; we will
be made all things to you, rather than that you shall be left behind."

Bunyan, Pilgrim's Progress

540.   " 'They that are strong ought to bear the infirmities of the
weak,' and not to please themselves. There's a text wants no

candle to show't; it shines by its own light. It's plain enough you get into the wrong road i' this life if you run after this and that only for the sake of making things easy and please yourself. A pig may poke his nose into the trough and think o' nothing outside it; but if you've got a man's heart and soul in you, you can't be easy a-making your own bed an' leaving the rest to lie on the stones. Nay, nay, I'll never slip my neck out o' the yoke, and leave the yoke to be drawn by the weak uns."

George Eliot, Adam Bede (Adam)

for the worker

541. *(The allusion is to the Spittalfield weavers in England, at the time of the Industrial Revolution.)*

Wages fell so low that in order to keep body and soul together the laborers, both in town and country, *and their children* had to work from thirteen to fifteen hours a day. Having no leisure, they naturally lost the art of making a profitable use of leisure. Then, to make matters worse, came a wave of puritanical Evangelicalism which swept over the country and carried with it the notion (much favored by the employers of labor) that all recreation, at any rate on the part of the working classes, was "carnal," and that the harder the poor worked and the less they enjoyed life, the more likely they were to be "saved." At last things came to such a pass that the public-house became the only place of recreation, and drinking the only distraction from the monotony of never-ending, ill-paid toil.

Edmond G. A. Holmes,
Freedom and Growth and Other Essays

542. *(Addressed to the masters of industry in Victorian England:)*

Your ideal of human life is that it should be passed in a pleasant undulating world, with iron and coal everywhere underneath it. On each pleasant bank of this world is to be a beautiful mansion, with two wings and stables and coach-houses. In this mansion are to live the favored votaries of the Goddess [of Getting-On]: the English gentleman, with his precious wife, and his beautiful family. At the bottom of the bank is to be the mill; not less than a quarter of a mile long with a steam engine at each end, and two in the middle, and a chimney three hundred feet high. In this mill are to be in constant employment from eight hundred to a thousand workers, who never drink, never strike, always go to church on Sunday, and always express themselves in respectable language.

Ruskin, *The Crown of Wild Olive,* "Traffic"

SOCIAL GATHERINGS

543. "I'd sooner ha' brewin' day an' washin' day together than one o' these pleasurin' days. There's no work so tirin' as danglin' about an' starin' an' not rightly knowin' what you're goin' to do next; and keepin' your face i' smilin' order like a grocer o' market-day for fear people shouldna think you civil enough. An' you've nothin' to show for't when it's done, if it isn't a yallow face wi' eatin' things that disagree."

George Eliot, *Adam Bede* (Mrs. Poyser)

SOCIAL INTERDEPENDENCE

544. Culture, like a mountain, should be broad-based if it is to rise to a lofty height. . . . The great mountain, as Ruskin has well said, lifts the lowlands to its sides. It is only by lifting the lowlands, by using them as the lower courses of its own structure, that it has been able to rise so high above them. The Eiffel Tower spurned the lowlands. It tried to take a short cut to heaven. But because it had made no attempt to identify itself with the lowlands, or to incorporate them in its own structure, it failed ignominiously and had to be cut off, lest it topple over when it had reached the level of one of the humblest of Nature's hills.

Edmond G. A. Holmes,
Freedom and Growth and Other Essays

SOCIAL JUSTICE *see also* INTOLERANCE, PREJUDICE, SOCIAL CASTE

a plea for

545. I am a Jew. Hath not a Jew eyes? hath not a Jew hands, organs, dimensions, senses, affections, passions? fed with the same food, hurt with the same weapons, subject to the same diseases, healed by the same means, warmed and cooled by the same winter

and summer, as a Christian is? If you prick us, do we not bleed? if
you tickle us, do we not laugh? if you poison us, do we not die?

Shakespeare, *The Merchant of Venice,*
Act III, Sc. 1 (Shylock)

SOLITUDE   *see also* REST
the ministry of

546. Rest is the condition of all true moral and spiritual recep-
tiveness. Half our failure to respond to spiritual realities is due
to our fussy obsession in merely external things, our incapacity
for rest. . . .

Great souls have found their inspiration in quietness. Religion
has been cradled in solitude. Its leaders in all ages have known
the worth of rest. They have sought it far from the crowded city
and the noise of the marketplace. The Founder of Christianity
confessed its necessity for Himself and for that communion with
the Divine Father which was the very breath of His life. He sought
it in the mountain heights, in the quiet hours of the night, or in
the house of God. He taught His disciples its infinite worth, and
that they learned their lesson is proved by the history of Christianity. In quietness the revelation came to them, and in the light it
gave they returned to their fellow-men with a message from God.

from *Selected Essays from The Times* (London)

547.   [*Expostulation:*]
              "Why, William, on that old gray stone,
              Thus, for the length of half a day,
              Why, William, sit you thus alone,
              And dream your time away?"

                          *   *   *

              [*Reply:*]
              "The eye—it cannot choose but see;
              We cannot bid the ear be still;
              Our bodies feel, where'er they be,
              Against or with our will.

              "Nor less I deem that there are Powers
              Which of themselves our minds impress;

That we can feed this mind of ours
In a wise passiveness.

"Think you, 'mid all this mighty sum
Of things for ever speaking,
That nothing of itself will come,
But we must still be seeking?"

Wordsworth, "Expostulation and Reply"

SORROW   *see also* SUFFERING
comfort in

548.   When some beloved voice that was to you
Both sound and sweetness, faileth suddenly,
And silence, against which you dare not cry,
Aches round you like a strong disease and new—
What hope? What help? What music will undo
That silence to your sense? Not friendship's sigh,
Not reason's subtle count . . .
Not songs of poets, nor of nightingales . . .

Nay, none of these,

Speak *Thou*, availing Christ!—and fill this pause.

Elizabeth Barrett Browning, "Substitution"

549.   *(When Coleridge learned that Mary Lamb in a fit of insanity
had slain her own mother, he wrote words of consolation to Charles
Lamb—the only letter of his to Lamb which has been preserved:)*
"I am not a man who would attempt to insult the greatness of
your anguish by any other consolation [than religious]. In storms
like these, that shake the dwelling and make the heart tremble,
there is no middle way between despair and yielding up of the
whole spirit to the guidance of faith. And surely it is a matter
of joy that your faith in Jesus has been preserved; the Comforter
that should relieve you is not far from you. But as you are a
Christian, in the name of the Saviour I conjure you to have re-
course in frequent prayer to 'his God and your God,' the God of
mercies and the Father of all comfort."

Quoted in Anne Gilchrist, *Mary Lamb*

impotence of words in time of

550.   I sometimes hold it half a sin
            To put in words the grief I feel;
            For words, like Nature, half reveal
        And half conceal the Soul within.

                *   *   *

        In words, like weeds, I'll wrap me o'er,
            Like coarsest clothes against the cold;
            But that large grief which these enfold
        Is given in outline and no more.
                          Tennyson, "In Memoriam"

life must be lived in spite of

551.   *(Mrs. Browning wrote these lines after the tragic death by drowning of her brother Edward, July 11, 1840. The sorrow almost took her life.)*
        The face which duly to the sun
        Rose up for me when life begun,
        To mark all bright hours of the day
        With hourly love, is dimmed away,—
        And yet my days go on, go on.

        The tongue which like a stream could run
        Smooth music from the roughest stone
        And every morning with "Good day"
        Make each day good, is hushed away,—
        And yet my days go on, go on.

        The heart which like a staff was one
        For mine to lean and rest upon;
        The strongest on the longest day
        With steadfast love is caught away,—
        And yet my days go on, go on.
             Elizabeth Barrett Browning, "De Profundis"

the loneliness of

552.   *(The Brontë family suffered much from ill-health. Within one short year the parsonage at Haworth witnessed the passing of*

*Branwell, Emily, and Anne, leaving Charlotte alone with her invalid
father. It was shortly after Anne's lingering death that Charlotte
wrote these words to an intimate friend:)*

"Sometimes when I awake in the morning and know that Solitude, Remembrance, and Longing are to be almost my sole companions all day through—that at night I shall go to bed with them,
that they will long keep me sleepless—sometimes I have a heavy
heart of it. But crushed I am not. I am aware I have many comforts,
many mercies. But I do hope and pray that never may you, or any
one I love, be placed as I am. To sit in a lonely room—the clock
ticking loud through a still house—and have open before the mind's
eye the record of the last year, with its shocks, sufferings, losses—
is a trial."

Mrs. Elizabeth Gaskell, *Life of Charlotte Brontë*

the ministry of

553. (*Margaret Ogilvie is one of the finest tributes ever paid to a
mother by her son. The first chapter is entitled, "How My Mother
Got Her Soft Face.")*

She had a son who was far away at school, a merry-faced boy
who ran like a squirrel up a tree and shook the cherries into my lap.
When he was thirteen and I was half his age the terrible news came.
The face of my mother was awful in its calmness as she set off to
get between death and her boy. We trooped with her down the brae
to the wooden station, and I think I was envying her the journey
in the mysterious wagons. Her ticket was taken; she had bidden us
good-bye with that fighting face, and then my father came out of
the telegraph office and said huskily, "He's gone!" Then we turned
very quietly and went home again up the little brae. The first thing
she expressed a wish to see was the christening robe, and she looked
long at it and then turned her face to the wall.

That is how she got her soft face and her pathetic ways and her
large charity, and why other mothers ran to her when they had lost
a child. "Dinna greet, poor Janet," she would say to them; and they
would answer, "Ah, Margaret, but you're greetin' yourself'."

Sir J. M. Barrie, *Margaret Ogilvie*

554.   "There is no God," the foolish saith,
                  But none, "There is no sorrow,"

And nature oft the cry of faith
    In bitter need will borrow.
Eyes which the preacher could not school,
    By wayside graves are raiséd;
And lips say, "God be pitiful,"
    Which ne'er said, "God be praiséd."

Elizabeth Barrett Browning,
"The Cry of the Human"

555.   I walked a mile with Pleasure;
                        She chatted all the way;
                    But left me none the wiser
                        For all she had to say.

                    I walked a mile with Sorrow,
                        And ne'er a word said she;
                    But, oh! the things I learnt from her,
                        When Sorrow walked with me.

Robert Browning Hamilton,
"Along the Road"

556.   *(Martha Lang was known in Levenford as a just and right-eous woman, but a woman to be feared. "Black Martha" some called her because of her sober dress. Left a widow when Geordie was just three she reared the boy with a rod of iron. He seemed to reach his teens with hardly a mind of his own on anything. When the winter of 1895 brought a deep freeze, Geordie was invited to represent the town in the annual skating race round the island of Ardmurren. It was a historic event, and the lad felt keenly the honor thrust upon him. All his pleading with his mother, however, met only with stern refusal. When the day of the race arrived, Geordie evidently had taken things into his own hands, for he took his place on the ice alongside the other competitors. All went well till near the end of the race. The local provost [mayor] continues the tale:)*

"At the half-mile from home, when Geordie was away in front o' the others, suddenly and without warnin' there came a crack that would have made your heart stand still, a fearsome sound that was like the crack o' doom, that cut the cheering like it had been severed.

. . . The ice broke, and Geordie Lang went through it like a stane. . . ."

(The provost and the minister braced themselves to break the news to Martha.)

"Martha was there right enough; standing behind her counter, waiting for the son that had disobeyed her. Ye could see from the look in her eye that she was ready to chastise him—not with whips but with scorpions. . . .

" 'It's no use, minister,' she cries out, 'there's no use your comin' to ask me to let him off. He maun dree his ain weird' [suffer his own fate].

"A kind of shiver went through me as I heard her.

" 'Martha, Martha woman,' says the minister in a quiet voice, 'ye must forgive your son.'. . .

"A twisted look drew ower Martha's face, and she flung out, 'Not till I've punished him for what he's done.'

" 'Punish him you will not,' says the minister in a sorrowful face. 'That's all by with now.' "

Then he told her what had happened.

(Late that same night the provost and some friends, passing by Martha's dwelling, glanced apprehensively in at the kitchen window.)

"The room was full of shadows, but by the thin light of the candle we saw Martha Lang walking up and doun like a woman demented. She had a shrunken shilpit look about her, and her hair had turned to the color of the driven snow. She was wringing her hands, like she was wrastlin' with something, and all the time moaning out Geordie's name. . . .

" 'Geordie! Geordie!' she went on crying out loud. Then all of a sudden she flung herself down on her knees by the low couch. She put one arm around her dead son's neck, and with the other hand she started fondling his cauld still face and smoothing back his plastered hair.

" 'Geordie! Geordie!' she cries out in a desperate voice, 'I never kenned I love ye till the noo, but I did, my son, I did.' On and on she went.

"Not one of us moved hand or foot. Rooted to the ground we stood in fear and sorrow. Through the drip, drip of the rain came

that strange and moving sound, which I will never to my dying
day forget. Ay, 'twas the fearsome sound of Martha's sobbing."
A. J. Cronin, "The Provost's Tale"

557.   Count each affliction, whether light or grave,
                God's messenger sent down to thee; do thou
                With courtesy receive him; rise and bow;
            And, ere his shadow pass thy threshold, crave
            Permission first his heavenly feet to lave;
                Then lay before him all thou hast; allow
                No cloud of passion to usurp thy brow,
            Or mar thy hospitality; no wave
            Of moral tumult to obliterate
                Thy soul's marmoreal calmness. Grief
                    should be
            Like joy, majestic, equable, sedate;
                Confirming, cleansing, raising, making free;
            Strong to consume small troubles; to
                commend
            Great thoughts, grave thoughts, thoughts
                lasting to the end.
Aubrey Thomas de Vere, "Sorrow"

558.   Adam Bede had not outlived his sorrow—had not felt it slip
from him as a temporary burden, and leave him the same man
again. Do any of us? God forbid. It would be a poor result of all
our anguish and wrestling, if we won nothing but our old selves
at the end of it—if we could return to the same blind loves, the
same light thoughts of human suffering, the same frivolous gossip
over blighted human lives, the same feeble sense of the Unknown
towards which we have sent forth irrepressible cries in our loneliness. Let us rather be thankful that sorrow lives in us as an inde-
structible force, only changing its form, as forces do, and passing
from pain into sympathy—the one poor word which includes all
our best insight and our best love.
George Eliot, *Adam Bede*

559.   The night before the end, George was carried out to his
corner in the garden, and Domsie [the local schoolmaster], whose

heart was nigh to breaking, sat with him. After a while George took a book from below his pillow, and began, like one thinking over his words:

"Maister Jamieson, will ye tak' this book for a keepsake from your grateful scholar? It's a Latin *Imitation,* and it's a bonnie printin'. Will ye read it, Dominie, for my sake, and maybe ye'll come tae see—" And George could not find words more.

But Domsie understood. "Ma laddie, ma laddie, that I love better than onythin' on earth! I'll read it till I die; and George, I'll tell ye what livin' man doesna ken. When I was your verra age I had a cruel trial, and ma heart was turned frae faith. The classics hae been my Bible, though I said naething tae ony man against Christ. He aye seemed beyond man, and noo the vision o' Him has come tae me in this garden. Laddie, ye hae done far mair for me than I ever did for you. Wull ye mak' a prayer for yir auld dominie afore we pairt?" There was a thrush singing in the birches and a sound of bees in the air when George prayed in a low, soft voice, with a little break in it:

"Lord Jesus, remember my dear maister, for he's been a kind freend tae me and mony another poor laddie in Drumtochty. Bind up his sair heart and give him licht at eventide, and may the maister and his scholars meet some mornin' where the school never skails [dismisses], in the kingdom o' oor Father."

When he passed out at the garden gate, the westering sun was shining golden, and the face of Domsie was like unto that of a little child.

Ian Maclaren, Beside the Bonnie Briar Bush

560. *(The Corn Laws, by keeping up the price of grain in England, so increased the cost of living that the poor found it hard to get enough to eat. It was during this time that John Bright suffered the greatest sorrow of his life.)*

"I was in the depths of grief. I might almost say of despair, for the light and sunshine of my house had been extinguished. All that was left on earth of my young wife, except the memory of a sainted life and a too brief happiness, was lying still and cold in the chamber above us. Mr. Cobden called upon me as his friend, and addressed me, as you might suppose, with words of condolence. After a time he looked up and said, 'There are thousands of houses in England at this moment where wives, mothers, and children are dying of hunger. Now,' he said, 'when the first paroxysm of your grief is past, I would advise you to come with me, and we will never rest till the Corn Law is repealed.'

"I accepted his invitation. I knew that the description he had given of the homes of thousands was not an exaggerated description. I felt in my conscience that there was a work which someone must do, and therefore I accepted his invitation, and from that time we never ceased to labor hard on behalf of the resolution which we made.

"Now, do you suppose that I wish you to imagine that he and I, when I say 'we,' were the only persons engaged in this great question? We were not even the first, though afterwards, perhaps, we became the foremost before the public. But there were others before us; and we were joined, not by scores, but by hundreds, and afterwards by thousands, and afterwards by countless multitudes; and afterwards famine itself, against which we warred, joined us; and a great minister (of the Crown) was converted, and minorities became majorities, and finally the barrier was entirely thrown down. And since then, though there has been suffering in many homes in England, yet no wife and no mother and no little child has been starved to death as the result of a famine made by law."

G. M. Trevelyan, Life and Times of John Bright

resignation in   *see also* SUBMISSION

561. *(After the death of her sister, Charlotte Brontë wrote to a friend:)*

"Emily suffers no more pain or weakness now. She never will suffer more in this world. We are very calm at present. Why should we be otherwise? The anguish of seeing her suffer is over; the spectacle of the pains of death is gone by; the funeral day is past. We feel she is at peace. No need now to tremble for the hard frost and the keen wind. Emily does not feel them. She died in a time of promise. We saw her taken from life in its prime. But it is God's will, and the place where she is gone is better than the place she has left."

Mrs. Elizabeth Gaskell, Life of Charlotte Brontë

the universality of

562.   That loss is common would not make
            My own less bitter, rather more;
            Too common! Never morning wore
            To evening, but some heart did break.

                                        Tennyson, "In Memoriam"

SOUL
impervious to attack

563.   The soul, secured in her existence, smiles
            At the drawn dagger, and defies its point.
            The stars shall fade away, the sun himself
            Grow dim with age, and nature sink in years;
            But thou shalt flourish in immortal youth,
            Unhurt amidst the war of elements,
            The wreck of matter, and the crush of worlds.

                        Addison, *Cato*, Act V, Sc. I (Cato's Soliloquy)

STRUGGLE   *see also* ENEMY
essential to victory

564.   We have before us an ordeal of the most grievous kind. We
have before us many, many long months of struggle and of suffering.
You ask, What is our policy? I will say: "It is to wage war, by sea,
land, and air, with all our might and with all the strength that
God can give us; to wage war against a monstrous tyranny, never
surpassed in the dark, lamentable catalogue of human crime. That
is our policy." You ask, What is our aim? I can answer in one word:
"Victory—victory at all costs, victory in spite of all terror, victory
however long and hard the road may be; for without victory there is
no survival."

                        Winston S. Churchill, *Blood, Sweat, and Tears*

a futile

565.   In the winter of 1824 there set in a great flood upon that
town—the tide rose to an incredible height: the waves rushed in
upon the houses, and everything was threatened with destruction. In
the midst of this sublime and terrible storm Dame Partington,

who lived upon the beach, was seen at the door of her house with mop and pattens, trundling her mop, squeezing out the sea water, and vigorously pushing out the Atlantic Ocean. The Atlantic was roused. Mrs. Partington's spirit was up; but I need not tell you that the contest was unequal. The Atlantic Ocean beat Mrs. Partington. She was excellent at a slop or a puddle, but she should not have meddled with a tempest.

Sydney Smith, Speech at Taunton (Oct., 1831)

man in a state of perpetual

566.   Ever and everywhere a mighty battle is raging around us, a battle in which we are all volunteers, ay, and enrolled soldiers on either side,—the great silent internal battle, of lust against purity, of truth against falsehood, of right against wrong. It needs no splendid occasion, no stately amphitheater, no pomp and prodigality of outward circumstances: for its seat is in the human heart. But its effects and issues are in the world.

F. W. Faber, *Treasure Thoughts of*, ed. by Rose Porter

SUBMISSION   *see also* DEATH—resignation in the face of, SOR-
ROW—resignation in

to God's will

567.   Begin therefore in the smallest matters, and most ordinary occasions, and accustom your mind to the daily exercise of this pious temper, in the lowest occurrences of life. And when a contempt, an affront, a little injury, loss, or disappointment, or the smallest events of every day, continually raise your mind to God in proper acts of resignation, then you may justly hope that you shall be numbered amongst those that are resigned and thankful to God in the greatest trials and afflictions.

William Law, *Serious Call*

SUFFERING
courage in   *see also* ADVERSITY, SORROW

568.   *(The Brontë sisters were remarkable not only for their talent but for the fortitude with which they faced life. Mrs. Gaskell quotes from Charlotte's letter telling of Emily's last illness:)*
"Day by day, when I saw with what a front she met suffering,

I looked on her with an anguish of wonder and love. I have seen
nothing like it. The awful point was that while full of compassion
for others, on herself she had no pity: the spirit was inexorable to
the flesh; from the trembling hands, the unnerved limbs, the fading
eyes, the same service was exacted as they rendered in health. To
stand by and witness this, and not dare to remonstrate, was a pain
no words can render."

Many a time [adds Mrs. Gaskell] did Charlotte and Anne drop
their sewing or cease from their writing to listen with wrung hearts
to the failing step, the labored breathing, the frequent pauses,
with which their sister climbed the short staircase; yet they dared
not notice what they observed. They sat still and silent.

Mrs. Elizabeth Gaskell, *Life of Charlotte Brontë*

569. *(Stevenson, the year before he died, wrote these words to
George Meredith:)*

Four fourteen years I have not had a day of real health. I have
wakened sick, and gone to bed weary; and I have done my work
unflinchingly. I have written in bed and out of bed, in hemorrhages,
in sickness; written torn by coughing, written when my head swam
for weakness; and for so long that it seems to me I have won my
wager and recovered my glove. . . . And the battle goes on—ill
or well is a trifle, so long as it goes. I was made for a contest, and
the Powers that be have so willed that my battlefield shall be this
dingy, inglorious one of the bed and the medicine bottle.

R. L. Stevenson, *Letters*

the lot of man

570.   A few seem favorites of Fate,
                In Pleasure's lap caressed;
            Yet, think not all the Rich and Great,
                Are likewise truly blest.
            But Oh! what crowds in every land,
                All wretched and forlorn,
            Thro' weary life this lesson learn,
                That Man was made to mourn!

            Many and sharp the num'rous ills
                Inwoven in our frame!

More pointed still we make ourselves
   Regret, Remorse, and Shame!
And Man, whose heav'n-erected face,
   The smiles of love adorn,
Man's inhumanity to Man
   Makes countless thousands mourn!

                    Burns, "Man Was Made to Mourn"

the ministry of

571.   I hoped that with the brave and strong
              My portioned task might lie;
            To toil amid the busy throng,
              With purpose pure and high;
            But God has fixed another part,
              And He has fixed it well,
            I said so with my breaking heart,
              When first this trouble fell.

            These weary hours will not be lost,
              These days of misery,
            These nights of darkness, anguish-tossed,
              Can I but turn to Thee:
            With secret labor to sustain
              In patience every blow
            To gather fortitude from pain,
              And holiness from woe.

            If Thou shouldst bring me back to life,
              More humble I should be,
            More wise, more strengthened for the strife,
              More apt to lean on Thee;
            Should death be standing at the gate,
              Thus should I keep my vow;
            But, Lord, whatever be my fate,
              O let me serve Thee now!

                    Anne Brontë (d. 1849, aged twenty-nine),
                        "He Doeth All Things Well"

572.   Most people have had a period or periods in their lives when they have felt thus forsaken; when, having long hoped against hope, and still seen the day of fruition deferred, their hearts have truly sickened within them. This is a terrible hour, but it is often that darkest point which precedes the rise of day; that turn of the year when the icy January wind carries over the waste at once the dirge of departing winter, and the prophecy of coming spring. The perishing birds, however, cannot thus understand the blast before which they shiver; and as little can the suffering soul recognize, in the climax of its affliction, the dawn of its deliverance. Yet, let whoever grieves still cling fast to love and faith in God; God will never deceive, never finally desert him. "Whom He loveth, He chasteneth." These words are true, and should not be forgotten.

Charlotte Brontë, *Shirley*

573.   (*Katherine Mansfield, pursued by ill-health most of her life, died of a pulmonary hemorrhage at the age of thirty-four.*)
"There is no limit to human suffering. When one thinks: 'Now I have touched the bottom of the sea—now I can go no deeper,' one goes deeper. [But] I do not want to die without leaving a record of my belief that suffering can be overcome. . . . What must one do? . . . One must *submit*. Do not resist. Take it. Make it a part of life. . . . I must put my agony into something, change it. 'Sorrow shall be changed into joy.' It is to lose oneself more utterly, to love more deeply, to feel oneself part of life—not separate."

Katherine Mansfield, *Journal of*, ed. by J. Middleton Murry

574.   Millions of human beings but for suffering would never develop an atom of affection. The man who would spare due suffering is not wise. It is folly to conclude a thing ought not to be because it hurts. There are powers to be born, creations to be perfected, sinners to be redeemed through the ministry of pain, that could be born, perfected, redeemed, in no other way.

George Macdonald

575.   (*Shortly after Romanes learned that not only his eyesight but his very life was threatened by a serious illness, he received a letter from Canon Scott Holland which moved him greatly. In it were these words:*)

"It is a tremendous moment when first one is called upon to join the great army of those who suffer. That vast world of love and pain opens suddenly to admit us one by one within its fortress. We are afraid to enter into the land; yet you will, I know, feel how high is the call. It is as a trumpet speaking to us, that cries aloud— 'It is your turn—endure.' Play your part. As they endured before you, so now, close up the ranks—be patient and strong as they were. Since Christ, this world of pain is no accident untoward or sinister, but a lawful department of life, with experiences, interests, adventures, hopes, delights, secrets of its own. These are all thrown open to us as we pass within the gates—things that we could never learn or know or see, so long as we were well.

"God help you to walk through this world now opened to you as through a kingdom, regal, royal, and wide and glorious."

The Life and Letters of George John Romanes

576.   There are those to whom a sense of religion has come in storm and tempest; there are those whom it has summoned amid scenes of revelry and idle vanity; there are those, too, who have heard its still small voice amid rural leisure and placid contentment. But perhaps the knowledge which causeth not to err, is most frequently impressed upon the mind during seasons of affliction; and tears are often the softened showers which cause the seed of Heaven to spring and take root in the human breast.

Scott, *The Monastery*

577.   *(The aged Lear, stunned by the base ingratitude of his daughters on whom he has lavished his entire fortune, quits their inhospitable roof in anger and goes into the night wild with storm. Suffering intensely in mind and body, he at length reaches a hovel which affords some slight shelter against the elements. It is only in the extremity of his plight, when he is almost on the verge of madness, that he thinks of others who may likewise be victims of such a night:)*

Poor naked wretches, whereso'er you are
That bide the pitiless storm—
I have ta'en too little care of this!

Shakespeare, *King Lear*, Act III, Sc. 4

578. *(When Robert Louis Stevenson saw the physical condition of the lepers in the hospital on Molokai [one of the Hawaiian Islands] he almost turned infidel. Faith returned, however, when he witnessed the loving care of the hospital attendants. This fragment he wrote in the guest book there:)*

> To see the infinite pity of this place,
> The mangled limb, the devastated face,
> The innocent sufferer smiling at the rod—
> A fool were tempted to deny his God.
> He sees, he shrinks. But if he gaze again,
> Lo, beauty springing from the breast of pain!
> He marks the sisters on the mournful shores;
> And even a fool is silent, and adores.

R. L. Stevenson

a part of God Himself

579. The good news of Christianity is that suffering is itself divine. It is not foreign to the experience of God Himself. "In all their affliction He was afflicted." "Surely He hath borne our griefs and carried our sorrows." "If thou be the Son of God," said His enemies, "come down from the Cross." No: not while any man remains unredeemed. It is the necessary form which divine love takes when it is brought into contact with evil. To overcome evil with good means to suffer unjustly and willingly.

William Ralph Inge, Speculum Animae

the problem of

580. *(Marget Howe was a proud woman when word reached her that her laddie had won his degree, with honors, at Edinburgh. But when young George Howe returned to the Glen he was mortally broken in body. It was not long before Kirsty Stewart, the "Job's comforter of the Glen," paid Marget a visit:)*

"Ay, ay, Marget, sae it's come tae this. Weel, we daurna complain. It's a sair blow after a' that was in the papers. Ay, ay, it's an awfu' lesson, Marget, no to mak' idols o' our bairns; for that's naethin' else than provokin' the Almighty."

It was at this point that Marget scandalised the village of Drumtochty, which held that "obtrusive prosperity" provoked the

higher powers, and that the deprecation of our children was a policy
of safety.

"Did ye say the Almighty? I'm thinkin' that's an ower grand name
for your God, Kirsty. What wud ye think o' a faither that brocht
hame some bonnie thing frae the fair for ane o' his bairns, and
when the puir bairn was pleased wi' it, tore it oot o' his hand and
flung it into the fire? Kirsty, wummin, when the Almighty sees a
mither bound up in her laddie, I tell ye He is sair pleased in His
Heaven, for mind ye how He loved His ain Son. Besides, I'm judgin'
that nane o' us can love anither withoot lovin' Him, or hurt anither
withoot hurtin' Him.

"Oh, I ken weel that George is gaein' to leave us; but it's no because the Almighty is jealous o' him or me. It cam' to me last nicht
that He needs my laddie for some grand work in the ither world,
and that's hoo George has his books brocht oot to the garden and
studies a' the day. He wants to be ready for His kingdom. I hoped
he would be a minister o' Christ's Gospel here, but he'll be judge
over many cities yonder. I'm no denyin', Kirsty, that it's a trial, but
I hae licht on it, an' naethin' but guid thochts o' the Almighty."

The village of Drumtochty understood that Kirsty had dealt
roundly with Marget for her pride and presumption. But when
Marget returned to her laddie and sat down beside him, her face
was shining.

Ian Maclaren, Beside the Bonnie Briar Bush (adapted)

581. *(Miranda, weeping, tells her father, Prospero, of a shipwreck
she has just witnessed from the shore:)*

                    O, I have suffer'd
With those I saw suffer: a brave vessel,
Who had no doubt some noble creature in her,
Dash'd all to pieces. O, the cry did knock
Against my very heart! Poor souls, they perished!
Had I been any god of power, I would
Have sunk the sea within the earth or ere
It should the good ship so have swallow'd and
The fraughting souls within her!

Shakespeare, The Tempest, Act I, Sc. 2

SUGGESTION
the power of

582. The most striking characteristic of the poetry of Milton is the extreme remoteness of the associations by means of which it acts on the reader. Its effect is produced, not so much by what it expresses, as by what it suggests; not so much by the ideas which it directly conveys, as by other ideas which are connected with them. He electrifies the mind through conductors. . . . He does not paint a finished picture, or play for a mere passive listener. He sketches, and leaves others to fill up the outline. He strikes the key-note, and expects his hearer to make out the melody.

Macaulay, "Essay on Milton"

SYMBOL
man's need of

583. He was a legend. With his old and tattered gown, his walk that was just beginning to break into a stumble, his mild eyes peering over the steel-rimmed spectacles, and his quaintly humorous sayings, Brookfield would not have had an atom of him different.

November 11, 1918. News came through in the morning; a whole holiday was decreed for the School, and the kitchen staff were implored to provide as cheerful a spread as war-time rationing permitted. There was much cheering and singing, and a bread fight across the Dining Hall. When Chips entered in the midst of the uproar there was an intense hush, and then wave upon wave of cheering; everyone gazed on him with eager, shining eyes, as on a symbol of victory.

James Hilton, *Good-bye, Mr. Chips*

584.
    And man is a spirit
      And symbols are his meat,
    So pull not down the steeple
      In your monied street.

    For money chimes feebly,
      Matter dare not sing—

> Man is a spirit,
> Let the bells ring.
>
> Louis MacNiece, *Holes in the Sky*

TEMPTATION
the significance of

585.   Was the trial sore?
> Temptation sharp! Thank God a second time!
> Why comes temptation but for man to meet
> And master and make crouch beneath his feet
> And so be pedestalled in triumph?
>
> Browning, *The Ring and the Book*

the subtlety of

586. *(The Argonauts, returning from their search for the Golden Fleece, came too near the fatal shores of the Sirens, fabulous creatures who by their seductive music drew men to destruction on the rocks.)*

They could see the Sirens of Anthemousa, the flowery isle; three fair maidens sitting on a beach, beneath the red rock in the setting sun, amid beds of crimson poppies and asphodel. Slowly they sang and sleepily, with silver voices mild and clear, which stole over the golden waters and into the hearts of all the heroes, in spite of Orpheus' song. And as they listened, the oars fell from their hands, and their heads drooped on their breasts, and they closed their heavy eyes; and they dreamed of bright still gardens, and of slumbers under murmuring pines, till all their toil seemed foolishness and they thought of their renown no more.

Charles Kingsley, *Heroes*

trifling with

587. He who dallies with temptation, he who tampers with evil, is never safe. People say that such and such a man had a sudden fall; but no fall is sudden. In every instance the crisis of the moment is decided only by the tenor of the life; nor, since the world began, has any man been dragged over into the domain of evil, who had not strayed carelessly, or gazed curiously, or lingered guiltily, beside its verge.

F. W. Faber, *Treasure Thoughts of*, ed. by Rose Porter

THANKSGIVING
see also PRAISE
in adversity

588.   Life is sweet, brother!"
      "Do you think so!"
      "There's night and day, brother, both sweet
         things; sun, moon, and stars, brother, all
         sweet things; there's likewise the wind on the
         heath. Life is very sweet, brother."
      "In sickness, Jasper?"
      "There's the sun and stars, brother!"
      "In blindness, Jasper?"
      "There's the wind on the heath, brother."

George Borrow, *Lavengro*

589.   "[If] I am fallen into the hands of publicans and sequestraters! They have taken all from me, What now! Let me look about me. They have left me the sun, the moon, a loving wife, many friends to pity me, some to relieve me. I can still discourse and write as I list: they have not taken from me my merry countenance, my good conscience, my cheerful spirit. They have left me the providence of God and all the promises of the gospel, my religion, my hopes of heaven, my charity to them too. Still I sleep and digest; I eat and drink; I read and meditate. And he that hath so many causes of joy, and so great, is very much in love with sorrow and punishment who leaves all these pleasures and chooses to sit down upon his little handful of thorns."

Jeremy Taylor, *Holy Living*

in devotions

590.   You are to consider this chanting of a psalm as a necessary beginning of your devotions, as something that is to awaken all that is good and holy within you, that is to call your spirits to their proper duty, to set you in your best posture towards heaven, and tune all the powers of your soul to worship and adoration.

For there is nothing that so clears a way for your prayers, nothing that so disperses dullness of heart, nothing that so purifies the soul from poor and careless passions, nothing that so opens heaven, or carries your heart so near it, as these songs of praise.

They create a sense of delight in God, they awaken holy desires, they teach you how to ask, and they prevail with God to give. They kindle a holy flame, they turn your heart into an altar, your prayers into incense, and carry them as a sweet-smelling savor to the throne of grace.

William Law, *Serious Call*

591. When all Thy mercies, O my God! my rising
          soul surveys,
      Transported with the view, I'm lost in wonder,
          love, and praise!
      Oh, how shall words, with equal warmth, the
          gratitude declare,
      That glows within my ravished breast? But
          Thou canst read it there.

              *   *   *

      Through every period of my life, Thy goodness
          I'll pursue;
      And after death, in distant worlds, the glorious
          theme renew.

Addison, from a hymn

592.   When I survey the wondrous cross
          On which the Prince of glory died,
          My richest gain I count but loss,
          And pour contempt on all my pride.

          Forbid it, Lord, that I should boast
          Save in the cross of Christ my God;
          All the vain things that charm me most,
          I sacrifice them to His blood.

          See from His head, His hands, His feet,
          Sorrow and love flow mingled down;
          Did e'er such love and sorrow meet,
          Or thorns compose so rich a crown?

          Were the whole realm of nature mine,
          That were an present far too small;

> Love so amazing, so divine,
> Demands my soul, my life, my all.
>> Isaac Watts, "When I Survey the Wondrous Cross"

inspired by nature

593. *(In a Swiss valley before sunrise the poet gazes at snow-covered Mt. Blanc towering above him—majestic, solitary, immovable—rising like a cloud of incense hymning the Creator's praise. Struck by the splendor of the scene he sings:)*

> Awake, my soul! not only passive praise
> Thou owest!

✦　✦　✦

>   Awake, my heart, awake!
> Green vales and icy cliffs, all join my hymn.
> Ye ice-falls! . . .
> Motionless torrents! silent cataracts!
> Who made you glorious as the Gates of Heaven
> Beneath the keen full moon? Who bade the sun
> Clothe you with rainbows? Who with living flowers
> Of loveliest blue, spread garlands at your feet?
> God? let the torrents, like a shout of nations,
> Answer! Let the ice-plains echo, God!
> And they too have a voice, yon piles of snow.
> And in their perilous flow shall thunder, God!
>> Coleridge, "Hymn Before Sunrise in the
>> Vale of Chamouni"

in praise of

594.   Would you know who is the greatest saint in the world? It is not he who prays most or fasts most; it is not he who gives most alms, or is most eminent for temperance, chastity, or justice; but it is he who is always thankful to God, who wills everything that God willeth, who receives everything as an instance of God's goodness, and has a heart always ready to praise God for it.
>> William Law, *Serious Call*

TIME
redeeming the

595.   'Tis not for man to trifle, life is brief
                And sin is here;
            Our age is but the falling of a leaf,
                A dropping tear.
            We have no time to sport away the hours,
            All must be earnest in a world like ours.

            Not many lives, but only one have we,
                One, only one.
            How earnest should that one life be,
                That narrow span,
            Day after day in blessed toil,
            Hour after hour still bringing in new spoil.
                        Browning, "Bishop Blougram's Apology"

TOLERANCE   *see also* SECTARIANISM, SOCIAL CASTE
the meaning of

596.   Tolerance means reverence for all the possibilities of Truth;
it means the acknowledgment that she dwells in diverse mansions,
and wears vestures of many colors, and speaks in strange tongues;
it means frank respect for freedom of indwelling conscience against
mechanic forms, official conventions, social force; it means the
charity that is greater than even faith and hope.
                        John Morley, *Life of William Ewart Gladstone*

TONGUE   *see also* CENSORIOUSNESS, CENSURE
a disciplined

597.   John Knox has the power of holding his peace over many
things which do not vitally concern him—"They? what are they?"
But the thing which does vitally concern him, that thing will he
speak of, and in a tone the whole world shall be made to hear: all
the more emphatic for his long silence.
                        Carlyle, *Heroes and Hero-Worship*

598.   We must look well to it that in our conversation be never
heard the serpent's hiss. We must speak no slander; no, nor listen

to it. The reputation of our enemies must be as sacred from our gossip as the reputation of our dearest relatives, and the absent must be as safe on our lips from secret malice as the dead.

F. W. Faber, *Treasure Thoughts of,* ed. by Rose Porter

a slanderous

599.   'Tis slander,
Whose edge is sharper than the sword, whose tongue
Outvenoms all the worms of Nile, whose breath
Rides on the posting winds and doth belie
All corners of the world: kings, queens, and states,
Maids, matrons, nay, the secrets of the grave
This viperous slander enters.

Shakespeare, *Cymbeline,* Act III, Sc. 4 (Pisanio)

600.   Good name in man and woman, dear my lord,
Is the immediate jewel of their souls:
Who steals my purse steals trash: 'tis something,
    nothing;
'Twas mine, 'tis his, and has been slave to
    thousands;
But he that filches from me my good name
Robs me of that which not enriches him
And makes me poor indeed.

Shakespeare, *Othello,* Act III, Sc. 3 (Iago)

TRUST   *see also* FAITH

601.   I do not ask, O Lord, that life may be
A pleasant road;
I do not ask that Thou wouldst take from me
Aught of its load;

I do not ask that flowers should always spring
Beneath my feet;
I know too well the poison and the sting
Of things too sweet.

For one thing only, Lord, dear Lord, I plead:
Lead me aright,

Though strength should falter, and though heart
    should bleed,
    Through peace to light.

I do not ask my cross to understand,
    My way to see;
Better in darkness just to feel Thy hand,
    And follow Thee.

             Adelaide Anne Proctor, from a hymn

TRUTH   *see also* HYPOCRISY
in dying men

602.   The tongues of dying men
        Enforce attention, like deep harmony:
        When words are scarce, they're seldom spent
          in vain;
        For they breathe truth that breathe their
          words in pain.

             Shakespeare, *King Richard II,*
             Act II, Sc. 1 (John of Gaunt)

the indestructible nature of

603.   *(His enemies, baffled in their designs against Wycliffe in his lifetime, consoled themselves by disinterring his bones and casting them into the River Swift.)*

Thus this brook hath converged his ashes into the Avon, the Avon into the Severn, the Severn into the narrow seas, they into the main ocean. And thus the ashes of Wycliffe are the emblem of his doctrine, which is now dispersed all over the world.

             Thomas Fuller, *Church History,* Sec. II, Bk. IV

604.   Here, in this little Bay,
        Full of tumultuous life and great repose,
        Where, twice a day,
        The purposeless, glad ocean comes and goes,
        Under high cliffs, and far from the huge town,
        I sit me down.
        For want of me the world's course will not fail:

When all its work is done, the lie shall rot;
The truth is great, and shall prevail,
When none cares whether it prevail or not.

                    Coventry Patmore, "Magna Est Veritas"

the infinitude of

605.   *(The poet quotes Isaac Newton, English physicist, philosopher.)*

"I know not how my work may seem to others—"
So wrote our mightiest mind—"but to myself
I seem a child that wandering all day long
Upon the sea-shore gathers here a shell,
And there a pebble, colored by the wave,
While the great ocean of truth, from sky to sky,
Stretches before him, boundless, unexplored."

                    Alfred Noyes, "Watchers of the Sky"

the power of embodied

606.   Perhaps none of the secondary causes which Gibbon has assigned for the rapidity with which Christianity spread over the world, while Judaism scarcely ever acquired a proselyte, operated more powerfully than this feeling [the desire of having some visible and tangible object of adoration]. God, the uncreated, the incomprehensible, the invisible, attracted few worshippers. A philosopher might adore so noble a conception; but the crowd turned away in disgust from words which presented no image to their minds. It was before Deity embodied in a human form, walking among men, partaking of their infirmities, weeping over their graves, slumbering in the manger, bleeding on the cross, that the prejudices of the Synagogue, . . . and the swords of thirty legions, were humbled in the dust.

                    Macaulay, "Essay on Milton"

VISION   *see also* BLINDNESS, FAITH—the vision of,
the blessedness of   GOD—the immanence of

607.   To see the World in a grain of sand,
And a Heaven in a wild flower;
Hold infinity in the palm of your hand,
And Eternity in an hour.

                    William Blake, "Auguries of Innocence"

608. At the time when Britain was weathering one of its most severe and perilous international storms, Jane Austen sat writing about genteel English parlors with not a glance at the outer world and with all her insight concentrated on the varied pulsing of hearts in the quietest of homes. Do we blame her now? Do we protest that she should have been rising to the Challenge of the Hour? Of course not.

Nor do we blame Wordsworth for making his observations on daisies and daffodils and on his drawing of morals from tranquil mountain scenery while Napoleon was raging across Europe. It would indeed be a victory for communism if authorship had now to behave as though nothing existed save evil and all traditional values had evaporated.

Ivor Brown, "On Writers and Writing"

609.   Earth's crammed with heaven,
           And every common bush afire with God;
           But only he who sees takes off his shoes;
           The rest sit round it and pluck blackberries.

Elizabeth Barrett Browning, "Aurora Leigh"

610. Carlyle has through some grim chapters been describing the horrors of the Reign of Terror, the panic, the bloodshed, the frivolity. You have been reading until you can bear no more; and Carlyle seems to have known what was passing in your mind. For it is just then that he begins a new chapter by telling us how, at that very time, away outside, there was a quiet scene, and ships with idle, flapping sails were swinging lightly in the tide! It is his wonderful way of telling us that, though all these horrors which he has been describing did indeed take place, still there was more in life than those horrors. There was the great sea, quiet and sun-lit!

John Hutton, The Dark Mile

611. I was sitting on the seashore, half listening to a friend arguing about something which merely bored me. Unconsciously I looked at a film of sand I had picked up on my hand, when I suddenly saw the exquisite beauty of every little grain of it; instead of being dull, I saw that each particle was made up on a perfect geometrical pattern, with sharp angles, from each of which a brilliant shaft of light was reflected, while each tiny crystal shone like a rainbow. Then, suddenly, I saw how the whole universe was made up of particles of material which, no matter how dull and lifeless they might seem, were nevertheless filled with this intense and vital beauty. For a second or two the whole world appeared as a blaze of glory. When it died down, it left me with something I have never forgotten and which constantly reminds me of the beauty locked up in every minute speck of material around us.

Aldous Huxley, Heaven and Hell

612.   O world invisible, we view thee,
           O world intangible, we touch thee,
           O world unknowable, we know thee,
           Inapprehensible, we clutch thee!

Francis Thompson, "In No Strange Land"

a constricted

613.   There stood a man who could look no way but downwards, with a muckrake in his hand. There stood also one over his head with a celestial crown in his hand, and he proffered him that crown for his muckrake; but the man did neither look up nor regard, but raked to himself the straws, the small sticks, and the dust of the floor.

Bunyan, Pilgrim's Progress

614.   "It's forty-four year next May since I first kept the books of Cherryble Brothers. I've opened the safe every morning all that time as the clock struck nine, and gone over the house every night at half-past ten to see the doors fastened and the fires out. I've never slept out of the back attic one single night. There's the same mignonette box in the middle of the window, and the same flower-pots, two on each side, that I brought with me when I first came. There ain't—I've said it again and again, and I'll maintain it—there ain't such a square as this in the world; I know there ain't. For pleasure or business, in summertime or winter—I don't care which—there's nothing like it. There's not such a spring in England as the pump under the archway. There's not such a view in England as the view out of my window; I've seen it every morning before I shaved, and I ought to know something about it. I have slept in

that room for four and forty year, and if it wasn't inconvenient and
didn't interfere with business, I should request leave to die there."
Dickens, *Nicholas Nickleby* (Mr. Linkwater)

615.   I believe in my father, and his father, and his father's father,
the makers and keepers of my estate, and I believe in myself and
my son and my son's son. And I believe that we have made the
country what it is. And I believe in the Public Schools, and especially the Public School that I was at. And I believe in my social
equals and the country house, and in things as they are, for ever
and ever. Amen.

John Galsworthy, *The Country House*

616.   A primrose by a river's brim
A yellow primrose was to him,
And it was nothing more.

Wordsworth, "Peter Bell"

illumination in moments of

617.   Oh, we're sunk enough here, God knows!
But not quite so sunk that moments,
Sure tho' seldom, are denied us,
When the spirit's true endowments
Stand out plainly from its false ones,
And apprise it if pursuing
Or the right way or the wrong way,
To its triumph or undoing.

There are flashes struck from midnights,
There are fire-flames noondays kindle,
Whereby piled-up honors perish,
Whereby swollen ambitions dwindle.

Browning, "Christina"

a man without

618.   So year after year Silas Marner had lived in this solitude,
his guineas rising in the iron pot, and his life narrowing and harden-
ing itself more and more into a mere pulsation of desire and satis-
faction which had no relation to any other being. His life had

reduced itself to the mere functions of weaving and hoarding without any contemplation of an end towards which the functions tended. The same sort of process has perhaps been undergone by wiser men when they have been cut off from faith and love—only instead of a loom and a heap of guineas, they have had some erudite research, some ingenious project, or some well-knit theory.

George Eliot, *Silas Marner*

man's need of

619. Depend upon it, you would gain unspeakably if you would learn with me to see some of the poetry and the pathos, the tragedy and the comedy, lying in the experience of the human soul that looks through dull gray eyes, and that speaks in a voice of quite ordinary tones.

George Eliot, *Amos Barton*

a near-sighted

620. Like all his contemporaries he examines nature with near-sighted eyes. The mountains of Wales are unseen by him. He has no word about the great outlines of the country-side, but in the articulations of an insect or the softness of the stalk of a violet nothing escaped him. He notes the elasticity and the tenderness of the young-ringed tendrils of a vine. For glow-worms, grasshoppers, butterflies, he has a searching eye. He notes all the vicissitudes in the life of an apple-tree, its gum, its sterile branches, the fragility of its blossoms. . . . Instances of Jeremy Taylor's sensorial style may be prolonged indefinitely.

Edmund Gosse, *Jeremy Taylor*

a saving

621. Bethink thee often of the swiftness with which the things that are, or are even now coming to be, are swept past thee. . . . Folly! to be lifted up, or sorrowful, or anxious by reason of things like these! Think of infinite matter, and thy portion—how tiny a particle of it! of infinite time, and thine own brief point there. . . . What multitudes, after their utmost striving—a little afterwards—were dissolved again into their dust.

Walter Pater, *Marius the Epicurean*

sustaining moments of

622.   (*The poem is based on the life of Paracelsus* (*b. 1493?*), *a*
Swiss physician possessed from childhood with an aspiration to dis-
cover the secrets of the world.)

"I am a wanderer: I remember well
One journey, how I feared the track was missed,
So long the city I desired to reach
Lay hid; when suddenly its spires afar
Flashed through the circling clouds; you may conceive
My transport. Soon the vapors closed again,
But I had seen the city, and one such glance
No darkness could obscure: nor shall the present—
A few dull hours, a passing shame or two,
Destroy the vivid memories of the past."

Browning, "Paracelsus"

623.   There are in our existence spots of time,
That with distinct pre-eminence retain
A renovating virtue, whence—depressed
By false opinion and contentious thought—
                        . . . our minds
Are nourished and invisibly repaired;
A virtue, by which pleasure is enhanced,
That penetrates, enables us to mount,
When high, more high, and lifts us up when fallen.
                    ❖   ❖   ❖
                        Such moments
Are scattered everywhere, taking their date
From our first childhood.

Wordsworth, *The Prelude*, Bk. XII

WAR   *see also* CONSCIENCE
conscience and

624.   But what shall we do if our country be actually invaded?
Some may think it would be a sin to defend themselves. Happy
are they if they can refrain from judging or condemning those
that are of a different persuasion. Certain it is that some have fought
and died in a just cause with a conscience void of offense. To

some, therefore, it may be a matter of duty to repel a Common
Enemy. They who are called to this should learn their drill with
prayers and hymns.

John Wesley, *Journal*

the inevitabilty of

625.   The temper of each new generation is a continual surprise.
The fates delight to contradict our most confident expectations.
Gibbon believed that the era of conquerors was at an end. Had
he lived out the full life of man he would have seen Europe at the
feet of Napoleon. But a few years ago we believed the world had
grown too civilized for war, and the Crystal Palace in Hyde Park
was to be the inauguration of a new era. Battles, bloody as
Napoleon's, are now the familar tale of every day; and the arts
which have made greatest progress are the arts of destruction. What
next?

J. A. Froude, *The Science of History* (1864)

a soldier's prayer

626.   God, I am travelling out to death's sea,
        I, who exulted in sunshine and laughter,
    Dreamed not of dying—death is such waste of me!—
        Grant me one prayer: Doom not the hereafter
    Of mankind to war, as though I had died not—
        I, who in battle, my comrade's arm linking,
    Shouted and sang, life in my pulses hot
        Throbbing and dancing! Let not my sinking
    In dark be for naught, my death a vain thing!
        God, let me know it the end of man's fever!
    Make my last breath a bugle call, carrying
        Peace o'er the valleys and cold hills for ever!

John Galsworthy, "Valley of the Shadow"

WILL   *see also* CHOICE, INDECISION, PROCRASTINATION

627.   Grant us the will to fashion as we feel,
        Grant us the strength to labor as we know,
        Grant us the purpose, ribbed and edged with steel,
            To strike the blow.

> Knowledge we ask not—knowledge Thou hast lent;
> But Lord, the will—there lies the bitter need.
> The deed, the deed.
>
> John Drinkwater, "A Prayer"

WITNESS
of a dying man

628. *(When Scott was nearing the end he called for Lockhart, his son-in-law.)*

I found him entirely himself, though in the last extreme of feebleness. His eye was clear and calm—every trace of the wild fire of delirium extinguished. "Lockhart," he said, "I may have but a minute to speak to you. My dear, be a good man. Nothing else will give you any comfort when you come to lie here."

John Gibson Lockhart, *Memoirs of Sir Walter Scott*, Vol. V

629. I have known what the enjoyments and advantages of this life are, and the refined pleasures which learning and intellectual power can bestow; and with all the experience that more than three-score years can give, I, now on the eve of my departure, declare to you that health is a great blessing, competence a great blessing, and a great blessing it is to have kind, faithful, and loving friends and relatives; but that the greatest of all blessings is to be indeed a Christian. . . . And I, on the very brink of the grave solemnly bear witness to you that the Almighty Redeemer, most gracious in His promises to them that truly seek Him, is faithful to perform what He has promised.

Coleridge, in a letter to his godson, a
few days before his death, July 13, 1834

unashamed

630. *(When John Kenyon, a distant cousin, remarked that the scriptural tone of some of her poetry was injurious to its popularity, Elizabeth Barrett wrote him as follows:)*

Certainly I would rather be a pagan whose religion was actual, earnest, continual—than I would be a Christian who, from whatever motive, shrank from hearing or uttering the name of Christ out of a "church." I am no fanatic, but I like truth and earnestness in all things, and I cannot choose but that such a Christian shows but ill beside such a pagan. What pagan poet ever thought of casting his gods out of his poetry? . . . And if I shrank from naming the name of my God lest it should not meet the sympathy of some readers, or lest it should offend the delicacies of other readers, or lest, generally, it should be unfit for the purposes of poetry, in what more forcible manner than by that act can I secure to myself unanswerable shame?

Elizabeth Barrett Browning, *Letters*

WOMEN
and Christianity

631.   I will say again that when Jesus was come, women rejoiced in him before either man or angel. I read not that ever any man did give unto Christ so much as one groat; but the women followed him, and ministered to him of their substance. It was a woman that washed his feet with tears, and a woman that anointed his body to the burial. They were women that wept when he was going to the cross, and women that followed him from the cross, and that sat by his sepulchre when he was buried. They were women that were first with him at his resurrection-morn, and women that brought tidings first to his disciples that he was risen from the dead. Women, therefore, are highly favored, and show by these things that they are sharers in the grace of life.

Bunyan, *Pilgrim's Progress*

WONDER   *see also* VISION, WORSHIP
the decay of

632.   Wonder is on all hands dying out: it is the sign of un-cultivation to wonder. Speak to any small man of a high, majestic Reformation, of a high, majestic Luther and forthwith he sets about "accounting" for it; how the "circumstances of the time" called for such a character, and found him we suppose, standing girt and road-ready, to do its errand; how the "circumstances of the time" created, fashioned, floated him quietly along into the result; how, in short, this small man, had he been there, could have performed the like himself! For it is the "force of circumstances" that does everything; the force of one man can do nothing.

Carlyle, *Critical and Miscellaneous Essays*

an element of worship

633.   The Sense of Wonder is obviously nearest to that spirit of worship which is the first instinct of religion. Wherever we have the sense of wonder, in however gross a form, we have one of the germs of that spiritual insight which sees the world and the most "everyday" fact in it bathed in that strange light which for some is never gone from sea or land. Anyone with the sense of wonder must be to some extent religious, must be emancipated in some measure from the dull materialism of his fellows.

Richard Le Gallienne, *The Religion of a Literary Man*

the lost sense of

634.   There was a time when my little soul shone and was uplifted at the starry enigma of the sky. That has gone; gone absolutely. I could not have imagined that it would ever go. While I was still a little fellow at Mowbray, I remember looking at the stars one night upon the terrace—it must have been a night in winter, because Orion was there—and I was in an ecstasy. I was rapt in a passion of wonder. I was lost to all other feeling. . . . But now I can go out and look at the stars, as I look at the pattern on the wallpaper of a railway station waiting-room. About them I have become prosaically reasonable. If they were not there, there would be something else as casual, as indifferently sublime. The more I have learnt about them, the more coldly aloof from me have they become.

H. G. Wells, *The World of William Clissold*
(William Clissold)

635.   There was a time when meadow, grove, and stream,
  The earth, and every common sight,
    To me did seem
   Apparelled in celestial light,
  The glory and the freshness of a dream.
It is not now as it hath been of yore;—
    Turn wheresoe'er I may,
     By night or day,
The things which I have seen I now can see no more.

   The Rainbow comes and goes,
   And lovely is the Rose,

The Moon doth with delight
Look round her when the heavens are bare,
   Waters on a starry night
   Are beautiful and fair;
   The sunshine is a glorious birth;
   But yet I know, where'er I go,
That there hath passed away a glory from the earth.
      Wordsworth, "Ode on Intimations of Immortality"

at nature   *see also* NATURE

636.   I wonder how a seed as good as dead
Comes forth a flower from out its earthy bed.
I wonder how an acorn very small
Can change itself into an oak so tall.
I often wonder how the silver moon
Can cause the gentle tide to change so soon.
I wonder how the little violets bloom
Within the precincts of the forest gloom.
I never see a bed of crimson clover
But what I want to sit and think things over.
      James Douglas, "Wonderment"

WORK   *see also* FAITHFULNESS, IDLENESS, SERVICE
the blessing of

637.   Thank God every morning when you get up that you have
something to do that day which must be done, whether you like it
or not. Being forced to work, and forced to do your best, will breed
in you temperance and self-control, diligence and strength of will,
cheerfulness and content, and a hundred virtues which the idle
never know.

      Charles Kingsley, in a letter

the dignity of

638.   I was introduced to old George, a Cotswold mason. He is in
his seventies but still at it. . . . He had spent all his long life among
stones. There were bits of stone all over him. He handled the stones
about him, at once easily and lovingly, as women handle their
babies. . . . He was a pious old man, this old George, and when
he was not talking about stone and walls, he talked in a very quiet

though evangelical strain about his religious beliefs, which were
old and simple. Being a real craftsman, he obviously enjoyed his
work, which was not so much toil exchanged for so many shillings
but the full expression of himself. . . . I have never done anything
in my life so thoroughly and truly as that old mason did his building. . . . Old George had always been a mason, and his father and
grandfather were masons before him. I do not know for what pit-
tances they worked, or how narrow and frugal their lives must have
been, but I do know that they were not unhappy men; they were
not taught algebra and chemistry and then flung into a world that
did not even want their casual labor; they were not robbed of all
sweetness and dignity of real work; they did not find themselves
lost and hopeless in a world that neither they nor anyone else
could understand; they did not feel themselves to be tiny cogs in
a vast machine that was running down; they had a good trade
to their fingers, solid work to do, and when it was done—and there
it was, with no mistake about it, ready to outlast whole dynasties—
they could take their wages and go home and be content. I am
glad I met old George and saw him at work.

J. B. Priestley, English Journey, "In the Cotswolds"

the joy of

639.   That thing which I understand by real art is the expression
by man of his pleasure in labor. I do not believe he can be happy
in his labor without expressing that happiness; and especially is
this so when he is at work at anything in which he excels. A most
kind gift is this of nature, since all men, nay, it seems all things,
too, must labor; so that not only does the dog take pleasure in
hunting and the horse in running, and the bird in flying, but so
natural does the idea seem to us, that we imagine to ourselves that
the earth and the very elements rejoice in doing their appointed
work; and the poets have told us of the spring meadows smiling,
of the exultations of the fire, of the countless laughter of the sea.

William Morris, The Art of the People

the sanctity of

640.   God provides the good things of the world to serve the needs
of nature by the labors of the plowman, the skill and pains of the
artisan, and the dangers and traffic of the merchant. These men

are in their calling the ministers of the divine providence and the stewards of the creation, and servants of a great family of God, the world. . . . So that no man can complain that his calling takes him off from religion: his calling itself and his very worldly employment in honest trades and offices is a serving of God.

Jeremy Taylor, *Holy Living*

the stewardship of

641. "I can't abide to see men throw away their tools i' that way, the minute the clock begins to strike, as if they took no pleasure i' their work, and was afraid o' doing a stroke too much. . . . I hate to see a man's arms drop down as if he was shot, before the clock's fairly struck, just as if he'd never a bit o' pride and delight in's work. The very grindstone 'ull go on turning a bit after you loose it."

George Eliot, *Adam Bede* (Adam)

WORLD   *see also* MAN—drifting further from God
the deterioration of the

642. Who that has once been young and now is middle-aged can have failed to observe the steady deterioration of the world in so far as men and women have altered it? I do not wish to indict the present age, but it is an age that has invaded *our* peaceful age with garish petrol pumps, with the odious odors of motor-bicycles, with bungalows, with the dance music of St. Vitus, with busses, with doubts, with psychoanalysis, with high taxation, with standardization of everything from tobacco to opinions, with advertisement and self-advertisment, with paint and powder, with prohibitions more puzzling than the riddle of the sphinx.

Robert Lynd, *Happy England*

an indictment against the

643.   O, that this too, too solid flesh would melt,
Thaw and resolve itself into a dew!
Or that the Everlasting had not fix'd
His cannon 'gainst self-slaughter! O God! God!
How weary, stale, flat and unprofitable,
Seem to me all the uses of this world!
Fie on 't! ah fie! 'tis an unweeded garden,

That grows to seed; things rank and gross in nature
Possess it merely.

Shakespeare, *Hamlet,* Act I, Sc. 2 (Hamlet)

satiated with the spirit of the

644.   From too much love of living,
                                From hope and fear, set free,
                        We thank with brief thanksgiving
                                Whatever gods may be,
                        That no life lives for ever;
                        That dead men rise up never;
                        That even the weariest river
                                Winds somewhere safe to sea.

Swinburne, "The Garden of Proserpine"

separation from the   *see also* CHRISTIANS

645.   He who has taken his stand, who has drawn a boundary
line, sharp and deep, about his religious life, who has marked off
all beyond as for ever forbidden ground to him, finds the yoke easy
and the burden light. For this forbidden environment comes to be
as it were not. His faculties falling out of correspondence, slowly
lose their sensibilities. And the balm of Death numbing his lower
nature releases him for the scarce disturbed communion of a higher
life. So even here to die is gain.

Henry Drummond, *Natural Law in the Spiritual World*

WORSHIP
acceptable

646.   Every time we perform an act of kindness to any human
being, aye, even to a dumb animal; every time we conquer our
worldliness, love of pleasure, ease, praise, ambition, money, for the
sake of doing what our conscience tells us to be our duty,—we are
indeed worshipping God the Father in spirit and in truth, and
offering Him a sacrifice which He will surely accept for the sake of
His beloved Son, by whose Spirit all good deeds and thoughts are
inspired.

Charles Kingsley, *Daily Thoughts*

the adoration of

647.   In such an hour
Of visitation from the living God,
Thought was not; in enjoyment it expired.
No thanks he breathed, he proffered no request;
Rapt into still communion that transcends
The imperfect offices of prayer and praise,
His mind was a thanksgiving to the power
That made him; it was blessedness and love!
                    Wordsworth, *The Excursion*, Bk. I

and the communion of saints

648.   We should try to be conscious of the Communion or Fellowship of saints, in which our own worship is actually offered. Whenever our own worship is genuine, the congregation in which we
offer it is not limited to the people gathered in the same building.
When we lift up our hearts to the Lord, forthwith it is with angels
and archangels and with all the company of heaven that we laud
and magnify God's glorious name. In this act of worship we do
indeed have communion with our loved ones who have gone before
us to the other world.
              William Temple, *The Christian Hope of Eternal Life*

defined

649.   To worship is to quicken the conscience by the holiness of
God, to feed the mind with the truth of God, to purge the imagina-
tion by the beauty of God, to open the heart to the love of God, to
devote the will to the purpose of God. All this is gathered up in
that emotion which cleanses us from selfishness because it is the
most selfless of all emotions—adoration.
                    William Temple, *The Hope of a New World*

reverence during   *see also* REVERENCE

650.   Now, and here, within these walls, and at this hour, comes
Christ unto you in the offer of this abundance; and with what
penuriousness of devotion and reverence do you meet him here?
God standeth, says David, God standeth in the Congregation; does

God stand there, and wilt thou sit? Sit, and never kneel? . . . I must say that there are come some persons to this Church, and persons of example to many that come with them, of whom I never saw master or servant kneel at his coming into this Church, or at any part of divine service. Kneeling is the sinner's posture, if thou come hither in the quality of a sinner, (and if thou do not so, what doest thou here? The whole need not the Physician). Put thyself into the posture of a sinner; kneel!

John Donne, *Sermons*

ritual in

651.   At bottom, worship is a spiritual activity; but we are not pure spirits, and therefore we cannot expect to do it in purely spiritual ways. That is the lesson of the Incarnation. Thus liturgies, music, symbols, sacraments, devotional articles and acts have their rightful part to play in the worshipping life; and it is both shallow and arrogant to reject them *en masse* and assume that there is something particularly religious in leaving out the senses when we turn to God. . . . People who talk contemptuously about "empty forms" forget that empty things can always be filled, and that it is up to them to do it. The silliest hymn and the most formal prayer can be made a great act of worship; if those who use it have worshipping instead of critical hearts.

John Stobbart, *The Wit of Evelyn Underhill*

the work of

652.   It is commonly assumed that, provided only we repair to our church or chapel, the performance of the work of adoration is a thing that may be taken for granted. But the work of Divine Worship, so far from being a thing of course even among those who outwardly address themselves to its performance, is one of the most arduous which the human spirit can possibly set about.

Gladstone, *The Might of Right*

YOUTH
the illusory strength of

653.   I need not tell you what it is to be knocking about in an open boat. I remember nights and days of calm when we pulled, we pulled, and the boat seemed to stand still, as if bewitched within the circle of the sea horizon. I remember the heat, the deluge of rain-squalls that kept us baling for dear life, and I remember sixteen hours on end with a mouth as dry as a cinder and a steering-oar over the stern to keep my first command head-on to a breaking sea. I did not know how good a man I was till then. I remember the drawn faces, the dejected figures of my two men, and I remember my youth and the feeling that will never come back any more—the feeling that I could last for ever, outlast the sea, the earth, and all men; the deceitful feeling that lures us on to joys, to perils, to love, to vain effort—to death; the triumphant conviction of strength, the heat of life in the handful of dust, the glow in the heart that with every year grows dim, grows cold, grows small, and expires, too soon—before life itself.

Joseph Conrad, Youth

ZEAL   see also AMBITION, APATHY, DISSENSION, INDIFFERENCE
an indiscriminate

654.   (*A candidate for a local office in Ireland tells of one of his campaign speeches.*)

The chief row was about Irish Home Rule and I thought I'd better have a whack at the Pope. Has it ever struck you that ecclesiastical language has a most sinister sound? I knew some of the words, though not their meaning; but I knew my audience would be just as ignorant. So I had a magnificent peroration.

"Will you, men of Kilclavers," I said, "endure to see a chasuble set up in your market place? Will you have your daughters sold into simony? Will you have celibacy practiced in the public streets?"

Gad, I had them all on their feet bellowing, "Never!"

John Buchan, The Three Hostages

an intemperate

655.   There is nothing so evident in life as that there are two sides to a question. History is one long illustration. . . . An enthusiast sways humanity by disregarding this great truth, and dinning it into our ears that this or that question has only one possible solution; and your enthusiast is a fine florid fellow, dominates things for a while and shakes the world out of a doze; but when

once he is gone, an army of quiet and uninfluential people set to
work to remind us of the other side and demolish the generous
imposture.

R. L. Stevenson,
Virginibus Puerisque, "Crabbed Youth and Age"

a misplaced

656.   She devoted herself to an extensive variety of public subjects
at various times, and is at present devoted to the subject of Africa;
with a view to the general cultivation of the coffee berry—and the
natives—and the happy settlement on the banks of the African
rivers of our superabundant home population. The room, which was
strewn with papers and nearly filled with a great writing table
covered with similar litter, was, I must say, not only very untidy
but very dirty. Mrs. Jellyby preserved the evenness of her disposition. She told us about Borrioboola-Gha and the natives; and received so many letters that Richard, who sat by her, saw four
envelopes in the gravy at once. During the whole evening Mr.
Jellyby sat in a corner with his head against the wall, as if he were
subject to low spirits.

Dickens, *Bleak House*

an unholy

657.   He who advocates the cause of Christianity should be particularly aware of fancying that his being religious will atone for
his being disagreeable; that his orthodoxy will justify his unchari-
tableness, or his zeal make up for his indiscretion. He must not
persuade himself that he has been serving God when he has only
been gratifying his own resentment—when he has actually, by a
fiery defence, prejudiced the cause which he might perhaps have
advanced by temperate argument and persuasive mildness.

Hannah More, *Practical Piety*

INDEX OF TOPICS

Listing is according to the number of the selection.

INDEX OF AUTHORS AND SOURCES

Listing is according to the number of the selection.

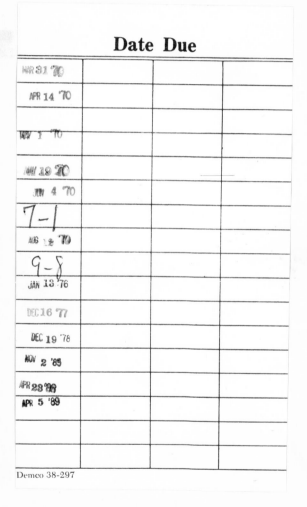